It Was Football, Stupid: The Untold Story of the XFL

Greg Parks

PublishAmerica
Baltimore

Hardcover 978-1-4512-0919-8
Softcover 978-1-60813-712-1
PUBLISHED BY PUBLISHAMERICA, LLLP
www.publishamerica.com
Baltimore

Printed in the United States of America

To My Parents, for nurturing the writer in me throughout the years. It finally paid off!

Growing up, I was always good at reading and writing and wanted to do something in those fields. Since there's not much you can do to get paid for reading, writing seemed the way to go. To that end, I figured it would be cool to write a book, to have something out there with my name on it that said, "I wrote this." And of course, to show off to everyone. So I'd first like to thank PublishAmerica for agreeing to take a risk and publish a book about, quite frankly, an unpopular subject. I sent out queries to many publishers throughout the past few years, with nary a bite coming back. I was so excited when I heard back and was able to set things into motion to actually write a book.

I guess I should thank all my English teachers coming up through grade school, who really fostered my love of writing and encouraged me to continue forward in that field. That's what led me, in part, to wanting to become an English teacher myself: To be able to develop the love of reading and writing in others, something that is too often not a priority with children these days. I'd like to thank my journalism professors in college, who did the same as my English teachers, only on a more advanced level—nourished the writer inside me.

The first two real writing jobs I had were for school newspapers, so I'd like to thank my editor of the New Courier at Genesee Community College, Kris Dassinger, and my editor for the Stylus at The College at Brockport, Ivo Chilev. They helped me get acquainted with newspaper writing, which is what I wanted to sink my teeth into at the time. Having moved on to teaching, I didn't want to leave writing behind, so I thank

Wade Keller of the Pro Wrestling Torch newsletter for allowing me to continue to hone my writing skills, and doing it covering something I'm passionate about.

I'd like to thank the friends and family who encouraged me in this project, a number far too numerous to name one-by-one, but you know who you are. My parents, of course, too. Whether it was writing or teaching, they've been right there to support whatever it was I wanted to do. Except when I was little and wanted to be a garbageman. But I think everyone went through that phase.

I guess I'd be remiss if I didn't thank Vince McMahon—without him, I'd have nothing to write about. I'd also like to thank Kevin Iole, Tim Lester, Kris Haines, and Bill Baker, all who were associated with the XFL and were kind enough to grant me interviews via e-mail so I'd have some new material to add to the book.

And I'd also like to thank all of you who bought this book: You are a participant in this dream of mine, this whirlwind book writing process. I thank you for taking an interest in the subject matter and my writing, something I love to do. Hopefully, like me, you'll also continue to help foster reading and writing in our young children as well. Hey, if you're going to set a good example by picking up a book and reading, it might as well be mine.

Greg Parks
Brockport, New York
July 22, 2009

I guess an explanation is in order for the title. It applies to two distinctly different groups: First, to the media. "It Was Football, Stupid," (suggested by a fan many years ago to me on thefanforce.com message board when I first thought of the book idea) is my way of putting some of the blame for the failure of the league on them, for treating the league like a circus act and covering everything but the football aspect of it. When the glitz and the glitter wore off, in the end, it was football, but some in the media were too worked up about dancing cheerleaders or cameras on the field to understand that. They vilified the league at every turn, and when they weren't doing that, they were ignoring it. Hard to gain acceptance when no one will cover you. Watch the last few games and you'll realize all the outside activities portrayed in the first week were gone, and it really was football. But by then, the sinking ratings were the only thing the media was interested in covering, not the actual football game itself. As a fan, it was frustrating to have to dig around the internet just to find information about goings-on in the league. The media didn't "get" that it was football, with a little icing on the cake.

The title also is addressed to the XFL itself. While I was a fan, it's hard not to look back and think of where they would be today if they had done a better job of promoting the product in the one year leading up to the first game. Everything was about cheerleaders, new rules, Jesse Ventura, and everything BUT the on-field action. Those in the league realized this and during the season, tried to make up for it by telling anyone who would listen that the football on the field was what was important to the league. If only they had pushed things that way out of the gate. Instead, they built the telecast up as something never seen before, something that would put other networks' sports coverage to shame. Everyone had high expectations going in, especially knowing Vince McMahon was behind it, and he was billed as a marketing genius. When week one of the season aired, the number one thing wrong with the league was the play on the field. The league was so busy trying to advertise all the extra shenanigans that the football suffered. They underestimated how many fans (or how few) would be willing to watch a second-rate football product. They should've tempered fans' expectations and been a little more down-to-earth in the months leading up to the first game. Most of the failure of the league could be pinned on week one and the fans who didn't come back for subsequent weeks. "It Was Football, Stupid" is just my way of saying that to the fans, it was about football; to the XFL, it seemed at the start, it was about everything else going on in the stadium. That's a huge reason things went south for the league.

As you read this book, going week-by-week through the league's development and the only regular season in XFL history, it will become clear that the league made mistakes, and that is one reason the media gave them such a short leash. When the payoff to the hype didn't come in week one, the media was more than happy to dance on the XFL's impending grave. Both entities share blame for what happened to the league; neither paid close enough attention to the football, and hence, the title.

CHAPTER ONE

I was in the ninth grade in February of 2000. After I came home from school one day and got on the internet, I remember going to a pro wrestling website that announced a press conference would be taking place the next day, February 3rd. It was called by Vince McMahon and had something to do with football, but no one knew exactly what. There was speculation that McMahon was possibly getting in bed with the National Football League with his company, the World Wrestling Federation (now World Wrestling Entertainment—WWE, which is what I'll refer to his company from here on out), perhaps becoming a major sponsor. The other rumor bandied about was that McMahon was going to buy into the Canadian Football League, or simply buy one of the teams. The latter made sense, as McMahon had, in 1999, attempted to buy the Toronto Argonauts of the CFL. In fact, McMahon went further than that and did consider running the CFL to help them in getting into the U.S. market in the mid-90s. According to an interview with the Toronto Sun, Vince wanted complete control of the league. Anyone who follows pro wrestling would not be surprised by that. In the end, the CFL Board of Directors shot down the idea. Still, I certainly, didn't see the bombshell that came less than 24 hours after I had first heard the football-related news: The creation of the XFL.

[handwritten margin notes: "Press conf 2/3/2000", "McMahon", "Argos", "CFL"]

Vince McMahon, who has been referred to as this generation's P.T. Barnum, took control of WWE from his father in 1982 and has run the company with an attitude ever since. He started by taking the promotion national, something most other pro wrestling promoters saw as a mistake. Instead, Vince gobbled up other territories (wrestling companies were basically split into territories at the time, with one running in Dallas, another running Florida, still another running the Carolinas, etc.) or their wrestlers in a bid to make his company the industry standard-bearer. His tactics in doing so were criticized by many in the industry and showed the ruthlessness he would later be known for. After hooking up with Hulk Hogan in the mid 80s, McMahon and his WWE were quickly becoming the top pro wrestling comapny in America. Vince attracted big stars like Cyndi Lauper, Mr. T, Muhammad Ali and others and debuted on pay-per view with The Wrestling Classic in 1985. In 1993, he went even bigger, creating Monday Night Raw and running it in prime-time on cable TV Monday nights. Both WrestleMania and Raw were big risks that paid off handsomely: Wrestlemania is now the Super Bowl of professional wrestling and Raw is entering it's 16th year on television. Clearly, McMahon isn't afraid to take risks. Throughout the mid-90s, he waged a war with Ted Turner's rival company, World Championship Wrestling (WCW). They even put their flagship show on Monday nights and challenged WWE in the pay-per view arena. For a while, WCW was winning the war, but WWE made a comeback, thanks in part to Vince's Mr. McMahon TV character. Vince ended up winning the war in 2001—how else?— by purchasing his opposition. I can't imagine the delight he felt that day, a day that guaranteed him a virtual monopoly on professional wrestling in America. He has been described as cocky, stubborn, arrogant and flamboyant. McMahon has often been prone to controversy inside the wrestling industry as well as in the mainstream light. From the steroid trial of the early '90s to sexual misconduct allegations of him and his employees, to the Chris Benoit murder-suicide of 2007, McMahon is a lighting rod of controversy and the face of a seedy industry.

Vince has always had a love-hate relationship with the mainstream media, going back to the days of his steroid trial, which was covered heavily by the national press. He has struggled to gain acceptance in their eyes and especially in the world of professional sports. His first foray into that field was with the World Bodybuilding Federation. The WBF, something the XFL was always compared to, was Vince taking what he knew from his time promoting professional wrestling and channeling it into the world of pro sports. The WBF only lasted two years and McMahon's own steroid trial had a hand in its death. It would've reflected poorly on McMahon for some many athletes in his company to appear "on the gas" during his trial, so he was forced to establish a drug-testing program. The bodies of his athletes shrunk and the WBF ceased operations in 1992. Vince took a hit from the national media once again and tried to climb the mountain of respectability in their eyes.

The XFL, less than ten years later, was another attempt at that. To those who follow pro wrestling closely, it's no secret that Vince McMahon's entire world revolves around his business and professional wrestling, so how much could the man know about starting up a football league? It made sense that he starteud up the WBF; chiseled bodies, charisma and good looks are three main ingredients in bodybuilding, and they also go for those in pro wrestling. But football? One wonders when the last time Vince McMahon actually sat down and watched an entire football game. But was the league about football, or was it about Vince McMahon and his need to be recognized as someone other than a purveyor of mindless violence?

In any event, as expected, the XFL announcement on February 3rd, 2000 was met with laughter and vitriol from the sports media. ESPN and CNN/SI, two major sports outlets, treated the story largely as a joke. "How dare they challenge the mighty NFL!" "Will the action be scripted or legitimate?" "I can't wait for a player to hit a referee with a folding chair!" As a pro wrestling fan, comments like these, which were common from sportswriters, were eye-roll inducing. Days after the announcement, McMahon was grilled by Fox News' Neil Cavuto on the new league and its possibly negative effects on WWE and its lack of TV partner (even though the league had a year to get one). Respected sports columnist Mitch Albom, a personal favorite of mine since his days on ESPN's Sports Reporters, scoffed at what society has become when WWE can put out a football product; and ESPN and CNN/SI didn't give much credence to the league either. If it were run by anyone but McMahon, there would've been a serious take and diligent reporting done. Instead, it was treated as a sideshow attraction. Fox News' Paula Zahn asked Vince McMahon if there would be drug testing in the XFL. If this were anyone but McMahon, would that be one of the top ten questions even asked of someone starting a pro football league? Top twenty questions? It probably wouldn't even be in the top 50. The sharks were already circling.

Even though I was in the ninth grade, it was amazing to see that I "got" pro wrestling in a way that many adults didn't get and still don't, to this day. And McMahon hoped to recruit his pro wrestling fans that often made his flagship show, Monday Night Raw, the top-rated show on cable. He even made reference to his penchant for hooking young male fans (a demographic the advertisers love) when talking about XFL's target viewers. Not only that, but WWE goes on the road 250 times a year, so McMahon certainly has the know-how in the live-event arena to make the stadium experience for fans one-of-a-kind. The press conference McMahon held that day does hold some historic value. There were many phrases he said that people still use today: "The No-Fun League," in reference to the NFL becoming more and more buttoned-down; "The Quarterbacks won't be wearing skirts," a shot again at the NFL for going overboard in protecting the QB (something still an issue even today); and the famous, "Where's my football? Where's my smashmouth football?," a slogan my friends and I repeat to this day.

The knocks on the NFL led one to wonder whether Vince actually wanted the league to succeed. He was putting down arguably the most popular professional sports entity in America in the National Football League; everything from TV ratings to attendance for the league dwarfed any other competitor in the major sports arena. Which brings us to a question previously asked: Why football, of all the sports he

Why choose F.B?

could choose from, would Vince dabble in? Did he think that because the NFL had such a populous fan base that there was room for another league because there were so many fans? Or was it because there was more talent available to populate a league, as opposed to baseball or basketball, where some of the top talent still play overseas? NFL-caliber players are cut each year from the league due to injuries, age, or the player's salary cap number. That doesn't mean they're not good enough to play in the league however, so the available talent is certainly stronger than other sports, where there is no salary cap or there are minor leagues for guys to play in. More on that later.

Either way, there had to be concerns about how other leagues fared that have attempted to cut into the NFL's audience. Currently, the Arena Football League (AFL) and CFL are number two behind the NFL, and calling them "number two" is being generous, as they are so far removed from the NFL in terms of talent it's really not comparable. But we've seen the USFL fail previous to the XFL and the USFL had much better players than the XFL. Like the XFL, the USFL didn't directly compete with the NFL as far as playing their games at the same time; they did compete for players though. McMahon was adamant that he was not competing with the NFL, that his brand was just different than the NFL brand and it's almost like they were going after two different fanbases. They may not have been in direct competition, but because they offer similar products, comparisons would always be made. It's eerily similar to the way WWE today is with Ultimate Fighting Championship (UFC); WWE claims they are not really competition, yet they're generally after the same target demographic and pay-per view revenue. WWE today says it competes with all forms of entertainment; I could see that argument being made with the XFL down the line as well.

Back to the USFL: The league went bankrupt, partly because of the money they spent on a lawsuit they fought against the NFL. This is of course not to mention the many leagues that were discussed and had plans of starting, but never got off the ground, such as a league rumored to start up with the combination of Ted Turner and NBC. Sportsline.com's Len Pasquarelli even wrote that Turner's company

Turn had plans for a league

had developed plans for the start-up league, but it fizzled out after a year of on-again-off-again planning. Of the leagues that came before the XFL though, they all made critical mistakes in some aspect of building/maintaining the league; it wasn't simply that "the NFL was better so they went out of business." In other words, it isn't impossible for a league not far removed from the NFL to start up and be relatively successful. We'll examine the comparisons between the USFL and XFL later on.

Another league the XFL was often compared to was the World Football League (WFL). They didn't last as long as the USFL, but did last slightly longer than the XFL. The WFL attracted some talent away from the NFL, but that did not help matters. Teams relocated in mid-season and before the first season was over, despite decent attendance numbers, most teams were running with a low cash flow. By the second season, instead of relocating, teams were folding as the season progressed, and eventually the entire league shut down in the middle of the season. Like the XFL, the WFL was ridiculed throughout its history and couldn't overcome the public's perception of it as a Mickey Mouse organization that would always play second-fiddle to the NFL.

Since the XFL and even as I write, leagues have popped up in an effort to cement themselves as a number two professional football league. The All-American Football League was started with teams and territories announced; instead of nicknames, they would simply be referred to as "Team Michigan" or "Team Florida," hoping to take advantage of college-like ties to areas. The league even had a draft, but has postponed the start of their season two years in a row. The United Football League was officially announced in 2009 to start play in the fall of that same year. That could oversaturate the market, which college and NFL games already taking place at that time. The UFL proposes to play on Thursdays and Fridays, which are prime high-school football nights. Seven teams in four cities have been announced for the league. With no TV deal yet, it reamins to be seen if this league is able to get off the ground.

Many of the leagues, whether at the start like the UFL or eventually, really hope to at some point become associated with the NFL. They hope to catch the NFL's eye and become a feeder system, a minor-league if you will like there is in baseball, or perhaps more accurately, like the NBA's relationship with the NBDL. Not only would this association almost guarantee long-term viability, but by the NFL associating with another league, it gives the "OK" for fans of the NFL to watch another league. "If the NFL is associated with it, it must be good football!" It would also improve the play on the field if actual NFL players played in the games. Of course, NFL Europe had this association with the NFL for a while, and even they had to fold. That had more to do with it being played overseas than anything else, though. The NFL has a loose association with the AFL, but the game is so different there that it can't truly be used as a feeder league. The XFL could've been that league eventually, even though that would go against Vince McMahon's renegade image that he cultivated for the league and himself. I could also see him spinning it as the NFL wanting to partner with him rather than go against him, so he could very well have the advantage were that situation to occur.

Vince McMahon was in usual McMahon form on February 3rd, the [2/3] day of the announcement: Take no prisoners. He called the NFL "an [Presser] overregulated, antiseptic brand of football" and said the XFL would "take you places where the NFL is afraid to go because, quite frankly, we are not afraid of anything." At least he gave sportswriters and TV people some great quotes and soundbites for stories. He also announced that it would take less than $100 million to start up the league and that he expected the league would be profitable within three years. McMahon made it clear in his remarks that this league would be the most fan-friendly in existence. He continued to bash the NFL in a Playboy interview released just before the league began play. He [Playboy interview] accused the owners of developing rules so as not to have their million-dollar athletes hurt, to go overboard in protecting them. He remarked that the NFL didn't know their audience, and asserted that the suits who run the league are too high on the corporate ladder to get a sense of what middle Americans like or want. Of course, Vince was a millionaire (perhaps even billionaire) at the time, so he wasn't exactly mowing his own lawn either. McMahon said that he understood the common folks; maybe he assumed that, coming from the rural background as he did. But anyone who watches his pro wrestling (sorry, "sports entertainment") shows knows that what Vince wants (and often gets) and what his fans want are often two totally different things.

The XFL immediately began to get plugged on WWE's top two TV shows, Raw and Smackdown. Clips from the announcement were shown and as each city was unveiled as receiving a franchise, those videos aired as well. Fans were inundated with XFL ads throughout the broadcasts, with saturation heavieset as opening day neared. It made sense to cross-promote the brands, especially since the target demographic the league was after was already watching their pro wrestling broadcasts. But eventually, so many ads ran, fans began to resent it and get tired of seeing it and one would assume they began to backfire as time wore on. While wrestling fans may also watch football, it doesn't mean football fans watch wrestling, something WWE learned by trying to promote their wrestling brand on the football broadcasts. It was not a two-way street, mostly because the football fans (and media who watched) looked down on that kind of sports entertainment.

Lost in the hoopla was the announcement via press release that the XFL would be run by Basil DeVito, a longtime WWE employee, who had experience in most every phase of the wrestling business, from pay-per view to advertising. Also on board were Mike Keller, who had assisted with the start-up of two previous football leagues that failed, as well as Michael Weisman, who would be in charge of the broadcasting end of the league; he had previously won awards as a producer and worked on seven Super Bowls. Former Major League Soccer GM and World League of American Footbal (WLAF) founder Billy Hicks was hired less than a month after the announcement of the league, to oversee day-to-day operations. Martin Mayhew, a former Washington Redskin defensive back, was named Director of Football Administration, and is now the General Manager of the Detroit Lions. Bill Baker, who was working for the Kansas City Chiefs, was brought aboard as director of player personnel and was responsible for signing all the players to league contracts, got a call from Keller when he was at the Hula Bowl in 2000. He said Keller was very vague about the league, but told him the number of teams that would be involved, and described to him that one man would own the league, but didn't say who. "I was excited because everything Mike said would happen did happen," Baker said. "The announcement was huge and I wanted to be a part a something new and big." Baker even praised McMahon as a person, saying, "(He was) awesome! Great person, great family and great business man. He is humble and polite and appreciated the effort on the football field. He hired people and let them work." Certainly a different man than the media portrayed not only during the XFL, but when covering his pro wrestling company as well.

Of course, this news somehow got passed the media outlets who preferred to mock and deride McMahon for his foray into "real" sports. Hell, it took Las Vegas until September, a full seven months after the initial announcement and countless media appearances by McMahon and company touting the league as legitimate, for them to decide to allow gambling on XFL games. The fear, of course, was that the games would be fixed. McMahon never said they would be; could Vegas have gotten the idea from the constant media negativity surrounding the league and its authenticity? Would a movie executive who started a football league face the same criticism as McMahon, as far as whether the action would be scripted? After all, he too would make a living selling fake stories to Americans, just like McMahon. The days when pro wrestling was touted as "real" to the public were put to rest at least a decade prior. Fans were "in" on the idea of pro wrestling not being real, yet the mainstream media was behind the times, still living in the era of wrestlers who would swear on a stack of Bibles that outcomes weren't pre-determined and wrestlers were really taking it to each other night-in and night-out.

Interestingly, the sites for all the teams were also announced on February 3rd, them being Los Angeles, Miami, New York, Orlando, San Francisco and Washington, D.C. Of those teams, two of them did not come to fruition and two others were added at a later date. Chicago, Dallas, Houston and Las Vegas were among others rumored to be the final two teams. Detroit didn't make the list because they had no viable open-air stadium; the XFL didn't want any teams to play in domes.

WWF stock low
Wrestlers worried XFL take money

The release also cited the playoff system and championship game to be held at a neutral site. Kind of like, well, real football. In a sign of how difficult things would be (and what would later become one of the reasons for the demise of the league), on the day the announcement was made, WWE stock (WWFE at the time) fell to an all-time low. Wrestlers inside the company, it was reported in the Pro Wrestling Torch newsletter, were worried about the XFL getting money that they would normally be getting. Right off the bat, it was evident this would be a tough sell to the public as well as WWE faithful.

The day the XFL was born, there were no players. There was no television outlet (FOX immediately went on record saying they weren't interested—not a surprise, as they had a TV contract with the NFL). And there were no rules. That would all come later. The image of the oversized, oddly-shaped black and red football sitting at the table in front of McMahon and also used in the league's logo, was, in the XFL's hope, a pre-cursor to those who would later find out: This ain't your daddy's football.

NBC in (handwritten)

CHAPTER TWO

Not long after that first press conference, it was announced that NBC would be partnering with the XFL and would air the games on Saturday nights in prime time. They also bought 50% into the league. NBC had lost out to CBS on the bidding for the NFL TV rights two years prior and was no doubt stinging from that loss. From McMahon's point-of-view, this was win-win: Getting the credibility of NBC along side your brand, and having a major television outlet airing the games, and in prime-time no less! WWE had been in business for decades and couldn't even sniff a weekly show on network TV and here was the XFL, less than two months in, getting a prime spot on the TV dial. Plus, the XFL would be advertised throughout the week on NBC, allowing the league to become a highly visible brand. On one hand, being broadcast on Saturday nights was a blessing as there would be no real pressure as most networks didn't put their top programs on Saturday nights and some would usually just play movies in the prime-time slot. The league and network had a modest goal of a 4.5 rating on Saturday nights. Plus, NBC hoped that the XFL's target demographic of young boys would stick around for Saturday Night Live right afterward. On the other hand, the reason for that becoming the norm is because Saturday nights had been a barren wasteland for television since the Golden Girls; this was an opportunity that McMahon and the

NBC big win! (handwritten)

Goal 4.5 (handwritten)

XFL couldn't pass up, in part because of his relationship with old friend and NBC Sports Chairman Dick Ebersol (who had helped bring WWE Saturday Night's Main Event to the network in the '80s, and who had close ties with WWE and XFL consultant Michael Weismann). But concerns abounded about whether they could get fans in the target demo to spend their Saturday nights home watching football. And they were valid concerns.

In the same press release that announced this partnership, it was also made public that an XFL Advisory Panel had been assembled, featuring lumanaries such as 14-year NFL veteran and former NFL Player's Association head George Martin and former Dallas Cowboy Drew Pearson, who would go on to become General Manager of the league's New York/New Jersey Hitmen. Wonder how the NFL reacted to so many of its former stars helping what some considered a rival group? Well, you weren't going to hear anything—no NFL execs would speak on the record about the XFL, but one NFL chief executive told Sports Illustrated that the XFL became legitimate in his eyes once the deal with NBC was reached.

On May 18th, the XFL announced that UPN had agreed to air games on Sunday nights, though some speculated that UPN was on board from the beginning. This was a more traditional football viewing time than Saturday nights, though UPN also didn't reach the number of households NBC did. UPN already aired WWE Smackdown!, so it was no surprise they got into bed with Vince for the XFL. Smackdown generally blew away the ratings of anything else aired by UPN and they no doubt hoped that the XFL would turn into a similar success for the fledgling network that was annually fighting The WB for last place among the network TV ratings. It was announced that former NFL caricature Brian Bosworth would be handling color commentary. "The Boz" was a colorful personality and an outspoken individual during his short time in the NFL, but in the end, was exposed as being an average player despite his collegiate accolades. The one player most fans probably remember him by is being run over by Bo Jackson. Brought in to do play-by-play for UPN telecasts (and to play the straight man to Boz) was Chris Marlowe, a veteran voice of the Olympics, college football and college basketball. They chose a sideline reporter with Olympic coverage experience as well in Michael Barkann, also a host of the sports network CSN. The other sidelines reporter was Chris Wragge, the youngster of the group with the look Vince McMahon likes in his announcers. Wragge, a former college football player, was a sports anchor in the Houston area.

TNN was the final network to come aboard, a cable network that would show games on Sunday afternoon, another traditional football timeslot. And again, cross-promotion was key, as WWE Monday Night Raw at the time aired on TNN. This made it easier for WWE's flagship shows to plug XFL action and vice-versa. Bob Golic (three time NFL Pro Bowler and co-star of "Saved By The Bell: The College Years," which is likely what he was best known for to the XFL's target demo) and Craig Minnervini (former WWE announcer, then Craig DeGeorge, with a sports background) were the main announcers. Lee Reherman, a former NFL player with a Ph.D. in Economics and a turn as an American Gladiator on his resume, was one of the sideline reporters, along with Kip Lewis, son of NFL Offensive Coordinator Sherm Lewis and then a sports announcer with the Cincinnati, Ohio NBC affiliate. It was rumored that former Chicago Bears greats Jim McMahon and Steve McMichael were considered for broadcast positions as well, but nothing came of the talk.

With the important stuff like TV rights were out of the way, it was time to start building the teams. On June 13, 2000, it was announced that Ken Valdiserri would be the Vice-President/General Manager of the Chicago club and that they would play at Soldier Field. The same Soldier Field occupied by the NFL's Chicago Bears during their season. That certainly put the XFL on par with the NFL, at least on one level. Valdiserri worked for the Bears for a number of years, as well as with the Chicago White Sox of Major League Baseball. He and Vince McMahon had a history: He was the point man for the Bears when WWE and McMahon contacted them about using Jim Covert and William "The Refrigerator" Perry in the Wrestlemania III Players vs. Wrestlers Battle Royal. However, Valdiserri lasted less than three months in the position, re-signing on September 10th due to personal reasons. He was replaced by Rich Rose, who was a Senior Consultant of Special Projects with the XFL before being named interim GM. The team nickname of "Enforcers" came after many other options were publicy bandied about, including Hitmen, Mob, Skyscrapers, Inferno and Breeze.

A little over a week later, it was oficially announced that Memphis would be getting a team in the XFL as well, and would play their home games at the Liberty Bowl. Two considerations went into giving a city a team, according to the XFL's VP of Corporate Communications: They wanted to be in either a city that's a top TV market (read: big cities) or in cities where there was not a pro football team currently. Memphis fell into that category. The fact that the Tennessee area has always been a hotbed for college football and that fans were still upset at the NFL that they were bypassed for an expansion team in 1993 may not have hurt their case either. The city that would become home to the Maniax had dabbled in pro football before. They were home to the Memphis Showboats of the USFL in 1984 and also the Memphis Mad Dogs, a CFL offering in 1996. McMahon's reasoning for coming to Memphis? It was always a great stop for WWE. One of the early signs that Vince had trouble separating the two distinctly different brands.

Also in June, comedian Dennis Miller was hired to join the ABC Monday Night Football broadcast as an analyst. Some figured that this was a pre-emptive strike on the XFL by the NFL, by trying to add a little color into the football game. It was as if they were trying to prove to the public, in response to the XFL's accusations, that they weren't stodgy and old-fashioned at that they could be proactive and make things more entertaining for viewers at home. Miller flamed out after a few years, but lasted long enough to hold up a He Hate Me jersey and take a few jabs on TV at the XFL once the league folded.

July 4th, Independence Day, was also the day Orlando got in on the ground floor of the XFL. Tom Veit, former executive for a Major League Soccer team, was named GM and the team would be playing at the Citrus Bowl. Will McClay was named Personnel Director. He had been with the league since 1999 as a scout, which was before the league was even announced. It was funny to read that in the Rage Post-Season

Media Guide, thinking of McMahon paying these guys but not letting what they were doing get out. The agreement between the XFL and the Citrus Bowl was a good one for the city of Orlando, which, thanks to the lease, made the city $50-55,000 per game with attendance in the low 20,000s. Three days later, Las Vegas was awarded a franchise to play at Sam Boyd Stadium. Three days after THAT, the Bay Area got a team when the XFL decided upon San Jose and Spartan Stadium. That one however, didn't last long. When the availability of playing at Pacific Bell Park, which would house nearly 12,000 more fans than Spartan Stadium, in San Francisco opened up, XFL officials jumped at the opportunity, signed a five-year lease and re-named the team the San Francisco Demons (though officials still claimed it was a team representing the entire bay area). The news of the change drew the ire of some San Francisco Giants baseball players, who were not happy about having to share a stadium with a football team again, after moving out of Candlestick Park, where the 49ers played at the time. Los Angeles got a team as well on July 12th, playing at the LA Coliseum, with J.K. McKay coming aboard as GM. McKay was probably best known as the son of the legendary John McKay, former head coach for USC and the Tampa Bay Bucaneers. August 1st was a busy day in Birmingham, as the team was established, a field to play on was decided (Legion Field), and head coach, VP/GM and Player Personnel Director were all named. Birmingham had a history of pro football, fielding teams in the USFL, WLAF and AFL. The deciding factor, according to the Birmingham News, to add Birmingham as a team was because NBC owned its affiliate in Birmingham. Two days later, New York/New Jersey (a combination needed to play at Giants Stadium) was revealed as the final team and piece of the XFL puzzle. Former Dallas Cowboy WR Drew Pearson was named VP and GM.

The announcement of the teams' nicknames were another occasion when the XFL could grab headlines. Vince McMahon seemed to make sure the XFL was in the headlines every week in the Summer of 2000, with press conferences or press releases to announce everything from Spalding being the first official license of the league, to BIKE being named the on-field helmet of choice and TOPPS as the official trading card of the XFL, all big names in the licensing industry. A cursory search by some fans online prior to the announcements led to finding team names that WWE had trademarked. Among the ones not used were "New York Chaos," (perhaps a back-up in case they couldn't get the trademark to Hitmen, since it was owned by the minor league affiliate of the Calgary Flames, the Calgary Hitmen) and the nicknames "Empire," "Crusaders," "Snake Eyes," "Warlords," "Vipers," "Rock," "Predators" and "Lazers." Chaos wasn't bad and nychaos.com was actually a domain name registered by WWE, but I think the ones they ended up with were better than these. Perhaps these were in preparation for expansion teams they had planned (although "Snake Eyes" would seem to only work with the Vegas squad). The actual team names were officially announced on August 24th, but some had leaked ahead of time. In fact, the Birmingham franchise was originally called "Birmingham Blast," but just two days before the XFL made the names public, it was changed due to anger from the Birmingham community over the name due to a 1963 bombing during the Civil Rights movement that killed four girls and a more recent abortion clinic bombing. According to the Birmingham News, 96 possible nicknames were shown to area residents (males age 12-24) and "Blast" was the one that was the most positively received. No secret as to what demographic the league was coveting there, and it almost caused them a lot of issues if no one had caught that oversight. Interestingly, the man who helped develop the team names, colors and logos was a former NFL Properties vice president who helped develop several NFL identities as well. The Silverman Group out of New Haven had a hand in designing logos for the Enforcers and Rage and were told by the XFL to make them specific to the area the team was based. Perhaps even more interesting: The XFL began to solicit information about team names a full two months BEFORE the XFL was even announced—they would poll football fans, under the guise of simply an anonymous football organization, pumping them for information about what they'd like to see in a football league. Of course, even the naming of teams couldn't pass through the media without write-ups containting quotes vilifying the names. On February 6th, 2001, Memphis GM Steve Erhart was sent a letter by the National

[handwritten margin note: B-ham Blast denied 4 little girls]

Mental Health Association, urging the team to change the nickname and logo, citing the fact that they were encouraging the stereotype connecting of mental illness with violence. The Jewish Defense League had people writing to them complaining that the Xtreme logo looked too much like a swastika for their liking. The Washington Times ran a piece quoting a naming consultant who ripped the choices, and also discussed why some other names were inappropriate (like the Hitmen, for the connotation with the Mafia). Yeah, it would've been much better to have names that are clearly racist (Washington Redskins, anyone?), named after boring animals or bordering on the absurd, like so many Minor-League Baseball teams (Connecticut Defenders? Montgomery Biscuits? Really?).

Schedules were next to be announced, on October 4th. The first XFL game was slated to be New York/New Jersey at Las Vegas. Not surprising that the team representing the biggest television market in America was on the schedule; rather, it was surprising the game wasn't held at Giants Stadium. Rather, it was to be played in the Entertainment Capital of the World. Knowing how the XFL was to operate, that decision made sense as well. Not only that, but the capacity of the stadium was about 40,000 less than Giants Stadium, so the crowd would no doubt come across better on television with fewer empty seats. A more intimate and more raucous crowd would play better on TV. The schedule itself was built by two mathematicians from the University of Vermont, who had to schedule the games around certain events already scheduled at the stadiums; and also around XFL office requests, such as wanting LA to host either NY or Chicago; SF playing at home in week one; and having one Eastern and one Pacific time zone game each week.

On October 24th, team uniforms were unveiled. Each were a bit off-beat, separating the XFL from the other leagues. Perhaps my favorite, and probably the most apt for the XFL, was the black-and-purple colors of the Chicago Enforcers. With the history of the Chicago Bears and the cold weather that's common in that area, black-and-blue was a color the fans could really get behind. Many of the unique patterns seem to have influenced a few NFL teams in their recent uniform changes, including the Buffalo Bills. Just one of the number of ways the XFL ended up impacting the NFL.

No Team owner

The XFL wisely addressed a few key issues that prevented other leagues from lasting. The USFL and WFL failed partly due to money issues as owners were quick to pull the plug on teams. The XFL solved that issue by not having any owners; all teams were run by the league. Since the pay structure was the same for each team, there would be no trying to out-bid other teams for players. There would be no power plays from owners or no relying on the owners themselves to provide *Salaries* money to pay for the franchises. Everything went through the XFL. It was the definition of "league-think," a phrase that led to the salary cap in the NFL and one of the most prosperous eras of any sports leagues. There was no free agency in the XFL to inflate salaries, as they were set by the league and if you were on a team, you were there until you opted out of the league. Everybody signs the same contract with the league upon entering and is put into an available player pool, then claimed or signed by a team. This is one complaint from sports fans in the salary cap era, that there are few players you can identify franchises with as there were back in the days of a Terry Bradshaw or a Willie Mays. In the XFL, you wouldn't have that complaint.

Of course, the haggles between teams and players, free agency, training camp holdouts and salary demands are what keeps the NFL in the news in the off-season. Players moving from team to team, looking for the big contract that will set them for life, is the lifeblood of the talk radio hosts throughout the Winter and Spring. It creates interest, controversy and keeps the league and teams at the forefront of the continuous sports cycle. Fans may say they hate the salaries, but they're glued to their TV or computer, reading about how their team is going to get under the salary cap. The fans craved this kind of news and by doing away with these types of controversies, the XFL was limiting themselves in terms of off-season information that they could provide to their fans.

The other player-related subject that set the XFL apart from the NFL was off-the-field player conduct. Vince McMahon mentioned

off the field rule

several times that if you get arrested and found guilty of something, you're out. It's one of the reason Lawrence Phillips never applied to the XFL despite rumors that he would try-out for the league. The NFL has cracked down on off-field behavior over the past few years and especially under new Commissioner Roger Goodell. Still, it seems that players cannot keep themselves out of trouble and when the punishment isn't that severe even if they DO get caught, I think a lot of players feel there isn't that much to worry about. The XFL Player Handbook, on page 13, states that XFL players are responsible for "presenting a positive image for the Team, the League and the sport of football, and serving as a role model for youth. Failure by a Player to conform to the requirements set forth in the Player Contract, this Handbook, and the rules and regulations of the League and/or Team may subject the Player to fines, suspensions, termination of the Player Contract and/or permanent disqualification from the XFL." While the Handbook is vague as to punishments not only for players being arrested, but for drug testing as well, McMahon had already made the rounds in the media noting he'd be tough on those who broke the law, and I'm sure the media would hold him to that. Luckily, the XFL didn't have to deal with anything of such a nature during their one year. Former NFL 1st round pick Lawrence Phillips was interested in joining the league and even had discussion with Las Vegas GM Bob Ackles, but nothing apparently came of it. Phillips was suspended while in college at Nebraska, and was arrested three times in his time with the St. Louis Rams, the team that drafted him. He bounced around with the Miami Dolphins and San Francisco 49ers, but was soon found himself out of the league and playing in NFL Europe.

By taking a hard line, McMahon was attacking another weakness of the NFL, much like he did with player celebrations. Len Pasquarelli noted that in doing research for the joint Turner/NBC league, the studies discovered that the biggest turn-offs of the NFL to the average fan were skyrocketing salaires, teams threatening to relocate, and players constantly getting busted by the law. The XFL took care of all three of these with uniform salary structures, league-owned teams and heavy consequences for negatrive off-field incidents.

Biggest complaints
① Salaries
② Teams threat to leave
③ Player conduct

No problem w/ XFL

The other issue is that the XFL didn't compete with the NFL for players, as the USFL and WFL did. The XFL allowed players at any time to leave the league if they had a contract waiting in the NFL; this occurred a few times during XFL team training camps. Obviously, since the pay structure for the XFL was much lower than the NFL's, they really couldn't even if they wanted to (though they could change the pay structure). But that also prevented the league from going bankrupt by trying to lure NFL stars. The closest the XFL came to dipping into the NFL talent pool was when they attempted to recruit big name college players who fell to the later rounds of the 2000 NFL draft. One name that was made public was Joe Hamilton, drafted by the Tampa Bay Buccaneers. Hamilton was an exciting college player for Georgia Tech who set all kinds of conference records and finished second in the Heisman Trophy voting in 1999. However, due to height issues, he fell to the 7th round, where he was drafted by Tampa Bay in 2000. According to Len Pasquarelli of Sportsline.com, the XFL's Mike Keller met with Hamilton's agent on the morning of May 2, 2000, in order to try to sell Hamilton and his agent on the league. While he would've taken a hit in pay, he also would've played right away in the XFL. Keller told Sportsline, "Whether or not Joe Hamilton ever plays in the NFL probably doesn't make a great deal of difference in that league's big picture. But I'll bet it makes a great deal of difference to Joe Hamilton, because he's a competitor." Clearly, Keller was appealing to Hamilton's competitive side and while his agent said all the right things about the possibility of his client going to the XFL (perhaps to try to get some more money out of the Buccaneers), Hamilton ended up choosing the NFL, but only ever played a handful of snaps in the league. He also spent time in the AFL and NFL Europe. It was the first public attempt at the XFL trying to make a splash and legitimize themselves as a real football league.

The XFL may not have competed outright with the NFL for players, but they did compete with other leagues. Like McMahon did when he took pro wrestling national, scooping up wrestlers from just about every regional promotion thereby weakening their talent roster, the XFL scoured the Arena leagues and CFL for players as well. The Arena

League season ran from April until July, so there was not really overlap with the XFL season. The CFL runs from June through November, so players, if they so choose, could play for both leagues, unrestrained. In fact, a few players did, with OL Jerry Crafts and WR Kevin Swayne famously playing non-stop, with Swayne playing 52 weeks in a row from the XFL, to the AFL then on to the NFL all in one year. Still, this didn't get in the way of bad blood developing between both the AFL and CFL and the XFL.

[handwritten margin note: Swayne no restrictn on one league]

The XFL held a supplemental draft not long after their initial player draft, to secure players who were released from their CFL contracts. They almost held another one just before the start of the league season, as CFL "free agency" didn't begin until February 15th, almost two weeks after the start of the XFL season, but that idea was subsequently scrapped. If they had held the second draft, increasing roster sizes for each team was considered. Mike Keller noted at the time that some CFL clubs were purposely not releasing the best players from their contracts to avoid allowing them to join the XFL. QB Keith Smith, drafted by the LA Xtreme, failed in an attempt to sue to be freed from his CFL contract to play for the XFL. The CFL teams who wouldn't let their players loose to play for the XFL were even barred from pre-season training camp for the new league, while other CFL teams that allowed their players the freedom to play were given access. Other teams had limited access.

But that was nothing compared to the problems the XFL had to deal with concerning the AFL. The AFL's collective bargaining agreement allowed players to play for multiple leagues. And yet, the AFL went to court to get a temporary restraining order to stop WR Calvin Schexnayder from playing in the XFL, saying he breached contract by going to the XFL without their consent. This was the most extreme case of the AFL leveraging themselves against the XFL. "Shakes," as Calvin was nicknamed, played only two games in the XFL as a result. Because of similar salaries and the stability of the league, many players opted to stay in the AFL, though it was reported that 410 AFL players were sent contracts by the XFL.

The XFL wanted to leave no stone unturned in its search for players. In fact, long-shot players trying to hook on with the upstart XFL allowed the league to grab some early headlines in small-town newspapers. At first, players with name value seemed hesitant to join a league run by a professional wrestling czar. They no doubt read the wild media speculation as to what the league would be about but soon came to realize that this was going to be real football. The league held tryouts across the country, and even had prospective players fill out applications to the league on the official website. Over 50,00 applied via the website, including a top Canadian college player, Fabian Rayne; and a woman, kicker Kathy Clope-Warren (a walk-on kicker at Louisville who held a soccer scholarship there). There are always tons of talented players left on the outside looking in every football season who for one reason or another, don't want to go up north to Canada to continuing playing or stay here in the states and play in the shoebox that is the Arena League. Finding talented football players is an imperfect science; in fact, two examples are the Pittsburgh Steelers, the defending Super Bowl Champions, who had five players in their starting lineup come aboard as undrafted free agents. Tom Brady, one of the greatest quarterbacks of this generation and a sure-fire Hall-of-Famer, wasn't drafted until the sixth round. WR Antonio Bryant, who had a break-out 2008 campaign for the Tampa Bay Bucaneers and was fourth in the NFC in receptions, didn't even play in 2007 because no team wanted him. So sometimes, scouts get it wrong and those playing in the NFL are not always "the best." There are guys just as good out there who could fill out the bottom of an NFL roster or even contribute significantly, and that's the kind of player the XFL was looking to accomodate. In fact, the following names were among those still unsigned as of June for the 2009 NFL Season: QB Rex Grossman, RB Warrick Dunn, RB Deuce McAllister, TE Bubba Franks, WR Marvin Harrison, WR Marty Booker, G Pete Kendall, DE Jason Taylor, CB Ken Lucas and S Roy Williams. Those are just a few of the big names still available. Most of the players listed above were salary cuts; they were just making too much money and at some levels, its cheaper to bring in rookies to do the job. Hundreds of players are salary cuts each

[handwritten margin note: League Tryouts]

season, as they make too much as veterans to latch on with another team. Ray Lewis, one of the greatest linebackers of all-time and coming off playing 16 games in 2008 and making 117 tackles, 3.5 sacks and three interceptions, re-signed with the Baltimore Ravens for 2009. Why? Because no other team showed interest in him in the free-agent market. Most likely because he's 34, but he showed he can still play. His high salary expectations and age is what kept teams away, and this happens to guys every year on the outside looking in. And their careers end with a whimper. The XFL would give these guys, many who still have gas left in the tank, a place to enjoy their final seasons without worrying about having too big of a contract for the team.

Bill Baker, the XFL Director of Player Personnel, wrote in the XFL game-day programs that players applied of all different experience levels, from former first-round NFL draft picks to those who had never even played competitively. He said the received 4,000 videotape submissions as well, some that didn't even specifiy a jersey number so they had no idea who to look for. Baker noted the decision of wanting each team to carry 70 players in camp, which alloted for 560 spots total. He said that they inivted 3,000 players to tryouts, taking the first 1,000 that responded. They had to discard 1,500 who responded too late. Tryouts took place in September and October and 400 players were selected to take part in the draft. Among the hundreds available in the draft, 14 were former NFL first-round picks.

The fact that there are many good, unemployed football players still out there leaves one to wonder what the XFL was thinking when, late in the first season of play, the New York Times reported that the XFL was considering allowing players to join the league out of high-school. This provision would provide for athletes who couldn't make the grades for college. Players wouldn't be able to join straight out of high-school; the minimum age would've been set at 19 years of age or one year after his high-school class would graduate. I think it's great that the league was considering giving those with talent who for whatever reason couldn't play at the collegiate level a chance. Of course, you have to weigh that against how likely the talent would be of being polished and ready to play against guys who, in some cases, have years of experience in the NFL. I suppose that would be weeded out when teams decide to bring in or not to bring in these young players. It wouldn't surprise me if the number of teams taking advantage of these players was quite low.

When the first XFL P.A.S.S (player allocation and selection system), or draft, took place on October 28, 2000, I admit that I played up an illness that day to get out of school and to follow the draft online. Territorial selections (up to 11 per team) were also made from three selected area colleges (the league decided on three schools after debating on as many as seven and as few as one), in order to make sure at least some players had ties to the city and to hopefully draw fans, since the history of the franchises couldn't draw because they were all expansion teams. Baker insisted that it was a difficult process deciding which schools to align with which teams, as they didn't want to be unfair and make players from too many powerhouse colleges available to only certain teams. Fifty-nine to sixty players were selected over three days in the XFL draft, while as many as 11 were secured via territorial selections and up to ten players per team were taken in the supplemental draft.

The great thing about leagues like this is the stories you get, players shooting for one more shot at glory. Some were profiled on XFL broadcasts, such as WR Jermaine Copeland working as a janitor at his former college before the XFL came calling; WR Anthony DiCosmo, who was one of more than 65 foster children taken in by Petrina DiCosmo and later was adopted by her; and K Jose Cortez working as a roofer while he actually received the call. TE Tyji Armstrong was drafted by the Enforcers and he'd be playing his home games back at Soldier Field, the same place where his mother died of a heart attack while watching her son in play in his rookie NFL season in 1992. LB Shawn Stuckey was an exotic dancer; TE Tremayne Allen a real-estate agent; TE Frank Leatherwood a construction worker; CB Donnell Day a security guard. America likes underdogs and these stories were really cool, seeing players leave their "real life" behind to chase their dream of playing professional football. RB Ryan Christopherson, a former NFL player, had taken a sales job with a major office services company and left behind an $80,000 a year salary to play football again. Outlaws WR Cedric Tillman, a former NFL player, was substitute teaching when he joined the league. WR Brian Roberson loved the game so much he played in the Indoor Football League, a basement-low level league and was paid $200 per game. Birmingham TE Alex Hass thought his career was over when he was cut by the St. Louis Rams in NFL training camp, but then signed up with the XFL to continue living his dream of playing pro football. DT Emile Palmer sent a five-foot tall red "E" to XFL's offices to get noticed by the league. S John Fisher was the stunt-double for Jamie Foxx in the football movie, "Any Given Sunday." NFL veterans like WR Alvin Harper and LB Kurt Gouviea, deemed too old by NFL standards, still had the competitive juices flowing and wanted to continue their football journey. Others, like QB Tim Lester of Western Michigan college, were prolific college players who never got the chance to stick in the NFL. Lester sent 17 passing records at the college but didn't get much of a sniff from the NFL. RB Brian Shay won the Division II equivalent of the Heisman Trophy (top player in the nation) but couldn't stick in the NFL due to his size (5'8"). Hitmen QB Corte McGuffey was a finalist for the Rhodes Scholarship at Northern Colordao, which gives students a chance to study at the presitgious Oxford University in England. These types of players found a home in the XFL.

Not only did you get great stories, but you got players who were able to express themselves. The NFL values its acronym and brand over any team and player. Likewise, they value the team over individual players. The league would rather have fans attached to franchises rather than the players themselves. This was especially key when free agency was instituted, and you didn't have players spending their entire career with one team. Teams wanted fans to cherish the franchise over the player so when that player that the fans loved for ten years decided to go elsewhere, they wouldn't follow the player and become a fan of THAT team, costing the original team money from merchandising and possibly ticket sales. In their ideal world, the players change but the fans support the TEAM. That's the leaguethink I mentioned in the previous chapter, on a smaller scale. The league doesn't market players so much as it markets teams. In the XFL, players and their personalities had to sell the tickets and get fans to tune in, because there was no fanbase already in place for the teams. Even if that wasn't a factor though, the XFL touted its player-friendly atmosphere and allowed athletes to express themselves like never before. We got up close and personal with players on the field both visually and auditorily, thanks to cameras and mics on the field and players. The players could be identified by the nicknames on the back of their jerseys (a last-minute decision by the XFL braintrust) and were allowed to celebrate. The "No Fun League," the handle given to the NFL due to its stringent penalties and fines for celebrations or acts of individualism, wouldn't let players show their emotions on the field. Some would argue that's a good thing and that by celebrating after TDs and dancing after sacks, you're disrespecting the game. I think anytime players enjoy the game so much as to make it their own and make their own mark on it, there's no higher respect given than that. But I can understand why some wouldn't like it. In the end, the question of "what harm does it really do?" could be asked. The XFL was for the FANS, and a great many fans, especially young ones (which it doesn't hurt to cater to when you're on national television, hoping to hook big-dollar advertisers) enjoy the antics of their favorite players, which is why guys like Terrell Owens and Chad "Ocho Cinco" Johnson are so popular. The players were allowed to be themselves without worrying about Big Brother looking over their shoulder.

As mentioned earlier in the chapter, the level of players who applied and were selected to play in the XFL gave the league a much-needed shot in the arm of credibility. Even before that though, the coaches who came on board had coaching backgrounds that ranged from College to the NFL to other professional leagues. Most of the front office heads were poached from the CFL, but they were turned down by at least one personnel man from north of the border, Hamilton Tiger-Cats personnel consultant Mike McCarthy (not the same McCarthy who now coaches the Green Bay Packers), who was offered a spot in the league in a comparable position. The coaches weren't the caliber of those recently selected to play in the United Football League (familiar names like Jim Haslett, Jim Fassell and Ted Cottrell), but they were selected from a combination of veteran and up-and-coming coaching candidates. They specifically scoured the ranks for African-American coaches who may have been disenfranchised with the NFL's lack of minority hiring. Coaches made between $150,000 and $200,000 for the one season. The NFL Coaches Association even offered to help the XFL out with their coaching search. Ironically, the first coach the XFL hired never even coached one game for the team. Dick Butkus was named head coach of the Chicago Enforcers squad on July 19th, no doubt as a way for the XFL to garner some extra press. It was no doubt on the top of the XFL's list to get Butkus involved, as Valdiserri approached Butkus with the offer to join the team in any capacity, from color commentator to head coach. Butkus certainly signified everything the XFL wanted to be. There were rumors that other big names, such as Buddy Ryan, Mike Ditka or Jim McMahon, all with ties to the city, could end up coaching the team, but none came to fruition. According to the Chicago Tribune, he was expected to try to coax former Bear Dan Hampton into joining his coaching staff. Interestingly, Hampton served as the NBC alternate game color commentator for the final week of the regular season.

Since Butkus had never coached at the pro level, they decided later to give him a Front Office position as Director of Competition, where he would represent the XFL at training camps and games as well as make sure everything was dont to ensure fairness of play. This allowed Butkus to still be a visible figure and face of the XFL without representing a certain team or having the pressure of producing results as a coach. The XFL hired Ron Meyer to coach Chicago on October 18. Meyer came from the TV studio, having worked for the now-defunct CNN/SI network since 1992. He still had coaching in his blood though and like so many before him in the NFL, he answered the call when the XFL came for him. Meyer had previous head coaching experience in the NFL with the New England Patriots and Indianapolis Colts from 1982-1984 and 1986-1991. He was the only head coach hired with NFL head coaching experience and was a former AFC Coach of the

Year. Enforcers player Tim Lester said he learned about how to coach in part from Meyer. "Wanting to someday be a coach myself, I tried to take full advantage of his experience. I think that he genuinely cared for us and our team success. I can see how he has had so much success in his coaching career." Among his assistant coaches were former Eastern Michigan defensive coordinator Tony Lombardi (defensive backs coach) and legendary Illinois high-school coach Bob Lombardi (assistant coach). Meyer has since returned to his broadcasting roots, working for The Score in Canada.

Gerry DiNardo was hired next, on July 31st, and he was given the option of coaching the Birmingham, New York or Memphis teams. He chose Birmingham. DiNardo had been the head coach of Vanderbilt University (1991-94) and NCAA powerhouse Louisiana State (1995-99). He led the Tigers to three consecutive post-season bowl games. Interestingly, one name bandied about in the local media that was in the running to coach the Birmingham franchise was Gene Stallings. Stallings was a legendary college coach in the state, having coached Alabama from 1990-96. DiNardo's assistants had loads of experience: Offensive Coordinator Dave Arslanian had been a college head coach for 11 years (Weber State and Utah State); brother Paul Arslanian had been coach for 25 years and was d-coordinator for San Jose State; running backs coach Lionel James had coached in the same position at one time for the Kansas City Chiefs; co-defensive coordinator Curley Hallman had been a head coach at LSU and Southern Miss; and Rick Rhoades, with 30 years of coaching tenure on his record. As for DiNardo, he went back to the college ranks after the XFL, and coached the University of Indiana from 2002-04. He now works as an analyst for the Big Ten Network.

On August 8, 34-year coaching veteran Galen Hall was named the head coach of the Orlando Rage. Rumors swirled that perhaps Jay Gruden (brother of NFL coach Jon Gruden), or former NFL head coaches Joe Bugel or Ted Marchibroda would lead the Rage. The reserve, rotund Hall, a longtime assistant at the University of Oklahoma, also was head coach in the Arena Football League, NFL Europe, and in the NCAA for the Florida Gators (1984-89). At the time of his hiring, he had just led the Rhein Fire to their second World Bowl Championship and fourth appearance under his guidance. Both of Hall's coordinators were head coaches in college—Charlie Bailey (defense) at UTEP and Mike Kelly (offense) at Valdosta State. Hall surrounded himself with coaches he had previously worked with in NFL Europe. He also bought aboard coaches from the Arena League. Hall is now Offensive Coordinator under Joe Paterno at Penn State University.

Another NFL Europe veteran was hired to lead the Las Vegas franchise. Jim Criner, the elder statesmen of head coaches at 60 when he was hired on August 11 (along with GM Bob Ackles and Director of Player Personnel Don Gregory), piloted the team Hall's Fire beat in the 2000 NFL Europe Championship game, the Scottish Claymores. He led that team for six years and prior to that had coached at Iowa State and Boise State. Criner's calm demeanor and fatherly touch hardly fit the profile of what was expected of XFL coaches. Two first-time coaches were on the Las Vegas staff: Secondary coach Rashid Gayle, and O-Line/TE Coach Mike Rockwood, notable for being the tallest player in Buffalo Bills history (6'11"). Criner also had two of his relatives join him in Vegas: His son Mark (defensive coordintaor) and nephew Scott (receivers coach). The head man in Vegas was described by Kevin Iole, who covered the team for the Las Vegas Review-Journal, as "great to deal with," and "very open and accessible." Criner most recently was a scout for the Kansas City Chiefs in the NFL under a former player of his, Dick Vermeil.

Kippy Brown was the first of two coaches to be plucked directly out of the NFL ranks when he was hired to lead the Memphis franchise on September 18, 2000. He was coaching the Green Bay Packers running backs at the time and had previous expereince in the same position with the New York Jets, Tampa Bay Bucs and Miami Dolphins. Brown fulfilled his duties with the Packers until the NFL season ended. He was also offensive coordinator for Miami from 1998-99. He was also an assistant in the college ranks for Louisville and Tennessee. Memphis was his first head-coaching gig, in the same city where he played college ball for the University of Memphis. Gene Stallings, legendary college football coach at the University of Alabama, also interviewed for the position and former University of Houston coach Kim Helton (who later was hired as Assistant to the Director of Player Personnel and interim QB Coach) was a third person considered along with Brown. Stallings had earlier turned down a chance to coach the Birmingham franchise. Among those who coached alongside Brown in Memphis were his brother Gerald (running backs coach), former Dallas Cowboys assistant Craig Boller (defensive line), and the man who led the Buffalo Bills defense during their Super Bowls (Walt Corey). Kippy Brown returned to the NFL after his stint in Memphis, working as an assistant with the Houston Texans and the Detroit Lions. Brown's hiring was preceded by the July 28th contracting of GM Steve Erhart (a former University of Colorado coach, President of the Colorado Rockies and GM of the CFL Memphis team) and Director of Player Personnel Steve Ortmayer (former VP of Football Operations for the NFL's LA Rams and GM of the San Diego Chargers).

Rusty Tillman spent 16 years coaching in the Seattle Seahawks organization, most notably their Special Teams unit. He also held the defensive coordinator position with Seattle, Tampa Bay and Indianapolis in the mid-to-late 90s. Tillman coached the New York Hitmen and was introduced as their head man on September 28. He was always the bridesmaid, never the bride, having interviewed for head coaching positions in the past, but never having gotten the green light. It was the allure of being a head coach and being in charge that led to him taking a pay cut and joining the XFL ranks. Tillman filled out his coaching staff before mini-camps began and surrounded himself with three other coaches with ties to the Oakland Raiders organization where he once coached. The grandson of the great Vince Lombardi, Joe Lombardi, was also on his staff as running backs coach. Ironically, Vince McMahon encouraged players to date cheerleaders, a no-no in the NFL. But Tillman himself is married to a former Seahawk cheerleader. Tillman went on to work with the Minnesota Vikings special teams in the years following the XFL.

The other two coaches hired by the XFL were Al Luginbill for Los Angeles and Jim Skipper for San Francisco. The Xtreme wanted to find a coach that had experience starting a football team, and Luginbill had just that, having been the first coach of NFL Europe's Amsterdam Admirals (where he was coaching when hired by LA). He also coached in college as head of Pasadena College's squad and was an assistant for Arizona State. The XFL was in the business of finding the next Kurt Warner, and it was partially because of Luginbill that Warner got a chance in the NFL—Luginbill facilitated the Rams signing Warner in 1997 as a favor to him. Luginbill's offensive coordinator Jim Barker was coming off his first season coaching the Toronto Argonauts of the CFL. Others of note were John Gill, L.A's D-line coach who coached in the same capacity the previous four years with the Carolina Panthers; and Al's son Tom, who now works for ESPN as a college football recruiting analyst. In 2003, Al Luginbill made his first foray into the AFL, and coached the Detroit Fury.

The no-nonsense Skipper (in which one Demon player referred to his camp as military-like) had 26 years of coaching experience under his belt when the XFL came calling on September 28th, and he was slated to be either coach of Memphis or San Jose (later San Francisco). He was brought aboard from his position as assistant head coach and running backs coach of the New York Giants. In 1997 and 98, he served as their offensive coordinator. Skipper spent 10 years coaching the running backs for the New Orleans Saints and also coached in the USFL and college ranks. Before hitching his wagon to the XFL's star, the only other time he had been head coach was of Duarte (CA.) High School's JV Team in 1973. He came to the XFL because he had two characteristics working against him as far as getting an NFL head coaching job: One, he was older (52), and many teams were opting for younger and younger coaches; and two, he was African-American, and it's been well-documented how the NFL hasn't historically given head coaching opportunities to African-Americans. Two of Skipper's assistants had experience coaching in the NFL with the San Francisco 49ers. Keith Millard, his defensive line coach with the Demons, manned the same post for the Oakland Raiders and Denver Broncos after the XFL. Unfortunately for Skipper, he left the Giants at the wrong time: They won the Super Bowl in 2001, the same year he led the Demons to the XFL Championship Game. However, he landed on his feet in the

NFL and currently is the assistant head coach to John Fox in Carolina and also coaches their running backs.

These coaches, like the players, added legitimacy to the XFL. While casual fans may not have recognized the names, the XFL was thinking more about the long haul with these hires, and also bringing aboard those with experience in the minor leagues of football. By bringing real football men aboard, the XFL proved they were as serious about their football as the fans were.

real coaches meant
Real football not WWF showbiz

CHAPTER THREE

The XFL made noise in the media based on rules that were different from the NFL. They wanted to be more physical, more "in-your-face." Even something as simple as the football was reinvigorated. Gone was the traditional brown pigskin; the XFL produced a rather plump ball *new ball* that was black and red and looked like an NFL football on steroids. The bump-and-run was allowed by defenders. The NFL once featured *Bump Run* this rule, but in an effort to open up the game and, it was disallowed. The result? More passing yards, higher-scoring games and thus, more eyeballs watching. To even things up for the offense, the XFL adopted *one foot* the college football rule of needing only one foot in-bounds for a catch to be legal. Like in Arena Football, one offensive player was allowed *Man in motion* to be moving forward, outside of the tackles, before the ball was snapped. No in-the-grasp for quarterbacks. The defenders were allowed *in the grasp* to treat the quarterback as an actual player rather than playing touch-football with them. The QB would be considered down if they slid, just like in the NFL, so there was some protection. Special Teams became more interesting, as the XFL eliminated the most boring play *Xtra point* in football, the extra-point. The offense had to go for a one-point conversion, much like teams go for two-point conversions in the NFL. They got to go from the two yard-line and if they fumbled or threw an interception, the defense could return it for one point of their own.

Also, no fair catches on punts. Of course, the dirty little secret the XFL didn't bother to tell the fans was the five-yard halo the returners were allowed, thus preventing the very thing fans were licking their lips for with this rule: the big hit. The NFL has only a two-yard halo because of the fair-catch allowance. Also, the punting team had to wait until the ball was kicked to release from the line of scrimmage, meaning the returner had more time to return the ball. The punting game had other rules as well. No punts out of bounds, as there would be a ten-yard penalty. The coffin corner punt wouldn't be utilized, as punts that went out of bounds inside the 20 yard-line would end up on the 30. Players were allowed to celebrate sacks and touchdowns and taunt the opposing team; in fact, this was encouraged. Any punt after 25 yards became live, so the returner (or someone on that team) HAD to reel it in. They could express themselves with nicknames on the back of their jerseys instead of just their last name. These advances went along with McMahon's mantra of wanting to make the players be seen as individuals and also to allow them to express themselves.

In overtime, the XFL took a page out of the college book, as no games could end in a tie. Each team got the ball at least once, and had four downs to score from their opponent's 20 yard line. If the first team scores, taking only two downs for example, the second team most follow suit and score in two downs or less. If they do, it would start all over again and it would continue until there was a winner. It made the overtime period more exciting than just simply a fifth quarter of football. Also, it gave both teams a crack on offense instead of the luck of the coin toss giving one team the ball and the better odds of scoring and winning the game, as in the NFL.

The league wanted to make the game fan-friendly, and planned to mic players and coaches, take the camera inside the locker room at halftime and also feature cameras on the field (called "Bubba Cams") and on players' helmets. This wasn't a totally unique idea: The NBA mic'd the benches during the All-Star Game and NFL Europe placed cameras on the officials during the World Bowl, their championship game. NFL Films has always mic'd sidelines and players. The difference is that these weren't broadcast during the game; only used on the Internet

[handwritten: Fans on TV could hear live mics]

or at a later date. Unlike the NFL, where coach-to-QB communications are turned off before the play on the field is run, the XFL didn't put any time limit on the communication; theoretically, the offensive coordinator could speak to the QB DURING the play—and fans at home could hear it. The week of the first games, the XFL came up with the scramble for the ball in lieu of the traditional coin-toss. Two players, one from each team, would dash 20 yards and whoever got possession of the ball would be equivalent to winning the coin-toss. The fan-friendliness reached out to the time of games, which often exceed three hours in the NFL. To speed up games (and also accomodate TV time), the XFL limited halftime to 10 minutes and the play clock to 35 seconds instead of 40 (25 seconds if there is no time stoppage after the play).

[handwritten: opening scramble]

[handwritten: Quicken game]

The XFL wanted to make the in-stadium experience second-to-none for the fan. Each stadium was equipped with a 25 x 50 foot video board, which, according to league officials, would be as clear as any TV screen. Every game would have 13 cameras and microphones on 16 players and/or coaches that would be available to hear over the loudspeakers. The league even planned to put mikes on the field to allow fans to hear the players racing down the sidelines. XFL President Basil DeVito said the goal for the fans live is to not know when the game is on a commercial break and to keep them occupied and entertained for the entire time they are in the stadium. They also planned to make tailgating a part of the league, providing music and festivities in the parking lots prior to games.

[handwritten: In stadium]

Another way in which the XFL wanted to make the game more fan-friendly is for tickets to be reasonably priced. The San Francisco Demons, for example, offered season ticket packages that were under $100. Two area NFL teams, the San Francisco 49ers and Oakland Raiders, sold season tickets that were more than four times that price. The average single-game ticket was more than 50% cheaper than their NFL counterparts. Seats on the 50 yard-line could be had for only $26. Not only that, but one fan on XFLBoard.com compared ticket prices from the Arena League and the XFL: Two tickets in the XFL cost him $40; two tickets at an AFL game were $105. Jerseys were $40 more expensive, and of the same quality. In all, he bought the same stuff at each game, concessions and everything, and spent $70 for two people at an XFL game, and $158 for two at an AFL game. In hindsight, the XFL should've pushed harder how fan-friendly they were compared to other leagues.

The Demons held a "Possess your seat day" during training camp in an effort to sell tickets and allow fans to watch practice. On that day, they drew about 6,000 people and sold 1,700 season ticket packages. While the XFL's goal was 6,000-7,500 season tickets sold per team, the Demons sold a reported 25,000 plus (even though the XFL wanted to keep season ticket numbers under wraps). The Las Vegas Outlaws, as of the first week in January, had sold about 5,000 season tickets. The week before the first game of the season, they sat at 8,000. Tickets flew off the proverbial shelves in Orlando, where the phone systems used to answer calls for season tickets crashed the first day they went on sale. Memphis was about middle-of-the-pack with a month to go before the first game. In Birmingham, five percent of season ticket sales were to out-of-towners as of early December, from as far away as Florida and South Carolina. They were lagging a bit behind though, with only 1,500 sold around that time. By early January though, the tickets started to sell a little faster and they reached about 2,800 at that time (coinciding with the signing of local star Jay Barker). Orlando had sold 5,000 season packages by mid-December (including one to a fan in London). Teams ramped up advertising for ticket sales in many cities as the first game drew nearer.

Another, small way that the XFL killed two birds with one stone was having the players travel from game-to-game in commercial, rather than charter, flights. This cut down on costs for the league, which spent a ton to upgrade stadiums and install the video boards and other gadgetry they planned to use. Plus, it made the players seem approachable to the general public who rode the flights along with them. You could converse with players and get their autographs and in general, have a positive experience. Word-of-mouth would then hopefully draw more fans to the product.

A good sign, no doubt, in one of the areas XFL officials must have been monitoring, that being attendance. The other would've been TV ratings. In my book (which this is), those two would be the biggest signs of how successful/unsuccesful the league would be. Putting butts in the seats and eyes in front of the TV give you a solid number of how many people are actually interested in the game. Of course, the XFL used a tried-and-true pro wrestling move to ensure the crowds looked good on TV regardless of how many people were in the stands: Tickets were cheaper opposite the "hard camera," or the main camera used for the action. That way, ideally, those seats would fill up faster and would make the place look packed. Unfortunately, one set of numbers was much, much more important than the other, and is one of the reasons the league ended up folding. But more on that later.

WWE continued to plug the XFL on its broadcasts, finding any way to get the name and the brand in the public's eye. WWE was garnering some of the highest ratings on cable TV, so many people were apt to see and hear about the new league. XFL ads starting running in about October, but they had been showing videos to that point of milestones in the league's history. They covered press conferences where team names were announced, when Dick Butkus was named head coach, and basically anything big they felt fans needed to know. In October, they also aired clips of the cheerleader tryouts, with announcer Jerry "The King" Lawler attending as a sort-of talent scout. Lalwer's affinity for young women was well-known by fans, so it certainly fit into his character. Cheerleader tryouts didn't get much coverage in the media, despite their more hyped-up presence in the XFL than other leagues. Las Vegas Weekly covered the Outlaws cheerleader tryouts, where 70 women showed up for 10 spots. Getting the chance to "shake it" on national television will draw those kinds of crowds. One young lady was a former Raider cheerleader, so they had experience. Judges ranged from the legitimate (assistant choreographer, a former 49er cheerleader) to the gimmicky (Lawler, who said they were looking for women who convey the "WWF Attitude," and a former UNLV baseballer who at the time played for the Montreal Expos). I guess they'd know what the males would be looking for in a cheerleader.

With coaches, teams and schedules set, there was but one rather large task left. Finding players to fill the teams. Teams would take 70 players to camp and hold 38 on the active roster during the season, with a seven-player practice squad (who couldn't even attend games). But finding players was perhaps the biggest test for the league, as the players chosen would set the tone for how seriously the league would be taken. If the players were of a high-school caliber, it would be a disaster. If the level was clearly professional, they had a chance. Nothing was more important than getting players who could dissuade people from the notion that the action would be "minor-league" or, worse, "scripted." But one thing that most media types and nay-sayers didn't take into consideration was that the front offices of the teams were staffed by people with extensive football backgrounds who knew what good players looked like. Among the notable players that were, at one time or another, linked with the league in terms of signing contracts but never actually were drafted or played, were QB's Dave Krieg, Jeff Hostetler, Bobby Hebert, Clint Stoerner and Billy Joe Tolliver, RB's James Stewart and Byron Hanspard, DE Chris Mims, WR Anthony Miller and CB Mark McMillian.

The XFL conducted combines, with the first official gathering of players on September 9th, then whittled things down and offered contracts to players. QB Tim Lester was offered a contract by the league after not hooking on with an NFL team after the college draft in April. He said he attended a combine in Chicago that others under contract participated in, so teams could get a look. He didn't participate until a legend asked him to. "During the final skills portion, Dick Butkis and another Chicago Enforcer executive asked me if I would throw for them. When Dick Butkis asks you to throw, YOU THROW. I went out there in tennis shoes and participated in the last 20 minutes or so of the combine." Those players eligible for the draft (likely between 600-700 players) were available to be worked out by individual teams at their own combines, under their coaching staff's eyes. At one point there was scheduled to be two supplemental drafts, one for players leaving the CFL and one for players available following the NFL season. They ended up having only one. Since each team could protect up to 11 territorial selections from three schools, those were players some teams focused on. Teams could make 15 protections throughout the season. This is something the AAFL (All-American Football League) picked up on in preparing their league for play in 2007. They held a draft, but have yet to play a down. According to the Las Vegas Review Journal, among those territorial possibilities the Outlaws worked out were DB's Toby Wright and Jamel Williams, OL Evan Pilgrim, Lonnie Palelei and Eric Bateman, LB Julius Jackson, and WR's Todd Floyd and Damon Williams. All but Pilgrim and Williams ended up with the team at some point.

The Orlando Rage had 60 players in for a free-agent tryout camp in mid-September, by invitation only. It was clear things were getting more serious and the ranks of players being looked at was thinning. Most of the drills the Rage conducted were very similar to the ones currently administered at the NFL Combine for NFL draft-eligible athletes. Oh, and the Rage hosted the camp in the middle of Hurricane Gordon, which was pelting Florida with wind and rain. Extreme weather conditions for an extreme league, I suppose. Los Angeles brought in some big names to Long Beach City College on September 28th to have a look at. Former NFL 1st round picks QB Tommy Maddox and WR Thomas Lewis were there, as was QB Steve Sarkisian, now head coach at the University of Washington. They were scheduled to have a work-out with another former 1st rounder, RB Rashaan Salaam, who would later go on to play for the Memphis Maniax.

The XFL Player Allocation and Selection System, or, P.A.S.S (the XFL's fancy way of saying "draft") was conducted in Chicago on October 28, 29 and 30, with the first ten rounds on day one and 15 on day two and the final 34 on day three. The league didn't pre-release the names of anyone available in the draft. Everything was done quite offically, as the Illinois Lottery Commission even held the random lottery to determine the order of selection. No television for this draft; however, they did update the selections on the XFL.com website. Bill Baker said they conducted a league meeting prior to the draft, with all the teams' representatives gathering for the first time: "quite a moral-booster," he said. Vince McMahon spoke at the meeting to everyone, then they broke out into individual groups to discuss marketing, talent, business, coaching and all different aspects of the league. The draft began on the last day of the meetings.

The LA Xtreme held the first overall draft pick, and selected a QB, but not one with a long NFL history. In fact, he almost didn't even sign with the XFL. Scott Milanovich, who wasn't drafted by an NFL team out of college, went number one overall. He had been in camps with the Cleveland Browns and Tampa Bay Buccaneers. Because the birth of his child was supposed to take place in February, Milanovich almost passed on the chance to play in the league in order to ensure he wouldn't miss the birth. Milanovich also spent time in NFL Europe, so Xtreme Coach Al Luginbill was no doubt familiar with him. Speaking of Luginbill, the Xtreme also drafted eight players who had experience playing under Luginbill in NFL Europe. Of their 60 picks, 30 finished the season on the Xtreme roster. They immediately had a QB controversy heading into training camp, as Tommy Maddox was protected via territorial selection.

The Birmingham Thunderbolts held the number two pick. They too went with a quarterback, Casey Weldon. The Florida State product was a runner-up for the Heisman Trophy in 1991. He bounced around the NFL with several teams, but was out of football in 2000 when the Bolts came calling. Among their other draft picks were former Dallas Cowboy WR Stepfret Williams, the NCAA's leading rusher in 1995 and 1996, RB Troy Davis (who went in round 28), and seven-year NFL veteran LB James Willis, who was a territorial selection. Birmingham had 59 draft picks. 27 ended the year on their roster.

Continuing the QB theme, the Memphis Maniax took Marcus Crandell with the third selection. Unlike the previous picks though, Crandell did not have any NFL experience to speak of. But at East Carolina, he set numerous passing records at the college and also led the squad to two bowl games. The Memphis draft was dotted with big names: One was a second rounder, former Buffalo Bill and Green Bay Packer RB Darick Holmes. Holmes had two years of 600+ yards rushing with the Bills. The QB position was addressed later in the draft by the team again, with former first-round NFL pick Jim Druckenmiller. Two more first rounders were taken later: DE Shante Carver (round 23) and RB Rashaan Salaam (round 26). CB Corey Sawyer and FB Roosevelt Potts, veterans of over 130 games in the NFL combined, rounded out some of the bigger names taken by the 'Ax. Super Bowl winning WR Alvin Harper (career numbers: 191 catches, 3,473 yards, 21 TDs), another NFL first-rounder, was protected in the territorial selection phase. 29 of 59 players drafted stuck through the end of the season.

The Orlando Rage went back to the QB well with the fourth pick, taking Jeff Brohm. A veteran of six NFL seasons, Brohm was taken after the Rage had narrowed their first-round options down to Brohm or Weldon, according to the Orlando Sentinel. When Weldon was taken two picks earlier, the decision was made. Despite drafting a QB with their first pick, a week after the draft, it was made public that Hall was pursuing CFL QB Kerwin Bell, who had played under Hall at the University of Florida. The deal never came to fruition and Bell stayed in the CFL due to fear of injury and the fact that he could make more money in the CFL. Five of the picks on the first day had played for head coach Galen Hall at one time or another. Hall also made four of the next eight picks linemen. All ten picks had experience at the very least in NFL training camps. Even more impressive, eight of the top ten selections for the Rage finished the season on the team, with the number being 33 out of 59.

The Las Vegas Outlaws held the fifth pick, and they took QB Chuck Clements. Clements played for Bill Parcells with the New York Jets in the NFL. Of the ten first day picks, head coach Jim Criner told the Las Vegas Review-Journal that he selected seven of the ten players they had targeted heading into the draft. The first XFL trade was made before the draft, when the Outlaws sent one of their territorial selections, LB Mike Croel (former first-round NFL pick) to the LA Xtreme for LB Joe Tuipala, one of their territorial protections. Other picks included a former four-year starter for the Oakland Raiders (G Isaac Davis), a player who had drawn interest from the Xtreme as well as the Outlaws in pre-draft workouts (G Pat Kesi), a player who held many NCAA track records and was an alternate in the 400-meter relay at the 2000

Olympic Games (WR Corey Nelson) and a former first-round pick of the Washington Redskins (DE Kelvin Kinney). The Outlaws focused on skill position players on day three of the draft after picking only one QB and two RB's on the first two days. Of the 59 draft picks, 27 were on the final roster.

It took six picks for a team to break from the run on QB's, and the San Francisco Demons did it with first-round NFL pick and RB Vaughan Dunbar. He played four seasons in the NFL with the New Orleans Saints and Jacksonville Jaguars. OL Scott Adams was their second pick, and he had an even more extensive NFL background with seven years in the league. In the 26th round, they took CB Dwayne Harper, who was a nine-year NFL starter and played 12 years in the league. A first-round pick of the Kansas City Chiefs, OT Trezelle Jenkins, was taken in round 20. Overall, 27 of the 59 picks finished the season on the team.

It was back to the QB position when the NY/NJ Hitmen went with Charles Puleri out of New Mexico State. He had seen it all, having been in training camp with the Dallas Cowboys as well as having tours of duty in the AFL, CFL and NFL Europe. The addition of Randall Cunningham to the Cowboys roster is what sent him packing during their training camp. The Hitmen chose the first defensive player in the draft in round two with DT Jermaine Smith. DE Dwayne Sabb, a 5th round pick, played in a Super Bowl with the New England Patriots. Others taken with NFL experience included RB Dino Philyaw (23 games in three seasons), WR Fred Brock (two seasons with the Arizona Cardinals) and LB Jude Waddy (eight NFL starts in two seasons). The Hitmen had what appeared to be a club with the least NFL experience. 31 of their 60 picks stuck with the club the entire year.

The final team to draft, the Chicago Enforcers, went the same route as the Demons, selecting a former first-round NFL RB. They took John Avery, late of the Miami Dolphins and Denver Broncos. Their next pick though was a QB, Paul Failla, who was out coaching a JV football team when Enforcers coach Ron Meyer tried to contact him to tell him he was drafted. Roell Preston, a WR and special teams demon in four NFL years, was taken in the 15th round. Another RB, LeShon Johnson, taken in round 45, and WR Aaron Bailey, selected in the 24th round, were both veterans of five NFL seasons. Their RB depth seemed solid, especially taking into consideration they protected Ray Zellars as a territorial selection, and he was a 16-game starter in the NFL for the New Orleans Saints. The club held on to 29 of the 60 players they drafted.

By the end of the P.A.S.S, each team was equipped with 70 players to head into mini-camp with. Some were too small (like 6'0" Enforcers QB Tim Lester or 5'8" Rage RB Brian Shay), too slow (like Outlaws WR Todd Floyd, who ran a 4.5 40-yard dash at the college combine, dropping his pro draft stock), too old (like 32-year old Rage C Cal Dixon, who had been out of football for three years due to a back injury and was the proud owner of a Dairy Queen franchise; or 34-year old Demons CB Dwayne Harper), from too-small a school (like Hitmen WR Kelvin Stevens, from Division II Shepherd College or Rage TE Terrance Huston, from Butte, a community college), became too expensive (like Outlaws S Brandon Sanders, a four-year NFL vet cut because his minimum salary was $440,000 and was summarily supplanted by a rookie making half as much) or too injury-prone (like Enforcers RB Charles Wiley, who battled knee injuries in college and in the pros and whose only experience was in NFL Europe) to make it in the National Football League. But with all their warts, they got a second chance to show their stuff in a pro football league, one last shot at glory. It was soon time to put on the pads, and nine months into the XFL experiment, finally hit someone.

CHAPTER FOUR

Even during the relative down-time before the camps started up, the media couldn't help but get their facts wrong when reporting on the XFL. An article by John Branch for the Knight-Ridder/Tribune News Service noted that the XFL stood for "Xtreme Football League," when Vince McMahon himself had been adamant that the "X" didn't stand for anything in particular. The same mistake was made by Mike Cobb of the Orlando Ledger and B.G. Brooks of the Rocky Mountain News. It's a little thing, but it just goes to show how little seriousness the media paid to this league. Other personnel and players had to convince their local media types and even family and friends that the XFL would be, as Jesse Ventura would famously say in commercials for the XFL, "real football." Rage RB Brian Shay kept getting pestered with the question from friends, "Is this [league] a joke?" Hitmen coach Rusty Tillman sent a letter to all 70 of his players before mini-camp that attempted to dissuade them from believing the speculation in the media about the XFL being a sideshow attraction. When a coach needs to convince his players of the authenticity of the league, someone is not doing their job. To me, it was the media that deserve most of the blame. From the first press conference on February 3rd, McMahon said it would be real football; no folding chairs, no phoniness, no gimmickry, no scripted action. And yet, the media continued to make jokes instead of even attempting to take the league seriously. GQ Magazine ran a story insinuating the XFL could be a place to drop off criminals who played in the NFL and The New York Times was the outlet where they suggested the XFL could wipe out the idea of sports as we know it. McMahon told the Orlando Sentinel's Jerry Greene in an interview that he felt the print media takes itself and sports in general more seriously than other media outlets, and he acknowledged a need to educate the press on the league and kind of hand-hold them through the process. He went quite easy on them there.

On January 24th, Mark Athitakis wrote a lengthy story called "Inner Demons" for the San Francisco Weekly. In it, he referred to teams as "fiefdoms" owned by the league and wrote "It's Vince McMahon's game. Nobody gets a vote." Well yes, in the sense that McMahon did own the league, but to infer that he didn't confer with his panel of league and team executives is just asinine. Then, in the coup de gras of his article, he speculated that after making a touchdown catch, a player could look into the camera and say, "Fuck you, Vince McMahon. Fuck yo for taking away the last shred of my dignity. Fuck you for taking my ambition and turning it into a laughingstock, a part of your 'sports entertainment' company store. Fuck you for making me your puppet, and fuck me for wearing the strings." And this is before a game is even played in the league! No player was being held in the league against his will. It was FOOTBALL, stupid! Closer to the NFL than many imagined. Saying that Vince would take away the dignity of the players, really? How exactly? By adding rules to make the game more exciting? By actually admitting the league features cheerleaders, instead of stuffing them into one corner of the stadium to be seen by the TV cameras only as a bumper into or out of a commercial break? This whole rant was seemingly precipitated solely on the fact that Vince was a pro wrestling proprietor, nothing more. Players as puppets for Vince? Come on. He also took a shot at salaries in his article, saying it would be adequate for lawyers, but not for guys getting shoved into the ground every week. Keep in mind, this pay was for four months of work. Not bad if you ask me, and a player in the article even says it's more than he'd make in NFL Europe. Yet I didn't see any shots at that league. Perhaps its relationship with the mighty NFL had something to do with it. Or it wasn't owned by a pro wrestling magnate, so it wasn't as easy a target.

November 8th was a historic day, and it really answered the question of how seriously the NFL and its teams would be looking at the XFL for players. The first player from an XFL team was signed by an NFL team as K Jeff Hall, a territorial selection of the Memphis Maniax, signed with the St. Louis Rams to fill-in for the injured Jeff Wilkins. He was released later in the month. Also signed by the Rams was another 'Ax, WR Derrius Blevins. He stuck with the Rams for the entire year along with WR James Kidd, a 50th round pick by the Xtreme, who was signed to the Rams practice squad in mid-November. WR Tony Gaiter, a territorial selection of the Orlando Rage, was signed by the New England Patriots to their practice squad for insurance as WR Dane Looker was placed on injured reserve on November 16th. Gaiter was released to play in the NFL, but his rights were held by the Rage were he to return. During his press conference that day, the master of playing games with the media, Patriots Head Coach Bill Belichick, skirted the question of whether NFL teams would scout the XFL, saying he didn't want to comment about individual teams' relationships with the XFL, or the NFL's relationship with the league for that matter. Gaiter was originally drafted by the Patriots in 1997. He made it back to play for the Rage in the XFL and finished the season on injured reserve. Clearly, the XFL was on the radar of NFL teams.

On November 16th, the XFL made another splash in the area of television presentation. While most teams were just starting up their mini-camps, the XFL announced that Jesse Ventura, Governor of Minnesota and former pro wrestler for WWE, would be doing color commentary for the NBC braodcast. Ventura not only had experience doing color commentary in WWE after his in-ring career is over, but he also served as analyst on Tampa Bay Buccaneers and Minnesota Vikings radio broadcasts in the past. The charismatic politician, who had also dabbled in film and starred along side future California Governor Arnold Schwarzenegger on the silver screen, was just the kind of voice the XFL wanted: Someone not afraid to speak his mind.

That attitude endeared him to Minnesota voters who were tired of getting the same run-around from traditional politicos and who vaulted him from throw-away third-party candidate to shocking winner of the Governors race in 1998. Never before had a sitting Governor ever done color commentary for pro football games but then again, few were ever as qualified as Ventura. At the press conference in Golden Valley, Minnesota, Ventura asked whether he thought he was a role model and whether teaming up with the XFL is consistent with that message he wants to send. Before the first game, some in the media had already made up their minds about the XFL: No one who considers themselves a role model would be affiliated with the XFL, despite not knowing at all what the finished product would be like. Some lawmakers in Minnesota were not happy at the perceived notion that Ventura was promoting the XFL during time he should've been governing. While the games didn't interfere with his job (because they were on Saturdays), he did come under fire for promoting the league after taking vacation time. Some questioned whether the XFL was taking priority for Ventura, though his approval rating was still at 70% in a Minnesota Star-Tribune poll. Ventura did say he wouldn't stick around in the XFL if he thought its content would reflect poorly on him as a Governor. At the same press conference, McMahon said he would forego skits with cheerleaders and players in favor of focusing on football, as the XFL would have enough hurdles to overcome without campy comedy. Yet on the first broadcast, that exact situation happened with an Outlaws cheerleader and QB Ryan Clement. Did McMahon think that, after seeing the action in training camps, that the football wasn't up-to-snuff, so he'd have to dress things up a bit?

A few days later, it was announced that Matt Vasgersian would join Ventura in the booth, with Fred Roggin and Mike Adamle roaming the sidelines on Saturday nights. Vasgersian was just what McMahon looks for in an announcer in WWE: young (Vasgersian was 33 at the time) and good-looking. Vasgersian was encouraged to be critical of players and even his own broadcast partners—anything that was off-limits in the NFL, such as criticizing players or calling them out, was open season in the XFL as McMahon continued his crusade to be everything that he felt the NFL wasn't. One of them, apparently, was "honest." Vasgersian had come from a baseball background, and actually juggled his duties calling games for the Milwaukee Brewers with his XFL commitments, missing only two Brewers games because of XFL obligations. According to NBC Sports President Ken Schanzer, Vasgersian was the first choice of the league and NBC, as Vasgersian's sense of humor, age, and announcing experience all combined to make him the perfect man for the job.

A press release was drawn up on November 29th announcing TNN as the third network and only cable station to broadcast XFL games. Word had leaked earlier that TNN was the likely cable destination of the league. TNN was in the transition face from The Nashville Network, a southern-based station with country music ties, to The National Network, gearing things toward a broader audience of young people. TNN was also broadcasting shows like WWE Monday Night Raw and repeats of Star Trek: The Next Generation. Three of the four games each weekend would be televised as the XFL was clearly going to be visible to all of America on the weekends.

On WWE TV, it was a down period for XFL stuff running. There were the usual ads, and they were finding ways to get the XFL subliminally on the broadcast, such as having the logo on something in the background of a backstage scene. Whenever they could, they had important XFL people in the crowd; when they were in Orlando in July, GM Tom Veit was shown in the front row. On December 4th, Hitmen coach Rusty Tillman and his assistants were at the show and shown on camera. They even brought the cheerleaders of the teams into the ring or backstage for segments on the show. By this point, wrestling fans were tiring of the hype and weren't keen on seeing the league invade WWE's broadcasts to such a degree.

Mini-camps started for most teams around November 14th. For the Chicago Enforcers, theirs was just held for five days with the offensive players, as the full team would come together less than a month later in the second mini-camp. John Avery said during mini-camp that he didn't even care to get paid; he just wanted a billboard of him erected in Chicago. The team obliged, and he ended up having four around the Chicago area by March, bearing his image. Mini-camp wasn't held in a big stadium or at a specially-built practice facility. The Enforcers were at Cornell Park in Chicago, near a softball field and a broadcasting tower. Fans and media were invited to watch the squad take the field for the first time. The team, readying themselves for the harsh Chicago weather in late Winter and early Spring, seemed to have the right mindset to start off the Enforcers brand of football.

The LA Xtreme players got to put on helmets for the first time on day two of their mini-camp, and shoulder-pads weren't to be used until their December full squad mini-camp. Then, mirroring the build-up and anticipation that the league itself has concocted, full pads were to be donne once training camp began in January. Players shuffled on and off the team during this mini-camp, with some players, as with most teams, not reporting to camp, having second thoughts about playing in the league after signing contracts and being drafted. That wasn't a big problem, as there were plenty of players still available to take their place. In addition to offense, the team's coaching staff got their first look at a kicker who would also be their punter. Because of roster limits, teams didn't have enough room to carry both a kicker and a punter, so must would have to pull double-duty. Jose Cortez, who was actually working as a roofer when he was called and told he was drafted (the Special Teams coach for the Xtreme, Chris Allen, told him just to make sure to not fall off the roof) and Brian Moorman, who would go on to be a Pro Bowl punter for the Buffalo Bills in the NFL, would vie for the job for LA. QB's Tommy Maddox and Scott Milanovich also began their battle for the starting job in Offensive Coordinator Jim Barker's high-octane offense.

The Orlando Rage's mini-camp, like others around the league, featured only wide receivers, quarterbacks, running backs, kickers and centers. They were "underwear practices," just a way to get the players familiar with the offense before the rest of the team would join them a month later. Because every team was starting from scratch in implementing a system, the more practice that were available, the better. For the Rage, they were so loaded at the WR position, they were forced to release three players after the November mini-camp. Head Coach Galen Hall singled out WR Kevin Swayne as someone who performed well during their first practice, and Swayne made Hall look like Nostradamus once the season got rolling.

For Las Vegas, speed was the order of the day in their first training session, with WR's Donald Sellers and Randall Lane looking particularly impressive. The size of their running backs also turned heads in camp. Perhaps practicing for cameras on the field during the season, an ABC affiliate's camera got a bit too close to QB Chris Kasteler, and he knocked the camera out of the cameraman's hands on the follow-through of one of his passes.

Kean University in Union, New Jersey, hosted the Hitmen mini-camp. In one of the lighter stories of the league to this point, the fourth day of camp cause a bit of commotion at the college. Four players posing for a Men's Journal magazine spread ended up causing the fire alarms in the locker room to go off when the photographer went a little to far with the fog machine. During practice, Head Coach Rusty Tillman professed the need to be versatile do to the small roster number. That led to RB Malcolm Thomas trying out as a long-snapper. That's something you don't see in the NFL right there. Practicing on the campus of a University could've been a disaster, but the Hitmen players were quite interactive with the student body during their time there. Of course, there were down sides to being in such an open facility. Many amateur footballers came to practices looking for a tryout and player agents also tried to appeal to those Hitmen who weren't represented by one already.

It wasn't all fun-and-games in the first mini-camp. At Pacific Bell Park, where the Demons were holding their mini-camp, TE Richard O'Donnell became the first player to get injured. He tore ligaments in his right thumb as he slipped on the turf. He was able to make it to December's mini-camp and participate there, however.

December mini-camps were another milestone for the league: The first time XFL teams met as a full squad. During the Xtreme's December camp, they brought aboard veteran NFL RB George Jones and LB

Brendon Ayanbadejo. Ayanbadejo is a great example of someone overlooked by the NFL, at least the first time around. Everyone was worried about the quality of players the XFL would have; well, Ayanbadejo failed to make the Xtreme roster, yet since then, he has made the Pro Bowl three times as a special teamer in the NFL. His case is similar to the aforementioned Moorman, a two-time Pro Bowler after failing to latch on with LA. It was already evident, even in the first scrimmage in the second mini-camp, that LA's offense would be dangerous. The offense put four TD's and a field goal on the board despite less-than-stellar weather conditions.

On the first day of December mini-camp, the Birmingham Thunderbolts were greeted by XFL President Basil DeVito at their temporary home, Birmingham-Southern College. Here, it was announced that 50% of TV advertising for the broadcasts had already been sold (going for about $50,000 per 30 second spot—though it was reported by Business Week in January that local ads were harder to come by being offered only one-year deals and advertisers were able to opt out of deals if the play on the field got too violent—yes, the worry was FOOTBALL was going to be too VIOLENT), but advertising stalled with a few days before the premiere, still at a respectable 63%. Yet, Mediaweek ran an article that some advertisers were scared off by comments made by Vince McMahon in various press conferences, including that cheerleaders would be encouraged to date players. McMahon has never been one to mince his words, but he also never had as much mainstream media exposure as he did in the months after the XFL was announced. Unforunately, "treading lightly" was not in Vince's vocabulary, but his words didn't seem to affect buyers all that much. The goal of having one million fans in the seats at the end of the year was 25% accomplished. Positive news for sure, and it must've created an upbeat atmosphere for the players, knowing that the league was heading in the right direction, at least, off the field. Unlike in other camps around the league, there was no QB controversey for the Bolts: Casey Weldon was the clear number one man. Behind him, three signal-callers (Mark Washington from Jackson State and Jon Nielsen of Fresno State, neither with any pro football experience; and Graham

Leigh, a camp arm for the Arizona Cardinals in 1999 who also played in NFL Europe) vied for the second and third-string jobs. Their offense was to employ a vertical passing game, much like the St. Louis Rams in the NFL at the time. In other words: No three yards and a cloud of dust. This was going to be exciting. Just what Dr. McMahon ordered.

The Orlando Rage lost their number one draft pick on the second day of their camp, as QB Jeff Brohm was signed by the Cleveland Browns, after the NFL team had to put their fourth QB on injured reserve. He never did get into a game with them and was only on the active roster for one contest, but he did garner a lot of press for the Rage and the XFL, as he was the first high-profile player to be signed by an NFL squad. It was the first wake-up call to the media that, hey, maybe these guys can play a little football themselves. Brohm wasn't the only player they lost to the NFL; DE Jonathan Brown and OL John Fuegill also signed before Brohm did. Along with the previously mentioned Tony Gaiter, it seemed the Rage players were, pardon the pun, all the "Rage" for NFL clubs. QB Aaron Garcia, a top-five passer all-time in the AFL, was brought aboard during camp to challenge the QB's in Brohm's wake. Director of Football Operations Mike Keller visited Orlando on their fifth day of mini-camp. With DeVito and Keller making the rounds, it was clear the XFL office wanted to keep tabs on how things were going and to make sure there were no problems or issues. The Rage also announced their radio partners for the season, and introduced Marc Lloyd as play-by-play man and former NFL DT Brad Culppeper as color commentator. Interestingly enough, Lloyd would later go on to work commentary for WWE.

The second mini-camp for the Demons was like test week for college students, as the players were in meetings and two-a-day practices, which added up to 12-hour days during the week of December 12th. At least the Demons had their head coach at the helm in December: The Memphis Maniax were without Kippy Brown, who was still honoring his contract as Green Bay Packers running backs coach for the rest of the 2000 season. Mini-camps in November and December were run by assistant head coach Rich McGeorge. Brown did get to address his team during mini-camp in December however, before taking back off for Green Bay.

The big news for the Las Vegas Outlaws occured after their December mini-camp wrapped, and that was the addition of LB Kurt Gouveia to the team. Gouveia was one of the handful of players in the league with no aspirations to make it back to the NFL; at 36 years old, it was more than a long-shot for him to get back in the league, but he was playing simply for the love of the game. Plus, he already had two Super Bowl rings from his 13 years in the league anyway. The Outlaws offense seemed to be geared around big running backs, of which they had several weighing in at over 220 pounds. On December 15th, they added veteran NFL OL Lonnie Palelei, who had played seven seasons in the NFL.

Rusty Tillman continued to field question from the New York media about the legitimacy of the league. In between answering questions about cheerleaders and wrestlers, he did manage to speak about his team, insisting that QB Charles Puleri had a better December mini-camp than the November one and that he expected offensive and defensive linemen to be the most hard to come by in the new league. He noted that the team would be looking for a cornerback who can provide tight coverage in the upcoming Supplemental Draft, and said his offense would have features of the West Coast variety. General Manager Drew Pearson also continued being a vocal supporter of the team, appearing at the team's practices and usually finding his way into the quotebook on the team's website for that day's practice and sometimes getting physically involved in the workouts. Like most football teams, animosity was in the air at times, which happens when teams get tired of hitting the same guys every day. LB Ron Merkerson and C Dustin Owen locked up in one battle during mini-camp, which DE Antonio Anderson credited the battle to the O-Line and their alleged penchant for holding. Could you imagine, two teammates going at it on the sidelines of an NBC telecast during the regular season, cameras and microphones there to catch every breath? McMahon must've been salivating at that idea.

While the teams were practicing for the games, the NFL was playing right into the XFL's hands. During the week of mini-camps, the NFL fined WR Travis McGriff $5,000 for a uniform violation having to do with his socks. They also brought the hammer down on several St. Louis Rams players, who celebrated for a brief time in the end zone, costing them $90,000. Speaking of celebrations, a few Indianapolis Colts decided to celebrate an interception in a key Monday night game. Their pocketbooks became $5,000 lighter after that. No Fun League indeed. John Branch got it right in his column, "Football fun? Not with Tagliabue," published in Knight Ridder newspapers. An excerpt:

"What the XFL will sell is personality, and the NFL should get in line at the register. The reason hardcore NFL fans enjoy those old NFL Films productions is because it takes us back to the days when the league's teams and players had unbridled personality and emotion, when stadiums were cloaked in spray-painted sheets hanging from the second deck.

"Players had nicknames, like Hacksaw, The Stork, Night Train. Teams, or parts of them, had nicknames, like the Steel Curtain, the Hogs, the Purple People Eaters. In today's NFL—sanitized for your protection—it's tough to muster that kind of emotion.

"Football doesn't have to be a circus act. But if the NFL is so hell-bent on adding rules, make one requiring football to be fun and spontaneous. For most of us, it is, after all, just a game."

And that's something McMahon had been preaching from the start: football is not "sacred," that it IS just a game. There is no reason to fine players for celebrating, or wearing their socks too high, or not wearing the right hat in the post-game press conference. It's about FOOTBALL. And more importantly, it's about making football entertaining for fans. The XFL attempted to bring the fans closer to the game in every way, while also letting the players show a little personality. Think of the top personalities in the NFL. Terrell Owens.Chad Ochocinco.Peyton Manning. Not only are they three of the top players in the league, but they are known for their actions on the field that are sometimes frowned upon by the NFL brass. Owens and Ochocinco for their celebrations and fact that they both share giant chips on their shoulders; and Manning for his gesticulations before the snap of the ball, which some in the NFL think takes away from the game. Say goodbye to gamesmanship.

The Supplemental Draft featured those players not available in the first draft, and would continue until each team passed when it was their turn to pick. About 200 players were available for the draft held via conference call on December 29th, and 65 were chosen. Among those available not chosen included RBs Vaughn Hebron, Lincoln Coleman (who hadn't played in the NFL since 1994) and Andre Collins, K Rick Tuten, and DBs Lance Brown and Eric Edwards. Some of the bigger names selected: The Xtreme shored up their offensive line by taking nine-year NFL Derrick Graham and five-year NFL vet Jerry Crafts. The Outlaws, who planned to selected six-to-eight players going in, selected DE Carl Simpson, who played in the NFL for seven years, QB Mike Cawley (who coach Jim Criner hoped would challenge Chuck Clements for the starting job), OT Jon Blackman (who, rumor has it, passed on a deal with the Carolina Panthers for the chance to play—and start—in the XFL; he transitioned from TE in 1998 and turned down a basketball scholarship from Penn State) and K Omar Cardenas (who sent film to the Outlaws from his time in a Mexican semi-pro league), among others. Heading into the draft, they were expected to go heavy on offense, already happy with their defense; and they did. The Demons took ten players, including DE Eric England, with a resume that includes extensive playing time in the NFL and CFL. The Rage took two kickers and two QB's among their picks. One QB, Steve Matthews, had been with three NFL teams and one kicker, Scott Blanton, kicked for the Washington Redskins for two seasons. Only one of the ten Chicago Enforcers picks ended the season on their roster, that being CB Troy Saunders. On the other hand, all three Hitmen picks made the team and played important roles: RB Joe Aska, a former Oakland Raider, was the team's leading rusher. TE Marcus Hinton was their starter at tight end and K Leo Araguz, who holds the NFL record for most punts in a game with 16, did double-duty for the Hitmen all season, handling punts and place-kicks. They didn't find that cover corner they were looking for though. The Bolts' went against the grain and picked players with little NFL experience; in fact, of the eight players they selected, the most familiar to NFL fans would've been Keith Franklin, who participated in two NFL contests. Like most squads, they went in hunting for more offensive linemen; they added two. OT Harry Boatswain was the first pick of the Maniax, a five-year NFL vet. They also chose 37 year-old DB Barry Wilburn, who had a Super Bowl ring from playing with the Washington Redskins. In 1987. Clearly, XFL teams wanted to load up on experience in the Supplemental Draft.

A few days before XFL training camps started, the Bolts fired their Defensive Coordinator Don Lindsey, who Head Coach Gerry DiNardo felt was headed to Ole Miss. He was asked permission by their head coach David Cutcliffe to talk to Lindsey and DiNardo was unhappy Cutcliffe tried to pry Lindsey away from him just four days before camp opened. Curley Hallman and Don Wnek, two coaches already on staff, served as co-defensive coordinators for the season. Wnek oversaw schemes and alignments and coached from the sidelines, and also worked with the line and linebackers. Hallman positioned himself in the press box, and was in charge of coverages and defensive backs. Because of this last-minute change, Birmingham's defense was a work-in-progress throughout training camp. The problems the Bolts faced on defense all year could point back to this situation before training camp.

By the end of December, and with a little over a month to go before the first XFL game, and with two mini-camps in the books, it was time to get one step closer to the night that promised to change professional sports. Hyperbole was always a calling card of Vince McMahon in pro wrestling, and it was evident as well in his formation and development of the XFL. But the professional sports media is a bit different than the pro wrestling media, in that they, like the NFL, can be very serious and stodgy, and are more apt to look closely at what you're presenting than those in the sports entertainment field. Was Vince McMahon ready for that type of criticism from "media elitists" as he referred to them at times? Would the XFL stand up to the questions that were about to be asked with one month to go before the big game? Would shining a light on the league expose its wrinkles, or would it help improve the legitimacy by simply having the media cover it? Like a petulant child, McMahon can often be starved for attention; but like it or not, he was about to get it.

CHAPTER FIVE

With one month to go before the start of the first XFL season and with training camps about to open with the calendar page turning to January, the question became, "is one month enough time to prepare the teams for the season?" Before training camp started, Outlaws coach Jim Criner, when asked what he wants most heading into training camp, responded that he'd like two more days. NFL teams typically start their training camps in late July and get one month to prepare for the season, but the differences is that (a) NFL teams are already established and have many hold-overs from the previous season who don't need to learn new rules or team playbooks, or how to work together as a team, and (b) NFL teams typically play four pre-season games to hone their skills and get ready for the regular season. XFL teams only had loosely-run scrimmages and no real exhibition games. It could be argued that February 3rd, the opening weekend of the XFL schedule and the most important game for the XFL, was really the first "real" game these athletes played in in the league. Some people thought the XFL should've waited another whole year before kicking off, giving teams plenty of time to hone their skills and put on the best football possible. The opening weekend saw some sloppy football, not the kind of play the XFL wanted to showcase to convince viewers that their players weren't that far of a drop-off from NFL players. About 1/3 through the season is when the play began to get up-to-snuff, but by then, they had lost most of their viewers.

Western Conference teams (Las Vegas, Memphis, Los Angeles and San Francisco) held their training camps in teh Vegas area, clustering together to make it easier for teams to have inter-squad scrimmages and dress-rehearsals for the real thing. Eastern Conference teams (Orlando, Chicago, New York and Birmingham) were sequestered in and around Orlando. Most practices were open to the public; of course, there were probably few Enforcer fans in the Orlando area, one of the problems of placing teams in the same area for training camps. At the end of training camp, January 28th to be exact, teams had to trim their roster from the 70 they carried in camp to 45 (first cut-down to 63 was January 14th; down to 55 on January 21st). For many players, that means the last time they'll suit up for a professional football team. The competition for the few spots available was no doubt intense. Most coaches, at least in the media, claimed they were very happy with the competition that existed at each position. Of course, the pre-season is always a time for optimists.

On January 15th, the XFL sent out a press release noting they had signed on with Sandbox to be their exclusive provider of Fantasy Football to its fans. There were 5.4 million users of Sandbox at the time the one-year contract was signed. These days, Sandbox is still operational, but most free fantasy football games are played on Yahoo or Fanball. I participated in one XFL Fantasy Football League. I can't remember exactly how well I did, but I'm assuming most in the league lost interest as the season went along, like everyone in America seemed to.

One day later, the XFL sent out a release officially highlighting rules that differed from those in the NFL and most other football leagues. Most of these had been reported earlier by other news outlets, but this was just another way to get XFL news flowing into the media stream and get it in the hands of newspapers and television stations that haven't report on the XFL to this point. And with less than three weeks until the first game, it was important to keep the league fresh in every fan's mind. The release quelled one main concern of the media as far as rule changes, that being that the QB could actually get hit. The press released noted that head slaps are illegal (I don't know why they had to put that in there; perhaps because of the encouraged taunting, of which head slaps could be considered, they felt the need) and QBs would be down by contact if they slid and couldn't be hit in that defenseless position. Otherwise, they were fair game.

The news of league expansion was already being discussed as of January 19th. The San Antonio Business Journal ran an article revealing that San Antonio was one of the first cities to speak with the XFL, but there were no open dates available in the Alamodome's schedule. XFL spokesmen said there were no plans for the XFL to expand, but Billy Hicks did say that by year three, there could be two expansion teams. The league also expressed the desire to play only in outdoor stadiums, but a representative from the Alamo Dome noted that those discussions never came up; Hicks countered by saying it was likely discussed before he came aboard and before the decree was to play outdoors only. Makes sense: If this was a throwback-type of football league, they wanted to play in the elements, just like all the old-timers did. There's nothing smashmouth about a temperature-controlled climate inside a stadium with a big cap on it.

With little time to go before the first game, the LA Xtreme were at 6,000 season tickets sold, below the expected 10,000. With each team getting $500,000 to market in their city, perhaps that should've been adjusted, as that kind of money can get you more in Memphis than it can in LA. Among others, the Xtreme had 200 billboards set up in the Southern California area. Other areas they advertised were TV, radio and print (English and Spanish), but with a limited budget, it was difficult for them to get too many spots.

January also saw mentions of the XFL ramped up on Raw and Smackdown. Whether it was Vince McMahon reading an article about the XFL on-camera backstage or Stephanie McMahon wearing an XFL jacket, McMahon was clearly trying to cross-brand his two products. The announcers also plugged the league and an XFL ad with model Carol Grow, who would later be featured in broadcasts of the game, aired near the end of January on Raw. Smackdown didn't have as much coverage, but then again, that show wasn't seen by as many viewers and didn't carry the same demographic numbers the XFL was so hotly after than did it's pro wrestling cousin.

The Birmingham Bolts suffered through some growing pains early on in training camp at the Citrus Bowl in Orlando as they searched for players to fit their West-Coast offensive scheme. Head coach Gerry DiNardo noted that effort was fine, but because everything is new, from teammates to rules, things were slow getting up to speed. The battle for the starting QB job was pared down by one early on in camp, when QB Jon Nielsen failed to report. The third day of camp saw things heat up with goal line drills, and while execution wasn't great, S Fred White probably caught the eye (or, ear) of XFL officials when he got vocal, shouting "This is football, not Barbie's Playhouse. I'm fixin' to bench press somebody. This is a demolition derby. This is football!" at his offensive teammates. The XFL could only hope for attitude like that once cameras started rolling. Other leagues wasted no time in sending scouts to check out the talent level of the XFL; Houston Texans and Atlanta Falcons representatives were present in the first week of Bolts camp, as well as scouts from the Edminton Eskimos and Hamilton Tiger-Cats of the CFL, and the San Jose SaberCats, Orlando Predators and Nashville Kats. The scout from the Falcons got an earful from XFL official Mike Keller that day—the XFL promised to allow access to practices for NFL clubs who allowed XFL scouts access to their games for the 2000 seasons; the Falcons were one of the teams who refused XFL entrance to their home games. For a league that many pundits decreed as minor-league and inferior to the NFL, the actions of teams from the number one league in America said otherwise.

Players continued to have to defend the league to the media. S Calvin Jackson of the Bolts went off on a UPN-TV reporter from Tampa when asked what he would say to someone who suggested the league wouldn't be above-the-board. On January 7th, a new QB was inserted into the mix: Area star Jay Barker, the all-time winningest QB in University of Alabama history. It was funny to read some of the Birmingham-area papers in covering the XFL, especially in the fall and winter months:

Every story seemed to have an update on Barker's status relative to the league, as he was still under CFL contract at the time but rumored to be signing with the XFL. So this was a big "get" for the Bolts not only on the field, but off, as they were one of the teams on the low-end of ticket sales at that point. It was also a bit of luck, as they happened to be first on the waiver wire list. Barker had tryouts with a few NFL teams around the time and it was possible he'd return to the CFL after the XFL season. He nearly didn't make it into the league though, as he was concerned about the authenticity of the play on the field at first. His first practice TD throw even made for a story in the local Birmingham paper.

A blimp in the shape of the league's unique Spalding football, used by the San Francisco Demons to promote the XFL, crashed in the Oakland area on January 10th. Many area papers covered the event, another way to get a laugh at the league that hadn't even begun play yet. In the end though, it was quite the metaphor for the league as a whole.

On January 13th, the Bolts' players got the day off, but did have to go to a meeting at a local hotel, to be addressed by Vince McMahon and NBC's Dick Ebersol. In a meeting with players, Rage CB Stephen Fisher noted that McMahon promised that they would have more exposure (due to being mic'd and where the camreas go) than any other team in football history. Vince had these meetings throughout training camp and if you could guess what else he would've said based on how he operates in pro wrestling, I'm sure he gave the players an "us vs. the world" speech. He probably noted how the media doesn't believe in the league and doesn't believe the players can put on a decent product. I'm sure it was a very "rah-rah" type of meeting, trying to get the players pumped up and make them want to run through a wall for him. McMahon certainly has the oratory ability to do so; but the XFL players weren't stuck in the "wrestling bubble" like so many of Vince's sports entertainers, where all they know is pro wrestling and they can't comprehend life outside the "bubble," or how things work in the "real world."

The first significant injury of camp was suffered by C Ryan Thomassie ten days into camp. He was expected to be out until the second week of the regular season after getting surgery on his knee. After a scrimmage with the Hitmen, CB Anthony Blevins needed surgery to repair a torn ACL. Scouts continued to monitor the Bolts, with the Tennessee Titans and Jacksonville Jaguars of the NFL represented as well as the Montreal Alouettes of the CFL. A scout for the Chicago Enforcers was even spotted at one practice. On January 16th, former Auburn coach Terry Bowden and XFL Director of Competition Dick Butkus were guests at practice, as was a WWE film crew, recording footage of special teams action for a "making of the XFL"-piece. Their first cuts on January 15th included three players who the Bolts had obtained in the Supplemental Draft.

Even two weeks into practice, DiNardo refused to mince words about his team's performances, especially in a January 17th scrimmage with the Orlando Rage, where he remarked that his team "got our butts kicked today, basically stunk the place up" (but luckily, XFL rules prohibited stats and scores from the preseason games, as well as keeping the public and media out, another example of the tight seal the XFL kept on some of its information). Only a handful of coaches in the NFL would be that blunt; Vince McMahon no doubt was hoping that would be the norm in the XFL. Three of their four TEs were injured during the game. It was getting to be that time of camp where players started to get dinged up and needed assistance from the training staff— half the players on the roster visited the trainers for treatment of injuries on January 18th. The media was ever-present, with two TV crews and reporters from up to three newspapers doing stories on the XFL and talking to players at Bolts camp. In addition to the QB competition, two kickers waged war for one roster spot—Brad Palazzo and Andy Russ dueled all the way until the last day of camp, when Palazzo, a semi-finalist for the Groza Award (awarded to the top kicker in the nation), officially won out. Palazzo hadn't punted since 1994. With two weeks left until the first week of the season, and one week of training camp left, positions still unsettled in camp included WR and secondary. On January 22nd, more cuts were made (including QB Mark

Washington, leaving the Bolts with the three they were going to go into battle with). They were left with many area players and a glut of WRs, with many of them susceptible to being cut at the end of January during the final phase of roster management dictated by the league. Also on that date, players filmed personality pieces to be used on XFL broadcasts during the season. Another effort to get the players over as stars, but at the same time, regular guys that fans can relate to, as opposed to multi-millionaires in the NFL.

Gerry DiNardo told Birminghambolts.com on January 24th that while the RB and QB positions are set, pretty much everything else was up for grabs. He named Stepfret Williams, Quincy Jackson and Jahine Arnold as WRs who were likely safe, but three to four receivers could be cut in the next few days. James Bostic and Curtis Alexander were the top two running backs, and Casey Weldon and Jay Barker the two quarterbacks atop the depth chart. Their final scrimmage was against the Enforcers on January 24th. The team didn't win, but DiNardo seemed pleased with the effort. The scoring by the Enforcers was done against the Bolts' second-team defense. One concern was the play of former Auburn guard Ed King, who was expected to win the left tackle job, but took longer than hoped to stave off the efforts of Ozell Powell.

Final cuts were made on January 29th, and among them was Arnold, who appeared safe a few days before. Also, RB Troy Davis, a prolific college runner who was a runner-up for the Heisman Trophy and a veteran of three NFL seasons was let go. K Andy Russ was released, leaving the Bolts with Brad Palazzo as their kicking specialist. Casey Weldon was entrenched as starter at QB, not so much because he beat out Jay Barker, but because he had more experience running the offense than Barker, who joined the team after training camp began. Who was going to protect the QBs was another matter altogether, as the OL was the biggest question mark on the team heading into the season. The defensive front was also a bit undersized, but the Thunderbolts were focused on speed for their defense.

I don't mean to sound like I'm constantly hating on the NFL—I watch the games every Sunday, I have a favorite team that I follow religiously, I play fantasy football and track each bit of news on the Internet. But the league isn't perfect. Neither was the XFL, but it made an effort to try to "fix" what people didn't like about the NFL, while offering a somewhat-similar on-field product. I can live with the NFL, warts and all, but there was certainly a place for another football league in America. Unfortunately, too few people agreed with me, especially in the media—and they held much more sway over the public than I did as a 17 year-old at the time.

The Memphis Maniax practiced at Foothill High School in Henderson, Nevada, a far cry from the posh facilities some former NFL players were used to for training camps. It was the first extended time that head coach Kippy Brown got to spend with his team on the practice field. Unlike most teams in training camp, it appeared the offense was ahead of the defense for the 'Ax, at least after the first scrimmage. Like most kickers in XFL camps, Maniax kickers had some adjusting to do. Most were used to doing field-goal kicking or punting, but not both. With the roster limit at 38 on game days, teams were looking for duel threats. Will Brice and Jeff Hall, the kickers in Maniax camp, came from opposite sides of the spectrum. While both punted and kicked in high-school, neither had done both since then. Brice was a punter, Hall a kicker, and for Brice, it was more difficult: He punts and kicks with different legs. Brice was an All-American punter at Virginia and punted in parts of two seasons in the NFL with the St. Louis Rams and Cincinnati Bengals. Hall kicked in four games with the Rams in 2000 and was the Southeastern Conference's all-time leading scorer in college. Both had the credentials any team would love to have in a kicker.

The kickers weren't the only ones trying new positions. Beau Morgan, a spread offense QB in college with the Air Force, worked during camp not only at QB, but at WR, DB, a holder on field goals and on special teams coverage and return units. Kippy Brown considered him a specialist that could be used anywhere on the field and another example of perhaps saving another roster spot by being able to use him at multiple positions.

The kicking game was a key difference between the XFL and most other football leagues. Memphis designated Kevin Prentiss, who, at just 5'7", was too small for the NFL, as their punt returner. Special Teams coach Chris Mattura formed a return game in the shape of a diamond, where two men would be lined up 25 yards from the line of scrimmage, with Prentiss back deep. That would provide blockers as well as serve as a safety net to make sure punts were returned after 25 yards since they were live.

In a scrimmage with the Las Vegas Outlaws over a week into camp, Brown was pleased with the defensive effort, aside from a few big plays given up the CBs. They got pressure on the QB and also held the Outlaws running game in check. RB Ketric Sanford, quiet during camp, surprised people by showing off some skills in the game. But at the time, he was already likely behind Rashaan Salaam and Rafael Cooper on the depth chart. Among those in the media on hand for the scrimmage were ESPN and Sports Illustrated.

Speaking of competition, like most teams, the Maniax QB battle was wide-open as well and each candidate brought something unique to the table. Marcus Crandall, their first-round draft choice, was a more mobile QB than the other two options. Jim Druckenmiller, an NFL first-rounder but drafted by Memphis in round ten, was known for his big arm and prototypical size. The darkhorse, Craig Whelihan, who impressed most in the scrimmage with the Outlaws, had the most NFL experience of the group and was the most accurate. All three were looking for a chance to get back into the NFL.

Not everyone wanted to be in Las Vegas for camp with the Maniax. WR Tyrone Goodson, picked in the Supplemental Draft, had submitted his name for the original P.A.S.S draft in late October after being released by the Green Bay Packers. But after not being selected (and not even being listed among those eligible for the P.A.S.S), Goodson was approached by the Washington Redskins, who wanted to sign him and send him to NFL Europe. But the problem came with the 'Ax refused to release him from his XFL contract. But after meeting with the coaching staff and management of the Maniax, he decided it wasn't for him and they released him on January 21st. Two weeks later, he signed with the Redskins.

Brown took the team through game-week preparation with 10 days left in camp, preparing them for the rigors of the regular season. Also, January 21st, in a scrimmage against the Demons, was the first time the Maniax would play with a running clock and the entire kicking game. And this is just two weeks before the regular season began. That sends alarm bells off for me that maybe things aren't going to go as smoothly as some would hope on the field come February 3rd and 4th. Luckily, they went all-out for that scrimmage as well as the LA vs. Las Vegas one later in the day, as these games were used as test sessions for NBC TV cameras and played in full game-like terms. Memphis was one of the few teams in the XFL who was happy with their depth on the OL and DL, leading to G Eric Schnupp and DL Kevin Sluder being cut with one week left in camp.

RB Rashaan Salaam was on a mission to prove doubters in the NFL wrong. He had been released by the Green Bay Packers after flaming out with the Chicago Bears, who had selected him in the first round. An ankle injury derailed his career, as well as the knock that he couldn't hold on to the football. Brown knew Salaam from his days in Green Bay and said he was still an NFL-level player when he was released. He was no doubt happy with Memphis, a power running team that was the only troupe in the league to carry two fullbacks on the final roster.

Only a week or two before the end of camp, the Memphis Maniax found their starting safety when Jack Kellogg came over from the CFL. He wasn't playing hoping to get into the NFL, instead, he was happy playing in the CFL and earning some extra money in the new American football league. He said a lot of players from that league could be playing in the XFL, but sounded like he thought CFL had the better players, saying the level of play there is as good as anywhere else and that he'd rather have to play against those in the XFL than in the CFL.

January 5th began the live action portion of the NY/NJ Hitmen practice and what's more exciting for players to practice than goal-line drills. The offense got four downs from the two to score, and the defense held, a good sign for a unit that was to run the 3-4 as its base. The first ever touchdown for the Hitmen went to FB Michael Blair, who scored from two yards out later in practice. A name familiar to NFL fans was brought in by the Hitmen to be a coaching intern for a week and to evaluate practice. Legendary Head Coach Chuck Knox, late of the Rams, Bills and Seahawks, coached with Hitmen head man Rusty Tillman in Seattle.

Speaking of Tillman, it was well-accepted that he was one of the fieriest coaches in the league. In fact, he showed his team movies such as "Braveheart," "Cool Hand Luke" and "Patton" to get them used to his coaching style.

The Birmingham team wasn't the only one being scouted during training camp. The Tennessee Titans, Atlanta Falcons, Jacksonville Jaguars dispatched NFL scouts to observe the Hitmen practice, and so did the CFL's Montreal Alouettes and San Jose Sabercats of the AFL. In what was seen no doubt as a good omen by XFL brass, the Hitmen and Enforcers actually had to cancel part of a scrimmage they conducted due to the chippiness of the players from both sides, starting when Hitmen DT Wilky Bazile delivered a possibly late hit on the Enforcers QB. Trashing talking ensued, tempers heated up and the two teams actually came to blows. When the dust settled, this was exactly the scenario the XFL would be hoping for on Saturday nights: Two teams wanting to win so badly and wanting to play so well that that desire would boil over into anger toward the other team, and frakases would break out numerous times.

The major battle in Hitmen training camp was for the starting RB job, where former Oakland Raider Joe Aska (4.5 yards per carry in his NFL career), Dino Philyaw (mostly a special teamer in the NFL, but did average 22.0 yards on 53 kick returns in 1999 for the New Orleans Saints) and Nathan Simmons (spent time with the Chicago Bears and now runs Nathan Simmons Wealth Solutions). All three made it difficult on the coaching staff, as they each had their moments in a scrimmage against the Birmingham Bolts. Both Simmons and Aska were cut as the Hitmen formed their final roster and looked for backs to fit their West-Coast system.

In late January, the Winnipeg Sun printed a note about LB Glen Young, who was in Hitmen camp for a brief time. He didn't have kind words to say about coach Rusty Tillman, who he referred to as "foul mouthed," or the league, which he called "crazier than you could imagine.It's nothing like I've ever seen. It's totally different." I'm sure the league was quite happy about that quote, which set the league apart from the NFL in at least one player's mind.

Tillman, in a test run for the NBC broadcast during a scrimmage against the Orlando Rage, reportedly told a cameraman, "Will you get your (bleep) ass out of my way?!?" Rusty said the NBC and XFL execs loved the reaction from him. Tillman told the Seattle Post-Intelligencer that he loved the idea of a no-holds barred approach to football and the fact that he can say anything he wants on TV, including profanities.

In Las Vegas, the Outlaws were one of two teams that got to practice at home. Despite being their number one pick, QB Chuck Clements was set to battle Ryan Clement (who had worked at Reebok the previous year) and Mike Cawley for the number one job. Head coach Jim Criner declared the job open to begin training camp. Clement had a leg-up on his competition, having been in the same offense for Criner with the Scottish Claymores of NFL Europe. Cawley began behind the eight-ball, as he was picked in the supplemental draft and didn't go through training camp with the playbook (or with the receivers) like the other two did. In a bit of synergy between WWE and the XFL, wrestlers The Dudley Boys and The Good-Father were available for autograph signings and a meet-and-greet at one of the first Outlaws' practices. On one hand, it got WWE fans a chance to sample the XFL, which is really where the league wanted to get its base of fans from, meaning the teen crowd that was into wrestling at the time. On the downside, it may have turned away football fans who were turned off by the wrestling aspect and saw this as another reason to think the action might not be on the up-and-up.

During camp, the Outlaws were able to shore up the TE position by claiming 34 year-old Keith Jennings, a veteran of eight NFL season and known mostly for his blocking prowess. Jennings reason for ending his two-year retirement? His kids had never seen him play football. He had no reservations about getting back to the NFL, but wanted to help build Vegas as a football city. This gave the Outlaws a solid veteran presence on the team, joining Gouveia and S Toby Wright as key guys looked on for leadership roles on the team. Wright was rehabbing a knee inury, and in his place, S Jamel Williams was impressing the coaching staff, making several interceptions. Both of them were cap casualties in the NFL, which meant not that they weren't good, but rather, that they plain made too much money.

G Lamont Burns had an interesting story in camp. He had given up the game of football, but then a priest told him he'd play football again, maybe not where he thought, but he'd play again. Burns said that almost a year to the day the priest told him that, he was offered a shot with the XFL. He revealed that in college, he played dirty, earning the nickname "Dirtbag." He'd fit right in in the XFL.

The QB competition heated up after the first scrimmage with the LA Xtreme, when coach Criner acknowledged the play of Ryan Clement as one who stood out. Clements soon experienced a sore throwing shoulder, giving Clement more reps as the competition became a two-man race. The Las Vegas Review-Journal estimated that about 3,000 fans showed up to watch, creating good exposure for the team. On defense, it was expected that the Outlaws would be a fierce, blitzing team. The team made a trade for some OL experience, acquiring David Diaz-Infante from the Demons in exchange for OT Harvey Goins. Infante, a member of two Super Bowl winning teams, was expected to push for the starting center job. After a scrimmage with the Memphis Maniax in muddy conditions, Criner even went so far as to note that Clements and Clement had moved ahead of Cawley and Lionel Hayes in the battle for the number one job. On defense, LB Toran James stood out, making stops on the first four offensive plays for Memphis. Vince McMahon, Dick Butkus and Basil DeVito all attended that scrimmage.

On January 12th, the QB competition became a little clearer when Chuck Clements heard a pop in his shoulder while practicing. Originally, it was diagnosed as a sprained shoulder, and he was expected to miss only three weeks. Cawley got the nod to backup Clement, even though he had been fourth on the depth chart, behind Lionel Hayes. Concerned at the lack of depth at the QB position with Clements down, the Outalws worked out QB Mike Buck, who had signed with the XFL, but only a day before the Supplemental Draft and hadn't committed to playing until afterward. Buck played 12 games in the NFL with the New Orleans Saints and Arizona Cardinals and had been serving as the Offensive Coordinator of the Pensacola Barricudas of the Arena 2 League (AF2). Criner spoke highly of Buck after seeing him work out, and the club claimed him just two days later, releasing another QB, Lionel Hayes, in the process. As of January 19th, Clement was all but annointed the starter and was expected to be more of a game-manager in the opener against the Hitmen. He still had to cleanly steer the team through an exhibition game or two as training camp winded down but it was his job to lose.

DT Antonio Dingle was a player made for the XFL: He promised to do a back-flip if he scored a TD in college, but didn't get the opportunity. The sight of a 320 pound man doing a back-flip would certainly gain the XFL some attention on highlight reels across the country. He even asked to be allowed to carry the ball in short-yardage situations, but coach Criner wasn't having that. He never got either chance, as he was released during final cuts on January 29th. Speaking of flips, the Vegas Cheerleaders got some national exposure when they appeared on *Live! With Regis* during January and while the players were preparing for the start of the league. It was a good way to keep word out there about the league, and also give fans a sneak peek at the cheerleaders, one of the more hyped aspects of the XFL.

One of the players expected to make a splash with the Outlaws was territorial selection LB Troy Dumas, who played 14 NFL games and was a third-round pick in the NFL Draft by the Kansas City Chiefs. While he impressed the coaches during a workout before the draft (including Criner saying it was one of the best workouts he'd seen in his 35 years in the game), he ended up being released in the first cut-down, beaten out by younger players Tony Ortiz and Marcel Willis. Another notable player who was let go was WR Cedric Tillman, who played in 52 NFL games and had 87 career receptions, but hadn't played a game in the league since 1995.

Donald Sellers, a former college QB and a WR expected to make the Outlaws out of training camp, became the first player in the league to face the long arm of the law. Sellers was indicted on January 19th in Arizona on nine charges of felony sexual misconduct, including sexual conduct with a minor. He was looking at up to 22 years in prison. Sellers never did play a game for the Outlaws, was placed on a reserve list on January 22nd and tragically, he passed away in a car accident in Arizona on February 11, 2001, just eight days after the Outlaws opened their season against the Hitmen.

Also on January 22nd, the Outlaws trimmed their roster to 56 by releasing, among others, veteran DEs Vince Amey and Sterling Palmer. Palmer, at 29, unsuccesfully tried to fend off younger players for a roster spot. Amey was a 'tweener, too small to play DT and too slow to play DE. K Marcus Williams was waived as well, leaving the Outlaws with K Paul McCallum, who played under Criner in NFL Europe. It was also announced that the voice of the Outlaws would be J.T. The Brick, a national sports talk-show, and former Oakland Raider RB Napolean McCallum would provide color commentary.

As of January 25th, Chrys Chukwuma appeared to be headed for the starting RB job, but coach Jim Criner refused to make a declaration on that front, as Criner also heaped praise on Rod Smart and Pepe Pearson after the team's final practice game. Chukwuma, with 4.45 speed and 232 pounds, seemed like the prototypical NFL RB. However, coming out of college, he got the reputation of not taking football seriously and didn't get much of a sniff from the NFL. Their final scrimmage with the Demons was chock full of penalties and they also struggled in the passing phase of the game, especially with Mike Cawley behind center, which pretty much sealed the deal for Ryan Clement to start.

As final cuts came down, there were a few surprises, such as Dingle, Pearson, Buck and LB Tony Ortiz. Criner, still concerned about the QB spot, said his roster was likely to be tweaked in the next few days, including adding another QB. Buck's downfall was his time off from the game and Cawley didn't play well in the final scrimmage. RB Vershan Jackson was placed on injured reserve, and coach Criner said that if he was healthy, he would've been a starter. Leaves one to wonder how the course of XFL history would've been changed if He Hate Me wasn't out there to take snaps at the RB position in week one. One man sad to see training camp end was DE Kelvin Kinney, who was always playing with a smile on his face. Kinney, who lost his unborn child when his wife was rear-ended while driving, was released from the Washington Redskins when then-head coach Norv Turner demanded he return to the team rather than stay with his wife. He noted that the Outlaws coaches treated the players like adults and encouraged input from the players.

A veteran the Xtreme were counting on to provide leadership and experience hung up the cleats during training camp. LB Mike Croel, bothered by various minor injuries for the previous few years, decided to call it quits. A big opportunity opened up when the team lined up for the first scrimmage against the Demons. Head coach Al Luginbill made it a point to emphasize the fact that every player had a chance to make the team, meaning that the scrimmage was the first time he'd see his players in game form against another team and a depth chart would be relased in the days following the scrimmage. Standing out in the scrimmage and leaping to the top of the depth chart became an important task for all of the players. Keeping players hungry sometimes can be the key to getting the most out of them. And it didn't matter who you knew: WR L.C. Stevens, who was the leading receiver for Luginbill's NFL Europe squad the previous year, was a victim of the first cutdown to 62 players.

With a week left of practice, the Xtreme had a strong scrimmage showing against the Outlaws, with their defensive line (which coach Luginbill called the strength of his team before the first game) and passing game in particular thriving. They did have a few fumbles, most coming during the center-to-QB exchange, another simplistic football play that was a casuality of the short time the teams had to work together. It was announced on January 29th that the Vegas sports books had pegged the Xtreme as the favorites to win the XFL Championship at 5-2 odds. Orlando was second at 4:1,w ith Memphis and Las Vegas at 5:1. Before final cuts were made, the Xtreme played one more scrimmage against hte Maniax. Tommy Maddox and Rashaan Shehee, the expected starters at QB and RB respectively, sat out the scrimmage. Unfortunately, they didn't come away from the practice game unscathed: G Ron Lewis was lost for the season with a broken right leg while attempting to make a block. Following training camp, the Xtreme moved on to Long Beach Community College, where they were set to practice in their week leading up to February 4th's matchup with the Demons.

Among those trimmed in the cut-down to 56 players was the single-season rushing leader for San Diego State, RB George Jones; CB Darwin Brown, a fifth-round pick by the Denver Broncos in 1999 and third-team All-Big 12 in his senior year at Texas Tech; and S Paris Johnson, who later went on to play with the Rhein Fire in NFL Europe, allocated by the Miami Dolphins. Clearly, these players had credentials to play pro football respectably, even the ones who were getting cut.

Bruce Beaton, an offensive guard who made the final roster with the Xtreme, was a Canadian import from the CFL. He even planned to go back to the Edmonton Eskimos once the XFL season ended and start back up in the CFL in June. That would be 28 games in a short period of time, though he would be a backup with LA and a starter with the Eskmos.

On January 31st, only four days before the first game against the Demons, the Xtreme named Tommy Maddox as the starting QB, over number one pick Scott Milanovich. According to coach Luginbill, Maddox played better in the scrimmages and was the catalyst behind more scores than Milanovich. Luginbill also said that Milanovich would play in the opener at some point.

The Rage lost two veterans early in training camp, as QB Steve Matthews and K Scott Blanton both left Orlando. The Rage did claim former San Diego Chargers 5th round pick DE Cedric Harden from the player pool to replace one of those players. He also had experience in NFL Europe and was a local player, having played college ball at Florida A&M University. Chicago teamed up with Orlando for a 60-play scrimmage and some kicking game work, giving the Rage their first live action of training camp against another squad. Their first cut-downs on January 15th didn't include many name players except TE Vince Marrow, who played 10 games in the NFL, and CB Tony Stargell, a veteran of five NFL teams and seven season in the league. He hadn't played football since 1998.

The Rage were not satisfied with their kicking game after Blanton and Daron Alcorn left camp, claiming University of Central Florida standout Charlie Pierce to compete with Jay Taylor. He didn't last long though, as he was cut just a week later as the Rage reduced their roster to 52. As the camp progressed, cut-downs became more and more difficult, with coach Galen Hall saying there were still battles to be won as of the middle of January and that some good football players would be on the outside looking in. Among those sent packing to get down to 56 players was former Vikings and Packers LB Kivuusama Mays and DBs Jay Hill and Brian Hinton. That put the DB numbers at 10, with more cuts in that area expected before the season began.

In the end, two DBs were cut in the last cut-down. Other notable veterans axed included TE Lonnie Johnson, DL Jerry Drake and DB Lawrence Wright. The three combined had 136 games of NFL experience. Highly touted QB Kerwin Bell was in talks to join the XFL and specifically, the Orlando Rage. He had conversations with Galen Hall and he had played under Rage offensive coordinator Mike Kelly in Winnipeg. The Rage did acquire DE Sterling Palmer from the Enforcers, making this his third stop already in the XFL before games even started. They traded an undisclosed 2001 pick for Palmer to strengthen their D-Line, which was key to the 4-3 defense they planned to run.

As expected, QB Jeff Brohm made it back from his short NFL stint to be with the club heading into the first game. The Rage planned on using a spread attack, utilizing three WRs and a running back in the starting lineup. Derrick Clark led the RB stable, but Brian Shay and Michael Black expected to see significant snaps as well.

After the first week of camp, the Demons got to scrimmage the Xtreme, but were without 11 of their 63 players, including three receivers, two running backs and three linebackers. That can make things difficult to evaluate, and head coach Jim Skipper acknowledged that after the contest. On January 18th, the Demons announced that they'd be practicing during the season at Diablo Valley College. The college got a good deal out of it, as the Demons were to conduct a joint football clinic during the summer with the college (which, for obvious reasons, never happened) and the team was to set an internship program to allow for sports administration majors to gain experience in their chosen field. San Francisco also wanted to aid in upgrading the facilities since both the college and the pro team would be using it.

After a scrimmage against the Memphis Maniax, Skipper was more pleased with his defense and special teams than his offense, but still said his team had a ways to go to get where he wanted them to be. Both offenses struggled in the scrimmage, though San Francisco played without two key receivers and a tight-end (first-stringer Sean Manuel, who was later placed on the four-week injured reserve). The Demons were bit by the injury (and illness) bug all camp long and were looking for a third-team QB after Kevin Feterik broke his thumb in the scrimmage. Perhaps because of these reasons, when the Philadelphia Eagles came calling for FB Jamie Reader, who they wanted to sign for the playoffs, the Demons refused to let him go. WR Jimmy Cunningham, who stood 5'8" and weighed only 165 pounds, was claimed during training camp to add WR depth. Unfortunately, the team didn't have shoulder pads his size and he had to wait 'til they were specially sent to him.

Unlike his acquaintance Kippy Brown, Jim Skipper, also hired straight out of the NFL, decided to forego staying in New York and decided to get right down to business and get his hands dirty with the Demons. No missing mini-camps or practices to finish his assignment with the Giants. The Super Bowl, which the Giants ended up playing in, was scheduled on the same day as the Demons would break training camp. Skipper lent credibility to the league for former NFL RB Vaughn

Dunbar, who had his doubts about the league until he heard that Skipper signed on as one of the coaches. Hindsight being 20/20 and all, one has to wonder whether Skipper would've jumped at the chance to coach in the XFL had he known it would only last one year, or coach in the Super Bowl with the Giants.

The Demons finished off their camp with a scrimmage against the Las Vegas Outlaws. It was supposed to take place at Sam Boyd Stadium, but the turf was in rough condition, so it was thought that the best idea was to leave the turf alone so it would be ready for the XFL season opener. Skipper noted that the final cuts would be difficult and some good players would be sent home. RB Vaughn Dunbar, who had been nagged by injuries since the first mini-camp, appeared to be fully healthy during the scrimmage. Another worrisome factor was that K Ignacio Brache missed four of five field goal attempts. Only C Curtis Macfarlane came away with an injury.

The Demons cut down their roster to 37 instead of 38 and were rumored to add CFL WR Robert Gordon to their roster, but never did. San Francisco decided to go with just two QBs on their roster for the first few weeks. The waived players included former Jacksonville Jaguar FB Ryan Christopherson and 1998 2nd Round NFL draft pick CB Cordell Taylor. Skipper kept his starting QB under wraps until the Tuesday before the first game, as well as the rest of the starting lineup. After Brache was cut, it seemed Francesco Biancamano would be their kicker heading into the first game. But viewers who tuned into the Sunday night UPN game during week one would find out that was not the case.

The offense under coordintaor Joe Paopao was expected to be explosive, with some creativity and variety. They were not the kind of team you'd see settle for a yard or two running the ball. Paopao was a QB during his time as a player and he coached in the CFL, where you get only three downs, so he certainly knew what it was like to need to pull off 10-and-12 yard chunks at a time. The defense would be a mirror of the offense—speed and quickness were prized. It wasn't revealed until all players made the roster, that two players on the team, WR Brian Roberson and RB Brandin Young were nephews of coach Skipper.

He only introduced them to everyone as such after they had made the team of their own accord, so there would be no question of nepotism.

Another scrimmage, another XFL head coach displeased with his team's performance. On January 17th, the Rage scrimmaged the Enforcers, and Chicago's Ron Meyer felt his team had an attitude going into the game, and got it adjusted by game's end. Still, he was happy with his running game and still looking for more consistency out of the QB position, saying they need "a lot of work." The defense was where he was particularly upset, even insinuating that they may not want to be around him for the next week, as he no doubt put them through the wringer for the following seven days. January 14th saw the Enforcers meet with Vince McMahon and Dick Ebersol, probably going over the same things the Bolts did during the meeting with these two a day earlier. QB Tim Lester said McMahon was "genuinely interested in the league and its success. He did not get too deep into his vision or expectations. He treated us like professionals and pretty much told us to do our jobs."

The Enforcers defense was expected to be stout, considering the conditions they would be playing in at Soldier Field, and knowing that Chicago football fans are used to a stifling defense. They ran a 3-4 (but just to show you how muddied the information was for the XFL: I found two different article, one saying they'd have a 3-4 and one saying they'd run a 4-3) with zone blitzing schemes that put a lot of pressure on the offense. LB Jamie Baisely was expected to be the leader of the defensive unit, relaying the plays from his ILB position. He played extensively in NFL Europe, and impressed the coaching staff during training camp.

Leading up to the first game, it appeared that Tim Lester had a leg up on the Enforcers' first round pick, Paul Failla, in the battle for the starting QB job. The Enforcers were set to run a one-back system with some use of the split-back, and a skilled offensive line was something else Meyer sought.

As training camps winded down and teams were in full exhibition mode, each team played a game that was a full dress-rehearsal for the kinds of games that would be provided by the XFL, including cameras on the field, microphones in players' faces and mics on the field. In addition to being able to scrimmage with each other with no preseason, this was another reason the XFL wanted teams to train in the same general area: so they could test out their top-secret gadgets they'd be using for the broadcasts. It was odd to keep things so close to the vest, but what would bring a lot of fans in on week one was seeing how the experience of watching on TV was truly different from the NFL; if they let this stuff get out, it wouldn't be nearly as fun. High-ranking XFL brass attended these closed sessions, including Vince McMahon, Dick Butkus, Jesse Ventura, Dick Ebersol and WWE Executive Producer Kevin Dunn. Talk about pressure on the players. But it wasn't just the players; it was the announcers learning the ropes as well. UPN sideline announcer Michael Barkann noted that Ebersol told him they only wanted the sideline guys to ask one question of the players; it didn't turn out that way once the real games started though. Ken Oxendine, a running back from the Xtreme (and MVP of the Orange Bowl as part of a 1-2 punch of RBs at Virginia Tech) noted that it was quite strange to have a reporter talk to you on the field. Xtreme VP J.K. McKay described an Outlaws defensive back who would constantly insult LA QB Tommy Maddox. In the end, apparently he didn't do too much damage on the field and when asked about it after the game, he told the announcer that it was just an exhibition game. In another game between the Outlaws and Xtreme, camreas in the locker room caught one of the coaches having lively discussions with his players, gesticulating and making a scene, while another coach was calm and did not get too emotional. No doubt the former was Coach Luginbill, the latter Coach Criner. All of the extracurricular activities during the games worried Enforcers Special Teams coach Kris Haines. "At first, yes I thought it was a bit of a distraction. But now, every sport on TV does it," he said.

With training camps over and most teams working on their game-week practice, poring over film of their first opponent, the league that promised to take football into the 21st Century was about to begin. The week before the season started, more good news for the XFL: Super Bowl XXXV was a stinker, a 34-7 snoozefest that saw the Ravens clobber the Giants. It was not a beautiful sight for offensive-minded fans, as the teams gained 244 and 152 total offensive yards respectively. Defense may win championships, but offense brings eyeballs to the TV: The Nielsen Rating dropped from the previous year. If the XFL succeeded, it would finally vault Vince McMahon into the ranks of legitimate businessmen and no longer would he be the butt of the joke in the sports-world. If it failed, it would be yet another sign that McMahon should stick to wrestling, and the media would have a field day. For McMahon's own ego, notoriously huge, I'm sure he encountered a few sleepless nights as February 3, 2001 neared.

CHAPTER SIX

The XFL sent out a press release on January 31st previewing each game of the coming weekend, and also giving information on teams and players (and throwing in some positive quotes from media outlets around the country). The tough thing for the XFL was to draw people in with casual fans having no emotional connection to the team or players. For the most part, there was little knowledge of the players as well. The first week was expected to draw based on the curiosity factor, but after that, the quality of football, new rules and technological advances would have to be the main pull for fans to tune in. Many NFL teams have an identity, one that can attract fans other than in the hometown. XFL teams had no such identity, as they hadn't even played a down yet. Same with the players; even if they were unique or had the attitude the XFL was looking for, there was no way of fans to know that yet because chances are, they hadn't seen them play yet. Thus, everything else had to be top-notch, or there was no emotional connection for the viewers.

Leading up to the first game, the fact that the XFL hadn't even played a game yet didn't stop some columnists from ripping on the league. Most made the mistake of predicting the XFL's failure, pointing to all other past leagues that have been left in the wind that tried to compete with the NFL. Only the XFL and Vince McMahon constantly said they weren't competing with the NFL. They would take players the NFL discarded and weren't playing head-to-head with the league. Heck, they weren't even competing for fans. There was no reason one could enjoy both leagues. The Associated Press's Jim Litke scoffed at the amount of money players were getting, some just $40,000, and insisted that was proof that the players wouldn't be up-to-snuff. Except several XFL players went on record to compliment the league's pay system and sounded more than happy they were making $40,000 for a few months of work. Litke also noted that the XFL was craving violence, wanting the most number of big hits possible. Well, yeah, except it's football. Do you think the NFL doesn't love the big hits they get on the field? The NFL is constantly tweaking its rules to make the game "safer," but they're also becoming less and less like football. They didn't have these rules, like you couldn't lead with the helmet, when Dick Butkus played, and that generation seemed to make out alright (except for the fact that the league failed to take care of its players after that generation left the game, but that has nothing to do with what happened on the field). The XFL wanted to maximize these hits and some people made it sound like they were taking advantage of these players. No one had a gun to their head and made them stay in the league. If they were afraid of the violence aspect (really, what football player is?), I'm sure they were free to leave at any time.

Even Newsweek ran a piece on the XFL in their January 29th edition. Of course, the first paragraph described a wrestler getting involved in the football game. Then in the second paragraph, they pronounce that a real football game will take place February 3rd. But when you put the idea of mixing wrestlers with football in football fans' heads, it can turn them off to the product before they even give it a chance. The article noted that buzz was strong for the league, geared toward male adolescents. But they also had an inset chart that compared the two New York teams, NFL and XFL. While the QB (Kerry Collins), RB (Tiki Barber) and WR (Amani Toomer) of the Giants were described with their eye-popping stats (the team did just compete in a Super Bowl) while the credentials of Charles Puleri, Joe Aska and Zola Davis looked miniscule by comparison. It wasn't fair and told fans that the

XFL was irrelevant. The worst thing you could do is compare the two leagues, let alone before the season even started. Is it shocking the NFL has better players? No. So why run this piece that so obviously and unnecessarily points it out? No one was saying the players would be on the same level. While the piece was positive, the comparison seemed out-of-place.

January 30th saw George Will, a Pulitzer Price-winning synicated columnist and noted conservative, weighed in on the XFL. And it was clear which side of the fence he was on: "XFL to coarsen culture even further" was his title. In between his use ten-dollar words and "better than everyone else" air projected in the column, Will took to task the XFL's increasing of the violence on the field, defending the NFL's rule of in-the-grasp by saying the QB is "in danger" when the play is stopped. In danger of what? Being hit? Like every other football player on the field? Yeah, don't want to risk injury to that $10 million-per-year arm. He termed the play "bush league football," again, before a game had even been played. Yes, it wasn't going to be NFL-caliber, and I don't know anyone that would've expected that from players that, for the most part, are only household names in their own household. But "bush league" doesn't simply mean "minor league"; it has a certain negative connotation that goes with it, unprofessional if you will (as in saying, "that's a bush league stunt"), and you can bet the award-winning Will knew exactly the connotation it had. League-wide, the XFL had 83% of its players play in the NFL at one time or another, and 79% of the players were in their 20s. So really, how bad could the football be? You'd think these were guys who were playing in beer leagues a few weeks before based on the way the media was expecting the league to be. It's funny to see the columnists dig into the bottom of the barrel for reasons to hate on the XFL, including the team nicknames. Yeah, "Enforcers" and "Outlaws" is terrible and will no doubt cause society to crumble around us. I'd much rather have teams named after animals or structures. It's different, and some people took at "different" as "threatening" (and here I go back to the fact that Will is a conservative). Will again took seriously McMahon's comment about going up to a cheerleader and asking her, if she was dating a player who made a bad play, if they did the "wild thing" last night. Some people shuddered at that thought, yet it was a simple example of taking a quote out of context: McMahon was simply providing an example of, not only allowing players and cheerleaders to date, but also how open the XFL was going to be as far as putting the mics in people's faces and getting some answers instead of speculation like the NFL provides.

On February 1st, Richard Sandomir wrote a piece for the New York Times that was titled, "XFL Is Reality Series That Promotes Bad Taste." He quoted Baltimore Ravens owner Art Modell, who accused the XFL of "selling sex." Yes, they acknowledge that cheerleaders will become a bigger part of the show than in the NFL. But don't NFL websites have sections devoted to their cheerleaders? Don't NFL teams sell calendars with cheerleaders in them? Didn't a few NFL cheerleaders recently (as in, 2000) pose for Playboy? And THAT's not selling sex? At least the XFL was honest about it. Sandomir wrote that ".those who believe he [Vince] cannot separate the WWF's values from the norms and practices of a real professional sports league." Of course, this is something Vince was more than happy to obliterate, that being the notion that there are certain "norms" that need to be followed in professional sports. It's a SPORT, not a religion. If someone comes by with a different vision of sports, whose to say that's wrong?

The media blitz got turned up on the weekend of February 3rd. CNNSI.com provided a team-by-team skill player analysis of each team. Even my hometown newspaper, the Rochester Democrat & Chronicle, had a big picture of Vince McMahon and a front-page (of the sports) story on the XFL, and they didn't have a dog in the fight. Most news outlets covered the rule changes, preparing fans for what they should expect, and the usual jokes about the pro wrestling-football connection. They'd also provide write-ups of hometown players in the league, usually with quotes about fans being surprised at the quality of football on the field and how they really believe the league will work (plus a story about why/how they didn't make it in the NFL and what led them to the XFL). With a day before the games, both Las Vegas and San Francisco had sold out their openers. A few other tidbits about the games that weren't officially announced (or sent out as press releases) trickled into the media that week before:

-The Scramble for the Ball was announced.

-The announcers were to be "one of the guys," and instead of being positioned in a comfy, cozy press box, they were to brave the elements along with all the expected crazed fans. A makeshift announce booth would be built into the stands where the announcers would call the games, exposed to the elements.

-The back-up NBC announcers were announced: Jim Ross, Jerry Lawler and Jonathan Coachman. All three pulled double-duty, as all three announced for McMahon's World Wrestling Entertainment (with Ross and Lawler as the announce team for Monday Night Raw, the flagship show of WWE and often the highest-rated cable program every week). Upon immediate inspection, it was an example of WWE's influence creeping into the broadcasts and was one of the reasons they didn't get one of the better commentary positions, as they had tried out during the original search. However, Ross had previous experience calling NFL games as the Atlanta Falcons radio play-by-play man. Coachman came from a sports announcing background, having worked for College Sports Television (CSTV) and the Madison Square Garden Network (MSG) in addition to his WWE duties. And it made no sense to hire sports announcers to simply sit around and wait for cut-ins in the main game and talk for 30 seconds. If there was a blow-out, they'd go to the alternate game, but there were probably few in the field who would want a job where they didn't even really do any announcing.

-Players would have the choice to have their last name, or a nickname, on the back of their jersey. Once again, this emphasized making players the stars and allowing them their individuality and letting their personality show.

-The NFL has the Super Bowl the XFL has…well….how does "The Big Game At The End" sound? Yes, the XFL still hadn't named their championship game. TBGATE had a certain ironic charm, but in order to be taken seriously, they needed to come up with something a little more creative.

On the football field, the Outlaws were wondering what kind of offense they'd see on the field after that third of the team didn't perform exceptionally well in the last scrimmage of training camp against the Demons. With strong-armed Ryan Clement at the helm, the Outlaws promised to be more than a dink-and-dunk West Coast offense. Despite winning the job at the tail end of camp, and only because Chuck Clements suffered an injury, Clement was given the go-ahead to call audibles at the line, needing to read defenses to do so. On the Thursday leading up to the game, QB Jim Ballard made his first appearance for Las Vegas after being released in the final cut-down by the Rage. Since waiving Mike Buck, the Outlaws were in need of a third QB until Chuck Clements was expected back.

The Xtreme had a deep receiving corps, but their main speed demon, Damon Dunn, would be held out with an injury, as would CB Donnell Day. That would make things a little more difficult for the Xtreme against their state rivals, the Demons. Of the 45 players on the roster, 22 played in NFL Europe and 18 have played in a regular season NFL game. Like most XFL teams, almost all the players had experience at least in an NFL training camp.

Two days before their opener, the Demons filled their final roster spot by activating WR Calvin Schexnayder, who had been held out due to his AFL committments. The spot was created late in training camp in hopes of finding a third QB to bring in, but in the end, they couldn't find one to their liking. With eight linebackers making the final roster, it was expected that the Demons would play a little 3-4 defense in addition to their base of the 4-3. Radio announcers were named by the Demons as well, as Roxy Bernstein would handle play-by-play and former San Francisco 49er, nine-year NFL veteran, and a man known for his unique dance after making big plays on defense, Merton Hanks, provided color commentary.

During a meeting with the media on the Monday before the XFL season began, Hitmen General Manager Drew Pearson made the proclamation that he expected the Hitmen to make the playoffs. He cited the team's play during the pre-season as a reason to be optimistic.

Not only that, but he speculated that Charles Puleri could be the best QB in the league. Anyone who knew Pearson would tell you that he was never one to come up short as far as hyperbole goes. Despite Pearson's feelings, the Las Vegas oddsmakers made the Outlaws a five-point favorite for the opener, while the Rage were an 8 1/2 point favorite over the Enforcers, largest of the weekend. .

Balance was the talk of the coaches before the season began. Every team had a chance to win the championship, and while each team had their individual strengths, no team looked like a sure-fire bet to win it all. That surely helped attendance figures as well, and credit the XFL for their draft system and ability to disperse talent for the fact that each coach felt like his team could be the first XFL champion. Director of Competition Dick Butkus, who saw each team play in training camp, felt that while each team may have its niche, none stood out head-and-shoulders above any other team. The other thing that evened out the competition was the lack of film each team had on others. They could only see what happened in training camp and during scrimmages. It's not like you have a history of this team, or this coach, or this QB to rely on. For the most part, coaches and players were flying blind in the first few weeks.

February 3rd had finally arrived. I had been waiting for this moment since the first I heard about the league. I had no idea what to expect, and I don't think a lot of casual fans had any idea, either. A week earlier, I had gone to one of my friends' house with about a half-dozen to a dozen people to watch the Super Bowl. This week, they gathered at my place, about five or six of them, to check out the debut of the XFL. They didn't have the interest in it that I did, but they were certainly curious. Even my dad stuck around to check it out. After tossing the football around in the dark outside, it was finally time for…well, at least SOME kind of football. Fans at the stadium were even more pumped, arriving as early as four hours before kickoff. They received programs at the games with messages from Vince McMahon and Dick Ebersol and basically provided a primer to fans on the league. The usual program stuff, such as rosters and coaches were included as well, and the opening week's programs detailed how the XFL got up and running and found players for the league.

The opening video package espoused the buzz words the XFL had been built on to this point: No Fair Catch, Controversey, Paid To Play—Paid More to Win. And the first person we saw after the opening? WWF's The Rock, touting the XFL. I wonder how many non-wrestling fans tuned right out after seeing him. The camera panned back and showed the video of The Rock talking on the video screen at Sam Boyd Stadium. Curiously, only the XFL logo was painted in the end zones and at mid-field rather than an Outlaws logo. This was the same at other stadiums. After another quick intro showing big hits, cheerleaders and the team's uniforms, the public address announcer introduced Vince McMahon to the racucous crowd. Vince McMahon was the first one on the field, welcoming everyone to the XFL in a now semi-famous scene. To those who hoped he would keep himself and wrestling on the back-burner, this was not a good sign. Wrestling fans know how much Vince likes to rely on himself as a performer when the ratings go down and he can be overexposed on WWE's shows. He welcomed fans to "our" brand of football and told fans to enjoy the all-access pass that other leagues have said were off-limits. He thanked the fans on behalf of players and coaches for the privilege of competing before them tonight. Each team came out seperately, just like wrestlers entering the arena to the cheers or jeers of the crowd. Actually, the NFL had the XFL beat in theatrics for this one (usually they'd introduce the players on at least one side of the ball individually and they'd come out of a big tunnel-like balloon). But the NFL rarely showed it on television. The Outlaws came out first to music, then the Hitmen. Matt Vasgersian and Jesse Ventura talked on camera, with Ventura cutting a wrestling-like promo talking about the sacrifices the players made to play in the league, like having to quit jobs to practice starting in November.

Down to Mike Adamle they went, who brought in Dick Butkus. Butkus took the mic (black and red, like the ball) and explained the Scramble rules. Adamle introduced the scramblers (boos for the Hitmen player, Donnie Caldwell, cheers for Jamel Williams of the Outlaws), then referee Randy Crystal (now a Division I college football referee) gave the players their marching orders. Both men sprinted to mid-field. Williams had the slight advantage on the dive, but the ball squirted another ten yards ahead, where Williams recovered it. Even though Caldwell lost, he didn't end up as badly as Orlando's Hassan Shamsid-Deen, who scrambled for his team in the other Saturday night game and suffered a separated shoulder. Those who predicted more injuries from this added attraction got to pat themselves on the back before the first play of the game. The PA announcer introduced the Outlaws cheerleaders, who danced in outfits no more revealing than any NFL teams. They showed the coaches in the locker room before the game, preparing their respective teams. It was the first wrinkle in the XFL coverage that they promised to deliver and they had 27 cameras and 26 wireless mics around the stadium to capture other moments like this. Coaches Criner and Tillman were shown addressing their teams. Of course, what goes on in the locker room isn't always interesting, and we saw that throughout the first few weeks. After showing the coaches on the sidelines, they showed a graphic describing the "play for pay" system.

In a play that, if I didn't know better, I'd think was scripted, the Outlaws received the opening kick and promptly ran a reverse to gain good field position off the bat, when Jason Kaiser handed it off to his safety-mate Jamel Williams. While giving the lineup for the Hitmen, Vasgersian made sure to give out the credentials of the players. The home team announced their own lineups before the game. This was one of those things likely added at the last minute to introduce the viewers personally to the players. It probably sounded like a good idea in the board room (or in the back of the van driving to the stadium, wherever this plan was hatched), but it didn't make for great TV. These guys were not public speakers and tried to give shout-outs after introducing themselves. Some guys took longer than others, which became a problem as the game tried to get started. Ryan Clement denounced the BCS, Todd Floyd called Vegas the city that really never sleeps, others sent shout-outs to their family and friends. Rod Smart, the starting RB, introduced himself and added, "they hate me baby, they hate me." Mike Furrey called himself not a receiver, but a threat. The NFL networks later utilized this in Sunday and Monday night football, having the starters do pre-taped introductions of themselves. Doing it in a controlled environment like that would probably be better, but the XFL hung its hat on spontaneity.

The camera went in the huddle on the first play, getting a glimpse and a listen to Clement giving instructions to his offense. He scrambled to the right on the first play, giving Ventura the opportunity to plug the fact that there is quarterbacks are treated as players in this league. Those watching the game were treated to a different view; the overhead camera was the main camera for the game, which again, was an attempt to present football in a different manner than most are used to. Unfortunately, this angle didn't provide very good depth perception for the fan and also didn't cover the full width of the field, leaving the split end receivers sometimes out of the picture. Because the camera was on a wire (the X-Cam), the picture was a bit shaky, making the presentation seem a bit minor-league. They played most of the game like this, which was quite an adjustment, and I'm sure many of the viewers preferred the traditional view (so much so that this was scrapped even as soon as the Sunday night UPN game). On play two, we heard the first coach-to-QB communication and Christian Maumalanga, DT for the Hitmen, jumped offsides and clotheslined Clement. He was taking a beating already. Vince McMahon must've been loving it.

After his first carry for a first down, Vasgersian wonderd aloud what was on the back of Smart's jersey. The camera on the field caught up with him to see "He Hate Me." After Clement's first completion, they showed Clement and a cheerleader, Crystal, in a pre-taped segment. Crystal asserted that Clement knew "how to score." The first double-entendre of the XFL had landed. Clement talked football-ese about scoring, and finished his spiel by noting the play would allow him to "penetrate" for the touchdown. Vince McMahon had actually promised NOT to run these exact types of pre-tapes during the game (and in one article, he mentioned a promo eerily similar to the line Crystal spoke). This was another complaint of fans and pundits the day after and again, it was removed by the second week. The on-screen graphics and chyron depicting the names of the players and the lineup was nothing special and the down and distance wasn't even included.

The first trash-talk session of the year went to Ty Talton of the Hitmen and Furrey of the Outlaws. The camera made sure to sidle up right next to the duo in an attempt to catch every word (seven-second delays were handy). The first drive of the game resulted in three points for the Outlaws. Jesse Ventura got off to a rocky start when he referred to Hitmen DB Brad Trout as "Ryan Trout." There were three penalties on the drive, one for offsides, one for delay of game (no surprise with the quicker clock) and pass interference. Even watching the first game again in research for this book, nine years later, the feeling I would use to describe it was "fun." It's just not as tight and wound-up as NFL broadcasts and games seem to be. It was a more relaxed atmosphere in the game, these guys playing with nothing to lose. That came across to the viewer—well, me at least. After the points, Fred Roggin caught up to Smart and asked him about "He Hate Me." Smart said, "they hate me, that's why." He also must've sworn, because they went silent for a few seconds. Adamle interviewed Tillman, who said he was unhappy with the yardage given up on that drive. Tillman later got angry at the cameramen on the sidelines, blocking his view of the field in an effort to catch an off-the-cuff remark or reaction shot.

No commercial in between possessions. No doubt they wanted to back-load them to hook the viewer off the bat. The Outlaws D introduced themselves as well, with Marcel Willis promising "raw footage," whatever that meant. CB Kory Blackwell told his wife that she completes him. The time it took to introduce players, while accomplishing the XFL's promise to get up-close and personal with them, also could've made football fans who tuned in to see only the game and how good the play on the field would be, restless. After the first Hitmen play from scrimmage, the camera eavesdropped on Rusty Tillman talking to his defense on the sidelines, using football lingo most likely unfamiliar to the casual fan. With the ball in their hands for the first time in regular season history, the Hitmen offense got a quick first-down then went three-and-out. This was our first look at the new punt return rules, but the play looked like any you'd see in the NFL. Just like much of the game, a penalty occurred on the play. Because of this, Las Vegas started deep in their own territory. Coming back from the first break, they showed a cheerleader at her workplace as she said a few words about being a Vegas cheerleader, then showed her cheering right in front of the fans at the stadium. Later, they got even more up-close and personal with fans, dancing in the aisles among the crowd.

WR Mike Furrey hauled in a long pass for 33 yards, the first big play of the game. He had 37 friends and family watching, including 14 at his apartment. This was also around the time of the first cut-in to the Orlando vs. Chicago game where they showed Jeff Brohm hooking up with WR Kevin Swayne on the first play from scrimmage, for the first touchdown in XFL history. Interesting, the Orlando Thunder of the WLAF in 1991 scored a TD on their first play as well. The coach then? Galen Hall. Also during the drive, a video package showed off big hits thus far, including one from the helmet cam of a player. Out of break, Dara Torres plugged the sponsors. This was a nice, simple way to ramp up the sex appeal without having to flaunt the cheerleaders to the viewers. Torres, an Olympic swimmer who has competed in five separate games, also had experience working as a sports reporter for ESPN, TNT and NBC. Two penalties, one from each team, on this drive. This is something you see in pre-season NFL football and could've been ironed out had there been more time in the pre-season for these guys. In the end, fans didn't see it that way: They saw it as sloppy football. Speaking of sloppy, the Outlaws scored their first touchdown on what Vasgersian called "sloppy seconds," after the pass was tipped by Hitmen LB Ben Hanks and then caught by TE Rickey Brady. This was also the first televised point-after attempt from the two yard-line. There was some confusion on where the point-after which end of the field the point after would occur from, since time had run out of the quarter. Brady dropped the pass, then told Clement "I'll make up for it." The dropped pass was shown on numerous highlight films after the game, including on ESPN's Sportscenter, in a montage of missed tackles, dropped passes, penalties and other bad plays, trying extra-hard to paint the XFL as truly minor league. That was certainly a low blow, as the play on the field wasn't as bad as the videos indicated.

Drive two for the Hitmen saw RT Jerome Daniels get hurt. He spent the rest of the season on injured reserve. The cameras showed David Spade in attendance at the game. I'm sure NBC wanted someone from one of their other shows to be at the game and provide the chance for cross-promotion by the announcers, as Spade was starring in the NBC sitcom "Just Shoot Me" at the time and also had the movie "Joe Dirt" coming out soon. The Hitmen punt on this drive resulted in the first five-yard halo penalty. He Hate Me caught a screen pass for a huge gain, breaking tackles along the way. Roggin tried to interview him after the play, but there was a play running on the field and afterward, Smart had to go right back into the game and had no time to talk. This added to his mystique. After a timeout, Stone Cold Steve Austin cut a pre-taped promo, bashing the NFL for calling the XFL a "non-issue." I feel like McMahon and his brain-trust had a difficult time balancing needs of the football fan with needs of the WWE fan in this first game, which is why we got wrestlers gushing, in character, about the league. Later on, it was explained that New York S Joey Eloms was given the name "Hurricane" that he wore on the back of his jersey from coach Rusty Tillman. Tillman was a darling of the NBC production crew, as they showed a montage of his mic'd up moments and he got much more camera time than his counterpart. During the third Hitmen drive, Carol Grow talked to fans in the stands about the game. Grow, wife of former NFL player Monty Grow, first gained fame as a beauty queen and model, but later became an actress and co-host of shows such as "Robot Wars: Extreme Wars" and ESPN2's fitness programs. Brandon Sanders made an interception and was also crushed on a hit out of bounds by OL Troy Stark. He came up smiling though, endearing him to The Body. They showed off the yard marker that was bent when the players collided with it. While talking to his teammates on the sideline, we heard the first curse word that slipped by the crack NBC censors, when he let the "shit" fly. It was the first, but not the last expletive that would air on an XFL broadcast. Now that the FCC has cracked down on what is acceptable for broadcast TV (thank you very much, Janet

Jackson), one would have to wonder what fines the XFL would be incurring today for those mistakes. With no penalty being called on the late hit by Stark, the Hitmen tried it again, with Trout walloping punt returner Mike Furrey out of bounds. The laundry flew on that one though. Just when things started to get stale with neither offense looking good, Clement hit WR Nakia Jenkins on a 27-yard pass play for a touchdown. The extra point was converted by OT Lonnie Palelei, an eligible receiver that Clement found in the end zone. "All day Joey, all day" said Clement in the face of Joey Eloms after the score. Palelei, when asked if it was the happiest moment of his life, joked (maybe?) that when he went deep next time, it'd be the happiest moment of his life.

Antonio Edwards of the Outlaws registered the first sack of the game near the end of the first half. At halftime, the scene in the locker room (sponsored by Burger King!) was about what you'd expect. Vegas WR Nakia Jenkins was listenting to music on headphones. There was no Tillman blow-up as Ventura had predicted. He didn't have kind words for the special teams, and said the Outlaws weren't beating them, they were beating themselves. Criner was talking to his offensive line and Rusty did do a little ripping on LB Tyrell Peters. I don't know what the XFL braintrust expected, but there wasn't a whole lot going on except coaches talking X's and O's and players sitting around.

As the second half opened, the score was 21-16 in Orlando, forcing some to wonder if that was the game that should've aired on the main broadcast with the outpouring of offense. The XFL gained more credibility when NFL DT and future FOX NFL analyst Tony Siragusa was interviewed on the sidelines. He got a cheer from the crowd when he said the Hitmen needed to get their heads out of their asses to come back. Goose even implored Tillman to get his club fired up. I'm sure the XFL loved having an NFL player touting their league on national television. Mics caught Tillman discussing a fake field goal in the third quarter, and on the same series, Puleri was hit and had to be checked for a concussion by the training staff. The anti-violence minions would've piled on Ventura, who said Puleri didn't even get hit that hard. This also gave more ammunition to the critics who thought the rule changes would end with the maiming of quarterbacks league-wide. WWE's Undertaker did a quick promo during a bumper before break. More injuries set the Hitmen back, as WR Kirby Dar Dar and DT Christian Maumalanga were hurt. With Puleri out, Corte McGuffey came in to relieve him and was sacked on his first play, a fourth-and-four opportunity. A pre-tape of Brandon Sanders and a cheerleader aired, much like the one earlier with Clement.

In the fourth quarter, with 13:55 to go and the game not totally out of reach but in danger of losing viewers, NBC switched to the back-up game, the Enforcers vs. the Rage. Lawler immediately made his priorirties known, saying he was there for the cheerleaders. Each team got three drives in front of a nationwide audience, including the first use of the receiver in motion toward the line of scrimmage, since neither the Outlaws nor the Hitmen employed that play. People who stuck around got to see some better QB play than in the first game, thanks to Jeff Brohm, who threw four touchdown passes for Orlando. Chicago scored late, but couldn't recover the onside kick, and the Rage ran out the clock, putting a "W" on the board, 33-29. Vegas held on to win 19-0 over New York. The ratings would tell though, that few viewers who tuned in had stuck around until the very end. In the main game overall, there were seven penalties against New York and nine against Las Vegas. While those numbers may seem high, and critics of the league pointed to penalties as a signifier of sloppy play, two NFL teams in 2008 averaged seven penalties per game, and four more, when rounded up, would reach seven. Even then, fans seemed to love the experience. Said Outlaws beat writer Kevin Iole about that first game: "The first XFL game was a great experience. The crowd was very excited and into it and it was very entertaining. I got the sense that the people really liked it a lot and were impressed by the quality of play."

Lending credibility to the product on the field were the advertisers they had lined up during commercial breaks. Among them were Burger King, the U.S. Army, Honda, Budweiser, Columbia Pictures, Ford, Verizon, Nissan, the U.S. Air Force, Castrol, Miller Genuine Draft, Pep Boys, Pennzoil, Pizza Hut, Snickers, 20th Century Fox, Stacker 2, Warner Brothers and Universal Studios, all major companies. The numbers would predictably thin as the season wore on, and others would get ads for free as the ratings went into a free-fall.

They say offense draws viewers, and there just wasn't a whole lot in the first game. Defenses usually develop quicker than offenses, so that explains that. Again, a full-fledged pre-season would've solved that and maybe in year two, with the XFL having nothing to hide as far as what the game was going to be like, it would've happened. But they were so concerned with keeping their gadgets and gizmos a secret that the football on the field suffered. But Vince McMahon, Dick Ebersol and Jesse Ventura, who held a press conference in Las Vegas following the broadcast, seemed pretty pleased with the results on the first night.

While the action may have been sub-par and the sideline interviews for the most part useless, while sitting back and reviewing the first game again in writing this book, it felt different than watching an NFL broadcast, even eight years later. It felt more relaxed, more fun and yes, more fan-friendly. And those are a few of the qualities the XFL wanted to set them apart from the NFL. The guys playing in the XFL weren't rich fat-cats half-assing it out there; they were giving it their all thanks to the $2,500 bonus going to each player on the winning team. And even though the action wasn't up to the NFL standards (and nobody in their right mind should've expected that), it was pretty decent.

In the newspapers the next day, Rust Tillman wasn't happy with the performance, but thought the effort was there. He was already talking about bringing in some fresh bodies, so it was clear he didn't like what he saw. Neither did Enforcers' coach Ron Meyer, who said his team made "a ton of mistakes." Rage coach Galen Hall was not the biggest fan of the scramble, hoping the XFL would take another look at it after his scrambler fell victim to injury on the play. The Outlaws were overjoyed after the game, with Lonnie Palelei, a veteran of seven NFL years, saying the crowd was more intense than in any NFL game he played in. Of course, some players (and coach Criner) had to answer questions from the throng of media credentialed in that first game about the quality of play. In another Review-Journal article the next day, fans were quoted as saying how much they enjoyed that action and atmosphere. They also ran a story detailing the domination of the team's defensive line and suggested a nickname for the four could be forthcoming if they keep it up. An interesting observation, as the Outlaws defense later in the season would get a nickname because of their conquering prowess. Coverage of the Enforcers featured quotes by John Avery, Chicago's RB, thanking Vince McMahon for having the courage to develop the league. The game story by Rupen Fofaria in the Chicago Tribune even mentioned the Orlando fans booing the QB for sliding for a first-down, rather than getting extra yardage and taking a hit. Oh, and it was the Rage QB. The crowd in Orlando was quite raucous, to the point that most of the fans stayed in their seats at halftime.

Not all was well in Orlando, as thousands of fans were left out of the stadium because of the capacity being set at 36,000 and the upper bowl being closed off. Many stadiums in the XFL didn't open the entire stadium, and it would appear that fact was left out of the media in Orlando, or at least fans didn't know that the capacity would be smaller than usual in an effort to make the atmosphere more intimate. One person even tried to get into the game by claiming he was the drummer for Creed and one man was arrested for trying to sneak in. It gave the XFL some bad press in the Orlando area, for a day at least.

The media was all over the league the next day, for various reasons. Even, and I kid you not, the priest at the Church I go to, the next day, spoke out against the XFL in his sermon. The Associated Press, in recapping the Rage vs. Enforcers game, focused on the injury to Deen and seemed to imply that it wasn't such a good idea. They also noted the quality of play was "spotty," pointing to the 17 penalties among the two teams. The article also mentioned how the fans at the stadium were largely ignored. OK, well, what would you like them to do? Everybody was worried that the focus of the league wouldn't be on football, then this article questions why fans weren't a bigger part of the game. What do NFL games do to get fans involved? About the only thing you can do is show them on the video screen. Is it that big a deal to make a note of it in a game recap though? Fans at the game made the comment that there was no net on field goal attempts, allowing fans to keep the ball that went through the uprights and into the stands. Also, they got to storm the field at the end without being cold-cocked by security. That sounds pretty fan-friendly. The AP's story did end by carrying a quote from a fan satisfied with the experience. And for what it's worth, the article spent four lines describing what happened in the game, in the entire recap. Clearly, the football play on the field didn't matter much to them despite going to such lengths to question whether it would matter to the XFL. It mattered so little in fact that noted sports blowhard Jim Rome (who, ironically, made a reputation for being loud and obnoxious) called the XFL entertainment, but not fooball. Then what was all that stuff going on on the field with the guys in helmets and pads? The New York Post and New York Times, two of the more widely-read news outlets, both decried the league, with the Post going so far as to call it "garbage." I really can't imagine what led to them calling a game of football "garbage," but then again, the Post is called a tabloid for a reason and neither it nor the Times are bastions of fair-and-balanced views.

Leonard Shapiro of the Washington Post wrote an article in the Monday edition titled "The XFL Bombs Away." He shamed NBC for selling out to "tawdry titillation and lousy football." Really, other than the cheerleaders, how was the game overtly sexual? You see cheerleaders at NFL games, even though they're not shown on TV that often. Does that mean that NFL games are home to the same kind of titillation? And it's not like they were wearing strippers outfits. They were pretty reasonably dressed, though I'm probably a bit younger than most of the stuffy media types who complained about the league. And "lousy" was not an opinion shared of other writers, like in the game recap at the Las Vegas Review-Journal, where they termed the play "quality football." Shapiro surmised that it wasn't really a football game, just an excuse to show the cheerleaders (again, it was in and out of breaks and that's about the extent of it) and show off gadgets. He went so far as to assume that Vince McMahon had to give away tickets to the game. With the buzz surrounding the league and the Las Vegas area getting a pro sports team that would be shown on national television, I'm sure that number is closer to zero than Shapiro would like to think. The lone compliment, a backhanded one at that, was that the game looked "real enough" and he took several snipes at Vince McMahon and scripting action. Again, if this were a movie producer or director, would he be facing the same accusations? I doubt it. He took issue with Ventura characterizing players as leaving jobs for an opportunity at glory, noting that they're only playing to get into the NFL to play for higher pay and more benefits. Yes, the higher pay that columnists usually complain so much about. And benefits? Yeah, until you're retired, as we've seen lately how bad off former NFL players are after leaving the football life behind. Complimenting McMahon, even in the slightest, meant complimenting everything he's done in the pro wrestling world, distasteful as it may be for proud journalists to acknowledge success in the "fake" sport of wrestling. The amount of negativity the day after was just ridiculous, like McMahon had spit in the NFL's face or something, and every media-type had to become the morality police and run to defend the league from the meanie who was taking football down a vulgar road.

Bob Raissman of the Daily News had a bit of a more even-handed look. While he termed the play on the field "awful" and classified Ventura's announcing as so bad that "he is stealing money" (he wasn't great, for sure—with all the inside looks at the game, the XFL needed someone to explain to the viewers as to what they were hearing as far as plays being called and football talk in general being caught by microphones), he also acknowledged that the broadcast featured the future of sports television with the technological advances shown, giving viewers an inside look at the game, a new perspective on an old sport.

Kevin Scarbinsky of the Birmingham News took the other side of the fence, saying the XFL WAS in fact, just a football game. He said you see more sex and violence on an episode of "The Sopranos." He really hit the nail on the head, saying, "you really should take a look at it before you look down on it." In a write-up for the Orlando Sentinel, L.C. Johnson even wrote that the XFL lived up to the hype. Too many columnists like Shapiro seemed to have the thing written before even watching the game (if they even went so far as to do that). Yes, it was an over-the-top presentation of football but in the end, it was just football. Too many media types bought into the idea that the violence would end society as we know it and the sex was so prevalent by reading some of the articles you would've thought an orgy was going on on the sidelines. Cheerleaders. And not even that scantily clad. And that was it for sexuality. Apparently, that was too much for some. Bill Baker said much of the attacks from the media was because of Vince McMahon's association with the league. "USA Today did not even run our scores but they had Women's Basketball and Tennis and Rugby . We outdrew all those sports both on TV and in attendance. I'm a bit jaded towards the media and the coverage."

Before leaving for Birmingham, the Memphis team invited fans to a walk-through practice, followed by players being available for autographs. In Birmingham, the newspapers detailed the XFL on the day of the Bolts' game, and GM Tim Berryman appeared to be doing everything he could to pump up attendance in a town that was lagging behind others, even being quoted in the paper as thinking the XFL would be family-friend and despite concerns about language with the live mics, that the players would represent the city with dignity.

For Los Angeles, the motivating factor prior to their game agains the Demons was the extra $2,500 that went to each player on the winning team. The article in the LA Times previewing the game did a nice job setting up each team's strengths and discussing football strategy and key players, rather than re-hashing the new rules like so many others had. Hey, it's been a year—if someone was interested in the XFL, I'm thinking they would've come across the changes by that point.

On Sunday, the debut of the XFL on UPN took place. Coverage began with clips of the games from the previous night (including the promo by The Rock-Austin and Undertaker cut one later in the program), as well as national and local television coverage of the league. For the most part, the script (no, not THAT script) from the night before was followed, with teams making their entrances, announcers Chris

Marlowe and Brian Bosworth talking about the coaches and a rivalry manufactured between UCLA's Tommy Maddox and Cal's Mike Pawlawski, each QB'ing their respective teams. Dick Butkus was once again on hand for the Scramble. We also learned that each player gets one false start on the Scramble. They featured some pre-taped segments with players, learning more about them, including Pawlawksi, Xtreme DL Jamal Duff and Demons OT Scott Adams, who discussed his father's death and the wrist-band he wears to represent him. Bosworth also mentioned that Adams gets so worked up before the game, he has to purge himself by puking.

More problems with game play ensued after the opening kick (which was even fumbled by returner Brandin Young), with many penalties being called early on. During introductions, one of the Demons players even stumbled over his own name. Hey, speaking on national TV is tough. They went with the more traditional sideline camera view for the player, but it wasn't clear if that was a permanent change on all broadcast, or if the X-Stream was exclusive to NBC. The Demons put pressure on the Xtreme right off the bat, as the first LA play from scrimmage was a Tommy Maddox fumble, forced by CB Dwayne Harper and recovered by DE Eric England. It was clear early on that Marlowe was definitely more reserve than I'm sure the XFL brass would've preferred, but loosened up a bit working with The Boz.

Despite the other Sunday game not being televised in the first week, TNN announcers Craig Minnervini and Bob Golic provided cut-ins to the Memphis vs. Birmingham game throughout the UPN broadcast. The Maniax pulled out a 22-20 win and if you had "less than a week" in the "how long before Birmingham fans demand Jay Barker in the game" in your office pool, you could collect your prize: Fans chanted "we want Barker" when Weldon struggled. In the stands in San Francisco, Stephanie McMahon (referred to only as "Stephanie" here), the daughter of Vince McMahon, interviewed fans in the stands. On a punt return near the end of the first quarter, we got our first fight. Xtreme WR Darnell McDonald went at it with Demons LB Jon Haskins. The camera on the field got a great view of it, as the two got tangled up and McDonald lost his helmet. Haskins kicked it across the field, much to the delight of the fans (and of course, Bosworth). Another Rock promo aired coming back from commercial. Of course, after coming back, Haskins was interviewed on the sidelines.

The Demons offense seemed content with going short pass after short pass down the field. Pawlawski unloaded 47 passes during the game, compared to only 18 rushing plays. Mike Panasuk, who made 11 of 12 field goals in his Demons tryout, missed the first field goal of the game and Michael Barkann even reminded him that this predecessor got nervous in sideline interviews during the exhibition games, but Panasuk said he could handle it. He was another great story, as he was teaching Speech at Lebanon High School in Lebanon Pennsylvannia earlier in the week before getting the call from San Fran on Saturday and kicking on national TV the next day. When he got the phone call for the XFL, he was actually expecting a very different person on the other end: He was a finalist for the game show "Who Wants To Be A Millionaire" and was waiting for a call to answer one question, and if he did, he'd get to be on the show in New York. His pro experience was limited, as he had failed to get signed in six NFL training camps and flamed out in the CFL. But Panasuk wasn't the only kicker struggling, as Jose Cortez of the Xtreme missed a chip-shot field goal as well. He came back to hit one later in the game—the first he missed attempting it barefoot; on the one he made, he had his shoe on. During the coach-to-QB communications, Bosworth could at least explain what some of the lingo meant. The lack of offense was once again a problem, as the teams went into halftime with the Xtreme up 7-6.

At the half, the camera caught Tommy Maddox talking with his teammates as well as Offensive Coordinator Jim Barker addressing his squad. In the home locker room, it was the Demons defensive coordinator Michael Church who held court with his guys. A production error led to being able to hear Marlowe talk to the guys in the truck while watching the locker room happenings, and he even dropped the F-bomb. Coaches Skipper and Luginbill gave their teams speeches that fans got to see before the teams headed to the field for the second half. Also at halftime they showed Carol Grow throwing XFL footballs into McCovey Cove, but none of the guys jumped in after it. It was likely scripted, because the guys acted distracted by the cheerleaders and Grow.

The Bay Area fans on hand seemed to be a combination of WWE fans and Raider fans, as there were loud "bullshit" chants after a pass interference call in the third quarter on Harper and a missed extra point in the fourth that. He came back the next play and crushed WR Latario Rachal with a clothesline. While neither coach had the kind of emotion that Rusty Tillman showed the night before when cameras were glued to him all night, the quarterbacks made up for it as Pawlawski and Maddox were both good interviews on the sidelines.

The score was 13-12 in the fourth quarter when the Demons began to drive with 2:00 to go. Panasuk was interviewed on the sidelines and it was clear he was getting in "game-winning kick" mode and seemed quite focused despite Barkann's questions. With time running out, no time outs left and at the buzzer, Panasuk, the schoolteacher from Pennsylvania, ran onto the field and kicked the game-winning field goal from 33 yards out as time expired and the crowd went bananas. That's the kind of finish they could've only dreamed of for the NBC game, but better late than never and quite the impression to make for the UPN viewers checking out the XFL for the first time. This time, Barkann was able to interview Pansuk after a little better performance.

In a nice change of pace, the San Francisco Chronicle, in the recap, covered it as an actual football, with hardly a mention of the much-ballyhooed wrinkles add to the festivities in the XFL. In fact, so did Steve Irvine of the LA Times. It was quite refreshing. People reading it, on the fence about the league, knew by the end that it was real football, rather than having been inundated with comments about everything BUT the game. Most of the articles covering the four games of the weekend featured positive reviews of the games from fans as well. Many equated the atmosphere at the games to a concert (certainly not a John Tesh concert anyway), and a Birmingham vendor said he sold more beer at the Bolts opener than any other football game.

A story in the Birmingham paper focused on long lines at ticket windows and concessions, as the Bolts were not expecting the large walk-up crowd that was attracted to the stadium. Some glitches in the sound system were mentioned as well, plus some occasional swearing by the players. It felt like an article that, instead of saying, "hey, great for this town and the XFL to have 35,000 fans at the game," it was more of, "35,000 had to wait in long lines all over the stadium." At least Clyde Bolton, the writer of the story, noted that the cheerleaders were about as bare as most of their NFL counterparts. A piece was included at the end about announcer Jim Ross, who was at the game. For some reason, it was included that he "provided commentary on the game." One, it wasn't televised, and two, when the cut-ins were shown, it was Golic and Minnervini announcing, so I'm not sure to whom Ross was commenting on the game to.

Because of the struggle at the stadium with the walk-up crowd and the fact that vendors ran out of beer in the third quarter, Birmingham vowed to make changes before the next home game to better accomodate fans. Many of the planned changes had to do with ticket sales and opening the upper deck of the stadium to fit more fans. Despite the crowds being rowdy and akin to pro wrestling or concerts, the manager of Legion Field said they have more arrests during college football games held at the stadium than they had during the XFL opener.

Joel Buschbaum of Pro Football Weekly was asked about the XFL's debut, and he chided the low-level football, society in general for latching on to the idea the XFL was promoting (here we go.) and the league for giving people a "sex show." I'm sorry, but really? A sex show? Where was that in the game, because I certainly missed it. Too many shots of the cheerleaders for ya, Joel? Or was it the sexual innuendos of the pre-tapes with Ryan Clement and Brandon Sanders, all of which lasted a grand total of 10 second? Football snobbery at its best, folks. It was like some of the columnists watched the highlights on SportsCenter or a similar show, where they showed miscues and mistakes by the players and based their opinions off that.

In the first broadcasts, the XFL threw everything at the wall, hoping something would stick. Some of it did. Of the XFL-exclusive content, most of the criticism in the media came down on the sideline reporters (only ask questions if they are needed.don't force it with dumb queries and wait until the guy catches his breath before asking him!), the scramble for the ball (which I like—it may be a bit unnecessary, but it's different from the NFL and that's what they were after) and nicknames on the back of jerseys (promoting individuality—I like it—it usually didn't take longer to figure out who was who). The league clearly had some work to do to retain fans for the second week after a so-so opening Saturday of actual football action. Baker said that some teams were simply further along in terms of knowing and being able to execute the plays than other teams. Weather conditions early on as well, though not so much in the first week, also contributed to some of the so-so football play. They come for the sizzle and stay for the steak. Just how many people came for the sizzle was released on Monday—the debut week ratings, ultra-critical for the media who were looking for anything to use and point to the league as if to say, "see, we were all right!" But they had to wait at least another week for that chance to come.

CHAPTER SEVEN

When the ratings came in, I'm sure there was much rejoicing at WWE and NBC headquarters. The rating was a 9.5 (14.6 million viewers), which was double the usual NBC Saturday night rating. For UPN's game, the preliminary rating was 4.2, which was almost two ratings points higher than the NHL All-Star Game on ABC (a bigger league and a bigger network—the final rating settled at 3.1). NBA Games and the Pro Bowl were also airing opposite the UPN game. The only downside was that the rating, at least for the NBC game, decreased throughout the game, meaning fans tuned in at the begin but for whatever reason, more and more tuned out as the game continued. About 18.5 million people were watching at the outset; that number declined to a still-respectable 12 million by the game's end. The demographic the XFL scored best in was their target demo, teen males. Despite the apparent success, the XFL drew even more comparisons to a past doomed football league, as the USFL got off to a hot ratings start out of the gate as well.

To tout the ratings and also put a lid on some of the criticism aimed at them after the first week, WWE sent out a Press Release hyping the week as "an Unqualified Success." The release publicized the fact that the average attendance for the four games was 35,115, an impressive number no matter which way you slice it. The question was, like the ratings, could the league sustain those numbers? According to the XFL, four cities saw huge ticket increases since the first games were played, so it appeared that wouldn't be so much of a worry as the televised portion. Despite the increase in ratings, WWE stock actually plummeted on the Monday after the first game, falling almost $2 by the close of business. Continuing to want to keep the XFL in the public's eye, or at least on the media's radar following the much-hyped debut, the XFL sent out a press release detailing week two's games, giving out injury reports and notes for each team.

WWE took advantage of the ratings success by mentioning it on their pro wrestling shows that week. Vince McMahon and The Rock both talked about the league briefly in promos they cut on Raw two days after the Saturday night game, and there were lots of promos for the XFL on TNN that would air the following Sunday. Highlight packages of the first week were shown and the announcers took a shot at USAToday columnist Rudy Martzke, who didn't have nice things to say about the XFL's announcers for the weekend. Of course, that's the kind of stuff that got Vince in trouble with the media in the first place; he can't leave well enough alone and when he feels he's been wronged, he has the need to fight back instead of let it go. Picking his battles, especially with the media, was not one of Vince's strong suits, and it needed to be if he were to run a league like the XFL.

For the Orlando Rage, who lost a player to injury before the game even started, they received word that CB Hassan Shamsid-deen would be out three-to-four weeks after dislocating his shoulder in the opening scramble against Chicago. He was told by doctors in the locker room that the pain he felt was equal to the pain felt by women while giving birth. Shamsid-deen vowed not to scramble upon his return.

The New York/New Jersey Hitmen went into week two keeping Charlie Puleri as their starting quarterback, despite his rough outing against the Outlaws where he completed only six of 19 passes. The Hitmen were also without starting RT Jerome Daniels after he fell victim to a season-ending knee injury; and starting RB Dino Philyaw, who was scheduled to miss four weeks due to a broken bone in his foot. In Philyaw's place, former Indianapolis Colts RB Keith Elias was to get the starting nod. There was a lot of pressure to win in front of their crowd in their home debut, and also from coach Rusty Tillman (who spoke out against the offense's performance during the week) and outspoken general manager Drew Pearson.

Keith Elias might have been one of the last people you'd expect to join the XFL. From the Jersey shore in Lacey Township, Elias graduated from the esteemed Princeton University with a degreee in History. From 1991 to 1993, Elias tore up the Ivy League, setting records for the Tigers in most career points and touchdowns, also both Ivy League records that still stand. Elias paced the nation in rushing yards per game as a junior and a senior. He was a two-time first-team All-American and was Ivy League MVP his senior season. Heading into the NFL draft, Elias had two things working against him: His height (only 5'9") and the fact that he didn't play in a conference known for its football acumen. The New York Giants signed him in 1994 after he went undrafted. He stuck with them for three seasons as a backup running back, getting into 26 games, mostly as a special teamer. After not playing at all in 1997 due to suffering a knee injury the season before, he went to the Indianapolis Colts, where he played in 27 games in two years. In 1999, he was the special teams captain of the Colts, but became a salary cap casualty the next season. He finished his NFL career with 42 carries and 22 receptions.

A no-nonsense player, it was then surprising when he decided to get in bed with the XFL after sitting out of pro football for the 2000 season. He ended up being the second RB the Hitmen selected in the XFL P.A.S.S, going in the 44th round, 346 overall. Elias revealed that he was skeptical of the league at first, but the more he read into it, the more he realized that major football people were involved and that it was going to be no joke. On the field, the then-28 year old Elias (who turned 29 on the day of the first XFL game) wasn't one to trash-talk or show-boat. He thought the game had too much of that anyway. An amateur screenwriter and novelist, Elias not only got to play pro football once again and make one final charge at getting NFL teams to take notice of him, but he got to play in his backyard at Giants Stadium. He didn't have pie-in-the-sky hopes of returning to the NFL though, acknowledging that he was getting old for a RB (even telling Mike Adamle during the inaugrual broadcast that "in pro football, I'm an old man pushing the envelope") and that he was mainly playing for the sociability and interaction that football provides.

Even as the seson began, Elias admitted that he felt more excitement before the first kickoff for the Hitmen, than he did when he played in the NFL. He said it was likely because he was actually getting the opportunity to play in this league. After starter Dino Philyaw went down with an injury in week one, Elias took the reigns and got the bulk of the carries for a few weeks. Elias saw his XFL dreams end after a week four knee injury against the Enforcers. But he took on an even bigger role after his injury, replacing Paul Butcher as special teams coach after Butcher left to tend to his business in California, which the team apparently knew about before the season began. Instead of Tillman taking over special teams as planned, he handed the reigns to Elias. His jobs included designing plays, scouting the opposing teams and being a go-between for the players and coaching staff. He finished the only XFL season, and his last in pro football, with 37 carries for 115 yards. Since 2001, he has been booked for speaking engagements at home and abroad and the spiritual Elias has participated in relief work after Hurricane Katrina. He also works with the New Jersey Youth Alliance and other youth groups to promote positive behavior.

The San Francisco Demons also suffered an injury setback in practice leading up to their game with the Rage on Saturday night. He led all receivers in the first week, nabbing 12 balls for 127 yards. Roberson made it clear that he wasn't thrilled with being asked questoins by sideline reporters during the game in an article in the San Francisco Chronicle, but coach Jim Skipper denied it was a distraction.

Things got testy for Birmingham leading up to their week two game against the Hitmen. On the Wednesday before the game, coach Gerry DiNardo kicked TE Nicky Savoie and LB Malcolm Hamilton out of practice for fighting, the second skirmish of the day. The offensive line, which struggled in the opening game like most lines around the league, got a week to get healthier, as they were bitten by the injury and food poisoning bugs. Toya Jones, Birmingham's designated scrambler, promised to win every scramble for the rest of the year as he headed into week two 1-0. He told the Birmingham News that he had a strategy that would guarantee him victory every time, but refused to share it for fear other teams would steal it.

Much of the buzz in Los Angeles was for pro football returning to the city and to the LA Coliseum for the first time since 1994. QB Tommy Maddox was with the NFL's Rams when they left Los Angeles to move to St. Louis, so he had previous LA football experience. The Xtreme, who were to face the Chicago Enforcers, were down two defensive linemen for the game, not a good sign as they had to contend with Enforcers RB John Avery, who scampered for 157 rushing yards and claimed the first-ever XFL Player of the Week honors during the first week. But WR Darnell McDonald wasn't worried—one of the more outspoken players (he and fellow WR Jermaine Copeland had promised a touchdown celebration dance when either of them scored) told reporters that he'd be surprised if the Xtreme lost another game all season after dropping their first. Al Luginbill's rule of giving the players 24 hours to sulk after a loss, then moving on, seemed to work, at least for McDonald.

The XFL may have made their first star on opening night. "He Hate Me" Rod Smart got all kinds of media attention during the week between games one and two and did 15 radio interviews leading up to the Outlaws' game with the Maniax. Smart was not a lock to make the roster as close as a week before the first game, but ended up winning the starting job over Chrys "Chuckwagon" Chukwuma in the final scrimmage against the Demons. He wanted "Who Is He" for the second game, but the equipment staff was notified too late, so he had to settle for "He Hate Me" again. He even began to be recognized in airports and He Hate Me was written on the scoresheets and used on the public address system in Memphis for the game. Another good sign was that while most coverage of the XFL's first week was negative, the Las Vegas Review-Journal did an interesting story on what kinds of diets the players on the Outlaws have in terms of eating throughout the week. OL Lonnie Palelei said he loses six to 12 pounds on the field, which he replaces with liquids. It was a fluff piece maybe, but it gave fans an inside look at the team at an angle no one else was taking. There's only so many times fans of the league (or non-fans even) can read people villifying the league.

The Maniax were without one of their most experienced players, WR Alvin Harper, in the first game due to a groin strain, but he was expected back against the Outlaws. The game was expected to match an offensive powerhouse (Memphis) against a defensive stalwart (Vegas).

The Chicago Enforcers quietly made a rather big move during the week leading up to the first game, when they dropped first-round pick QB Paul Failla to third on the depth chart, and moved Kevin McDougal up to back-up. Failla did see action in game one, completing one pass for five yards. It was surprising enough that he lost out on the #1 QB position to the unheralded Tim Lester, but Lester did well in the first week, completing 13 of 21 passes.

For the most part, in cities that were opening up their XFL season with home games, most of the media focused on ticket sales and there appeared to be little in the way of previewing the actual games. Those who did though used the space to run human interest stories about the players, in an effort to get them over as, if not characters, than regular guys living out a dream. Which was right up the XFL's alley.

The XFL certainly scheduled their NBC prime-time games well for at least the first two weeks: Opening up the league with the biggest media market in the nation playing, following it up in week two with a city getting their first outside pro football game in six years. Unfortunately, the league didn't get the message from fans and pundits across the country to discontinue the relationship between wrestling and football that occured in week one—the first person on the field during NBC's telecast of the LA vs. Chicago game was The Rock, long before he had become a cross-over star. He got the crowd fired up against the NFL for taking away their football team. Fans watching also heard a different voice introducing the game: Jim Ross was promoted from the B-squad to tha A-game and Matt Vasgersian was sent to work with Jerry "The King" Lawler. JR, good as an announcer as he was (and still is), gave the XFL another pro wrestling connection on the broadcast. Working with Jesse Ventura only enhanced the notion that things were turning into WWE: Football. This, in my opinion, was the exact opposite tact to take. Vasgersian did fine on the opening broadcast and if anyone needed to be moved, it was Ventura (but, as big a star as he was, that wasn't going to happen). Vince McMahon has been notoriously hard on announcers during his time in WWE, ironic because he broke in as an announcer and held that position until the early-to-mid '90s. Brett Forrest noted in his book "Long Bomb," that Vasgersian was demoted for not "selling" fans on the XFL enough in the first week, so McMahon brought on a confidant in Ross who knew what he wanted from his announcers.

The storyline started out in the pre-game, as Scott Milanovich, Xtreme QB, was awaiting the birth of his first child, who was already four days overdue. Since his wife could've gone into labor at any time, the XFL had a helicopter on stand-by to take Milanovich to the hospital, and Stephanie McMahon (she got a last name this week) provided the details on the situation. Milanovich was grateful to the XFL for this, and told the LA Times that the NFL wouldn't have been so thoughtful to do something like that. No word on if cameras would've followed the Milanoviches during the actual birth.

After the now-familiar scramble and pep talks from the head coaches in the locker room, viewers saw the screen go dark. It was the worst nightmare of the XFL brass as there was a power outage at the stadium and it took a few minutes for the network to switch to the San Francisco vs. Orlando game. People may have taken that opportunity to change channels and not come back, which was not something the XFL, wanting to show that the first week's rating wasn't a fluke, could afford. The Demons and Rage were about to kickoff, but there was about a minute or two of standing around before Mike Panasuk put the ball in the air to open the game, more down-time the viewer had to sit through. They stuck with player introductions, but each player just gave their name, position and college, which I'm sure was a decree from the higher-ups in the XFL so as not to take up any more time than necessary.

Because it was the alternate game, there weren't as many mics or cameras to catch the action. With 3:14 left in the first quarter of the Rage vs. Demons game, power was finally restored in LA and the coverage switched back. Orlando went on to claim victory, 26-14.

It was 12-6 when the game went back to LA, and all that offense could've helped viewers stick around. A few minutes later, another short outage took the game out for another minute or two. Terrible luck for a league that needed all the luck it could get. Instead of relying solely on the X-Cam, they did have some traditional side-shots as the play occured. Rashan Shehee was profiled in a video package and seemed to be one of the players and stories the XFL tried to get over. In the opening quarter, they also seemed to cut down on the intrusive questions by the sideline reporters. In fact, Ron Meyer and Al Luginbill didn't get nearly the face time Rusty Tillman did in week one. The Enforcers went up 18-6 in the 2nd quarter on a blocked punt recovered in the end zone by Brian Rodgers. The Xtreme seemed in disarray on offense, defense and special teams. But fans in LA seemed to be enjoying their time at the Coliseum, especially those in the hot tub featured beyond one of the end zones. Hilariously, the women in the tub ended up being strippers, and the Xtreme had no idea afterward who hired them and sent them there. The Xtreme scored to make it 18-13 late in the first and yes, Darnell McDonald and his offensive mates did the "Booty Call" touchdown dance despite McDonald's sore ribs. After scoring another touchdown to run the score to 25-13 Chicago heading into the half, RB LeShon Johnson threw the ball into the stands after netting the touchdown and extra point (like Wrigley Field in Chicago, an LA fan threw the ball back).

At halftime, The Rock joined the announcers to talk about the XFL and we got another All Access pass into the locker rooms. Another glitch occured when they sent it to Vasgersian and Lawler to give a report during halftime of the B-game, but there was no audio. All of the problems this week added up to making the XFL seem quite minor league, but that tends to happen when you rely so much on technology for the games. Coach Luginbill got a pop from the crowd when, asked why he went for a 4th-and-1 in his own territory, an attempt that failed, he responded, "I thought we needed a push, we didn't get it, it was the wrong call; hell, if we make it, it's a great decision." Of course, the announcers sung the praises of the XFL for allowing the ability for fans to see that kind of insight. While the announcers certainly were encouraged to "tell it like it is," way too often they were overly complimentary of the league for everything from its pay structure to game coverage. It felt like the league was insecure about itself and made sure the announcers relayed the positives of the league to the fans as much as possible.

Instead of mixing cheerleaders with players in pre-tapes, they had a few players cut pro wrestling-like promos, most notably LA DL Jamal Duff explaining his Deathblow nickname. In the third quarter, OT Octavious Bishop was seriously injured and an ambulance had to come onto the field to take him off, causing yet another delay during the game. Stephanie interviewed Rashan Shehee's mom in the crowd and as the camera tried to film the training staff tending to Bishop on the field, some of the players drew the "all access" line there and tried to usher the camera away from the scene. During the downtime, the crowd got restless, and while it wasn't captured on TV, many fans started throwing things and starting fights. Ventura, never one to mince words and when he finds someone to rag on he doesn't give up, tried to paint Tommy Maddox as a complainer, noting that he tried to get on the refs about getting some more calls. LA got some good field position after an unsuccessful quick-kick (the first time it was utilized in an XFL game), but were still down 12 as the third quarter wound down.

The action started to heat up in the second half. Unfortunately, as the game was getting good and it reached the half-way point of the fourth quarter, they reached 11:00 EST. The game got chippy at this point too as Leomont Evans of the Xtreme got in a scuffle with a few Enforcers and had to be restrained by teammates. As he reached the sidelines, he tipped over a water bucket in anger and told Fred Roggin that he was on the receiving end of a cheap-shot by a player that, in his mind, tried to take his career from him. Evans told him it wasn't over between them. Dick Butkus was on commentary during the fourth quarter and Ventura took the time to take a shot back at the "pukes" as

122

he called them, those who have been negative about the league and who likely, in his mind, had never played the game. That wouldn't endear the league to the media types. With 6:00 remaining, the Xtreme were still down two touchdowns. Jermaine Copeland was the main receiving threat, with 12 catches at that point. With 3:30 to go, the Xtreme converted a fourth down deep in Chicago territory. They scored on the next play, from eight yards out, on a pass to Damon Dunn, who got blasted in the back of the end zone by Corey Ivy, but held on long enough to garner six. It was the kind of hit that the XFL dreamed of, with Ivy leading with his shoulder and Dunn getting knocked parallel to the ground. The conversion was no good, leaving LA down by six with 2:36 remaining.

The Xtreme got the ball back with about 1:30 remaining in regulation. On 4th-and-10, with :39 to go, Tommy Maddox, who provided many great mic'd moments (including telling the coaches in his California drawl that "if he (Cortez) can't make it, let's don't kick it!") found Jermaine Copeland for 23 yards down to the one-yard line. RB Ken Oxendine punched it in from the one to tie things up. The extra point was again missed, and Al Luginbill was planning for overtime already. It was a first look at the new overtime rules. Chicago scored on three plays and converted the extra point. On LA's third play of overtime, where they needed to score or they'd lose, Maddox heaved a pass into the end zone that was hauled in by who else, Jermaine Copeland. Copeland scored on a slant to tie it up again and sent the football into the crowd. That's three for the game. LA got to go first in the second OT, and they scored on three plays again, this time on a 20-yard pass to Darnell McDonald and yes, the booty dance was witnessed again. The extra point was good. It was Maddox's 65th pass attempt of the game and Jermaine Copeland made history, pulling in 17 passes for 190 yards. Chicago, down to their final play, from the 15-yard line, was overthrown in the end zone, intended for WR Fred Coleman. The two final pictures that represented the game perfectly: Damon Dunn celebrating in the crowd with the Xtreme fans; juxtaposed with John Avery, left face down on the field, showing the pain of a game that got away.

Sunday afternoon, TNN aired their first XFL game, and it was the first Birmingham Bolts nationally-televised game and the Hitmen's first home game. Play-by-play was handled by former WWE announcer Craig Minnervini (who went by Craig DeGeorge then; he also had experience calling legitimate sports), with Bob Golic, the former Raider, on color commentary. Sideline reporters were Kip Lewis and Lee Reherman, both former NFL players. Reherman was even an American Gladiator once-upon-a-time and had a running bet, jokingly (maybe) about how many times a player would punch him because of his questions. Once teams made their way into Giants Stadium, Vince McMahon trotted out to mid-field. He likely made the trip for this one because New York City is close to WWE's home base of Stamford, Connecticut; and the fact that TNN was the home of WWE Raw at the time, so they may have asked Vince to introduce things. McMahon stated the rules for the scramble and made his appearance short. Minnervini noted that the Hitmen went undefeated during training camp, but started off sluggish last week. He also said that Tillman cried after the game last week because it was so important and he felt so bad for the guys afterward.

Unlike their counterparts on the NBC and UPN telecasts, Minnervini and Golic were short on bluster, which made them perhaps the best announcing combination all year. The broadcast didn't feature the player introductions like the previous three games that were televised. Overall it was a more conservative broadcast, even as it was in regards to cheerleaders and gratuitous shots of them. After a Mike Archie 2-yard TD run, Brad Palazzo got his first punt partially blocked. On his second kick, it was fully blocked. Two turnovers in the first quarter by New York prevented them from adding on. Near the end of the quarter, a profile aired on Anthony DiCosmo, who was adopted by a woman who raised 80 foster children in her lifteime. She was in the crowd for the game. Almost on cue, he caught passes on the next two plays.

The extra $2,500 was again much of the focus on the broadcast, and they asked Hitmen in pre-tapes what they'd do with them. Hurricane Eloms had perhaps the most unique answer: "Buy a whole lot of sammiches." Well, this helped the characters and players get over.but I'm not sure exactly what that said about Eloms' character. In another pre-tape, Tillman took issue with Ventura and Siragusa's comments in the previous week about not firing his team up enough. He was quite honest, saying he didn't care what anyone said, he's doing the job to the best of his abilities. On 4th-and-goal from the one yard-line, Keith Elias was stopped short and the Hitmen turned the ball over. The previous play, after a nice gain, Elias screamed that he didn't know the play and those in the huddle needed to communicate better. On the ensuing Bolts drive, DE Israel Raybon showed off his celebratory antics by dunking over the crossbar after sacking Weldon at the one. Eloms did what he could to insure his share of sandwiches by intercepting a long bomb, predicted by Tillman, on that drive. Another expletive was let loose when Birmingham RB James Bostic yelled "shit!" after being hurt and walking around on the sidelines. The Thunderbolts finally made a big play offensively, when New York S Brad Trout fell down, allowing former Dallas Cowboy Stepfret Williams to haul in a long bomb for 70 yards, down inside the five. Another "shit," this time from Tillman. While Birmingham was able to score, Casey Weldon began to get harrassed in the backfield after taking a number of hard shots the week before against Memphis.

The Hitmen really tried to tee off on Weldon in the second half, taking advantage of Birmingham's weak offensive line. Dwayne Sabb, who played four years with the New England Patriots including participating in Super Bowl XXXI in particular was often chasing Weldon in the backfield. The first punt return for a TD in XFL history occured in the 3rd, with Stepfret Williams running back a Leo Araguz punt 95 yards to un-tie the game. For a special teams maven like Tillman, that had to hurt. The boo birds came out when Puleri led his team on another three-and-out following the Bolts score. He was 3-of-10 passing at that point too. After surviving through "take him out" chants by the Giants Stadium crowd, Puleri led the Hitmen on a 14-play drive that finished with a Mike Archie score. The conversion was unsuccessful, and Puleri called a time out before it and complained to Tillman that his voice, calling the play, was on the loudspeaker for everyone to hear. Tillman, predictably, replied that he didn't care and to just run the play.

New York turned away Birmingham at their doorstep, fourth-and-goal on the one with 5:00 to go. The Hitmen's momentum was short-lived though, as the Bolts stripped the ball from Anthony DiCosmo, who thought forward progress was stopped, a few plays later and Birmingham scored to put them on top 19-12. Three penalties and a sack in Birmingham's territory made it 2nd-and-40 with 1:27 remaining. Tillman called a timeout and gathered his troops. This was something the XFL cameras were waiting for. He told them "we are going to do this" and that they'd win in overtime. After a catch-and-run by Zola Davis, 4th-and15 ensued. On a slippery field, Puleri chucked it into the end zone, but Fred Brock, cloaked by two defenders, couldn't come down with the ball.

After Gerry DiNardo (New York City-born himself) argued with the referees about the amount of timeouts the Hitmen had left, Kip Lewis caught up with Charlie Puleri, and asked him about the "Charlie sucks" chants. In his thick Bronx accent, he made his XFL all-access moment, passionately replying: "That's OK, I'm a grown man, I can take it. They have their opinion, that's fine, we didn't win today so they can say whatever they want, which is fine, I'm from New York, I'm a big boy, I can take it. You can keep booing, I love it baby. I'll be back next week, and the week after." That brought the boos down louder. But it showed off a little heel (bad-guy, in pro wrestling lingo) persona while also showing that he cared about the on-field results and was looking forward for redemption the next week. It was exactly what the XFL had in mind in having sideline reporters pestering players during the game.

The Memphis Maniax also made their national TV debut in week two, in their home opener against the Outlaws on UPN. After entrances, Michael Barkann warmed up the crowd on a cold night, then welcomed Memphis native Jerry Lawler, who introduced the scramble. The first player interviewed on the field before the game? Why, He Hate Me of course, to which the fans in the stands chanted, "We hate you." All this hate likely didn't endear the league to the media who were already piling on the league. On the first play from scrimmage, Rod Smart dashed for 22 yards down the sideline, causing the fans to spew even more vitriol toward him. Fans were all over him every time he touched the ball. It was evident they were loving it at the Liberty Bowl, already re-named "The Asylum" for the 'Ax (matching the "Hell Hole," the nickname given to Pac Bell Park for the Demons). Ryan Clement ran for a long gain on third-and-10 and was clobbered by Corey Sawyer and Anthony Marshall. Clement showed a little of that XFL attitude, getting right in the face of Marshall. It ended up being brought back due to holding on the play, once again a factor all game long.

The key for Smart and the XFL was, while it was nice to have an apparent star to hang their hat on early on, it only mattered if Smart was actually good and could back up the hype. He didn't break 100 yards in the first three games COMBINED and was in danger of becoming just a name, and an example of the XFL's hype machine propping up a player who just wasn't very good. But as the season hit the mid-way mark, Smart found his stride and put up some respectable numbers, including two 100 yard rushing days.

Maniax FB Roosevelt Potts relayed a funny story about the jersey nicknames, saying that his wife got after him after hearing about him putting a nickname on the jersey in the first week and told him that he better put "Potts" on the back for the second week. For the Maniax, it appeared UPN decided to focus on Salaam and Alvin Harper on offense and LB Paul Lacoste on defense. According to Boz, Lacoste epitomized the Maniax name and was a former CFL Rookie of the Year and Collegiate All-American selection. The controversy about the Manaix name and logo was addressed by Steve Ortmayer when asked of the situation by Dara Torres. While Burger King sponsored the All Access part of the game, Busch Beer was the sponsor of the Rules of the Game, where the announcers relayed the new rule changes to the fans. Near the end of the first quarter, Clement was nailed by 'Ax DE Shante Carver and writhed on the field. It was a borderline dirty hit, but the crowd loved every second of it. Clement, angry, got up and went after Shante in the Maniax huddle. As he walked off the field before the trainers could get to him, he told them the shoulder was separated. Bosworth, surprisingly, stuck up for Clement by calling it a late hit and said Carver unnecessarily drove him into the ground. Another QB bit the dust early in league play, which had to be a concern to teams and XFL management. They even showed Clement being looked at on the trainer's table in the locker room. Mike Cawley replaced Clement.

Speaking of concerns, the score was tied 3-3 at the end of the first quarter and for the most part, defense dominated once again. While there were a number of hard hits that may have satisfied the fans watching on TV, the offenses continuing to stumble didn't make for the most aesthetically pleasing game. Both teams struggled with the wet ball in the first half. The big hits continued, with Jamel Williams stuffing Maniax QB Marcus Crandell right in the face, jumping because he expected a pass and ended up in Crandell's grill, causing a fumble. While the mics on the field basically picked up chatter and grunts, Vegas DE Antonio Edwards taunted Rashaan Salaam, saying "you along way from 150," referencing his rushing total from the week before. The story for the Outlaws was the lack of offense once Cawley took over, and he was clearly struggling early on. There were 24 total penalties by the end of the game, preventing the game from getting into a flow. It seemed like there was laundry on the field every other play. Dropped passes were also prevalent. Also present were many post-play altercations in the first half, mostly just pushing and shoving or trash talking. Anytime they tried to catch the chatter or somebody firing up his teammates on teh sidelines, it seemed like the censors would be out and you'd see them screaming, but you'd hear nothing but silence.

At halftime, Lawler and his long-time girlfriend (and WWE performer) Stacy "The Kat" Carter joined the broadcasters. The Maniax team got in the red zone in the 3rd quarter, but coughed up a fumble that Kurt Gouveia brought back for a 98-yard touchdown rumble. It was put on the turf by Salaam, whose fumble-itis drove him out fo the NFL. He was visibly upset about it on the sidelines when asked if it was indeed a fumbe; he didn't provide an answer. Memphis's coaching staff disagreed with the fumble, as the audio caught Kippy Brown telling the refs, "you guys are screwing this whole damn thing up." The crowd cheered loudly for that. Not sure what his wife thought—even she was interviewed near the sidelines during the game.

Smart suffered from cramps in the second half and wasn't active on the field as much. But the Outlaws didn't need him, as they made their final score on a nine-yard Chrys Chukwuma TD run (who then riled up the crowd by reminding them he played at the University of Arkasas, a Memphis rival). It was 22-3 in the third and after tacking on three in the final stanza, the score ended at 25-3. In the fourth quarter, the Maniax installed Craig Whelihan to try and breathe some life into the offense. But he failed to lead the team to a score. In a switch from.well, every other sport on TV, the XFL showed a fan who ran onto the field instead of turning the camera away so as not to draw attention to the nuts. The announcers were disappointed when security didn't give him a lick when they caught him. They showed Boz dancing with the cheerleaders before the game, to which his broadcast partner Chris Marlowe noted it was why some animals eat their young. He even danced with them again late in the fourth. I guess that's what you've gotta do to enterain yourself when the game is out of hand. I would imagine the XFL brass knew that, in the event of a blowout, which was bound to happen, the gimmicks like mic'd players and rule changes would keep fans watchin on TV and in the stands. They wouldn't be sticking around because they have team loyalty or because of big name players or top-notch quality football like fans would in the NFL, so the XFL had to have a battle-plan for blowouts.

The Hitmen were upset at their lack of finishing drives after the game. In the Daily News the next day, Keith Elias frustratingly said that the game should've been over in the first quarter, thinking that the team should've been able to put enough points on the board then to put the game out of reach. Tim Leonard of the Bergen Record, in his write-up of the game, which don't usually feature editorializing, noted that many fans left during the game because "maybe they realized there wasn't much substance behind the hype." No other league would that be said about. But the XFL was an easy target.

In San Francisco, Jim Skipper showe off his usual even-keel self in post-game quotes printed the next day. The players seemed to think the momentum shifted early on in the game when a fumble was recovered for a touchdown by Rage S Omar Brown in the first quarter. WR Calvin Schexnayder called for the league to institute instant replay after a perceived TD catch that would've put the Demons within six points was ruled an interception by the Rage. This, coupled with DiCosmo's fumble lost for a TD in the Hitmen game, shone a light on the referees in week two in a way that the XFL would've liked to have avoided. Another problem for the Demons was when TE Brian Roche, a threat in the passing game, was felled with a leg injury against Orlando.

XFL officials were probably looking closely at the Orlando game, as on Saturday night, their game was the first to feature a second home game for a team. Attendance dipped in Orlando quite a bit, by about 11,000. If that was to be equated with television ratings, meaning the curiosity factor fell significantly in the second week, then it was not a good sign for ratings.

Defense was the word in Las Vegas after their game, with coach Criner remarking that it was among the best defensive performances he had ever witnessed. They played with a chip on their shoulder against Rashaan Salaam, who had predicted another 150 yard rushing day prior to the game. The QB situation got muddier when it appeared that Ryan Clement could miss up to three weeks with a shoulder injury. On the Tuesday following the second weekend of games, it was announced that the Outlaws' original starting QB and first-round pick, Chuck Clements, would be lost for the season after being forced to undergo shoulder surgery. Clement was expected to miss four games with his own shoulder ailment. Criner was working the horn, searching for another QB in the days after their game. Las Vegas was going to go with Mike Cawley or Jim Ballard, whoever performed best in practice, as their starter in week three. To rub salt into the wounds, the XFL's offiical supervisor, Carl Paganelli, also told the Outlaws that the hit by Shante Carver that took Clement out of the game was a legal hit. That didn't ease the anger felt by Criner and Clement. Clement, in particular, was not happy with the league allowing all the free shots at the QB.

The Bolts won their first game of the year despite a barrage of obscenties being sent the Bolts way by the fans at Giants Stadium. LB James Willis simply replied to the middle fingers fans were offering with a familiar catchphrase: "What you talking about, Willis?" The Bolts put all three phases of the game together, with RB James Bostic rushing for 104 yards and Casey Weldon throwing for 190. The defense also held the Hitmen to 225 total yards.

Week two saw the most exciting game to date in the LA vs. Chicago contest, and I'd argue, the most exciting game of the season. Just as important as the first week's ratings were the second. How many people came back for seconds? And how much media coverage would week two get, positive or negative, after the novelty wore off?

CHAPTER EIGHT

"XFL, Week 2: Sacked!" was the headline on the current events website Salon.com on February 12th. It was in reference to the week two ratings, which plunged to a 4.6, less than half of week one's rating. It was still, however, ahead of the 4.5 NBC promised advertisers, but the question became, "was this the bottom?" Like week one, viewers left in droves as the game wore on, despite it becoming closer in score and the final few minutes of regulation and overtime being the most exciting football you'll see anywhere. While the media all but buried the XFL after week one, this likely had an effect on fans tuning in for week two. Or was it the fact that the league concentrated more on football the second week and less on the surroundings? That wouldn't play well among the media types, who had been disparaging the league for not focusing enough on football. That was unlikely to be the reason though. It didn't help that the power went out in Los Angeles, causing a black screen to come up not long after the television cameras went on, giving fans the opportunity to switch over to another show. Most disturbingly, the teen male crowd that the XFL was coveting was, for the most part, absent during week two, as two-thirds of those who watched week one apparently found something better to do with the Saturday nights. UPN's rating was a 2.1, down from the 3.1 the first week, but the XFL was going up against the NBA All-Star game. The first game on TNN netted a 2.4 cable rating, a big number for the network, the only good ratings news for the week.

Another problem resulted when the game went into overtime. Because local late newscasts make the area stations so much money, they weren't candidates to be cut short in favor of getting to Saturday Night Live closer to its 11:35 timeslot. In the end, SNL didn't start until after midnight on the East Coast. That drew the ire of Live head Lorne Michaels, who was furious that his show got started so late. In fact, sources told the New York Times that Michaels was concerned from the outset about the XFL games running over, and had been assured by Dick Ebersol numerous times that the games would not affect SNL's start time. According to reports, Michaels was so upset that he briefly flirted with the idea of simply airing a previous episode rather than starting a live one so late. All of the ad time and hype surrounding host Jennifer Lopez and what was expected to be the biggest show of the year helped Michaels in deciding against that. The show didn't air live, but was taped live, and no one in the cast or in the studio audience didn't know it wasn't airing live. Ebersol and NBC head Jeff Zucker, in New York the next day to sooth the situation over, both bowed down apologetically to the throne of Lorne, which led to changes in the XFL, such as the game starting five minutes earlier, instituting a shorter halftime and having the game clock running when the ball is placed rather than when it is snapped on turnovers and incomplete passes.

It's hard to believe that any other sporting event would've garnered so much negative reaction from Michaels or anyone else. Zucker and Ebersol didn't seem to stand up for the XFL here, the first sign that perhaps the realtionship between the league and the network were beginning to strain. The adjustments made to accomodate SNL isn't a big deal, but the signal it sends is an interesting one. I'm sure it's not just seniority that Lorne Michaels was treated like the victim here, instead of rolling with the punches. I thought about taking the time to take a cheap shot at SNL's expense here, making a joke about the quality of the show declining in recent years anyway, but then I realized how hyporcitical that would've been in a book touting the XFL. So, moving on.

With two weeks in the books, the XFL was still getting ample media coverage in some places. One of those places was in the pages of Sports Illustrated, where the league even made the cover of the February 12th issue. "Cheap Thrills: Will sleazy gimmicks and low-rent football work for the XFL?" was plastered on the cover, along with a photo of Demons WR James Hundon going up for a pass, guarded by an Xtreme defender. Not exactly a ringing endorsement. Inside, eight pages were devoted to the league. The story, written by Leigh Montville, was mostly positive, even getting Bob Caporale, a former USFL team owner, quoted as saying he thought the league would fly mainly because the franchises were owned by the league, preventing owners from bolting from the league or declaring they've lost too much money and stepping away from the project. Then, once the article started talking about the first game between the Outlaws and Hitmen, decrying the boring gameand sideline reporters. In the end, they actually gave the action a B, noting that it was absurd to expect an NFL-level of play. An inset story to the main story, taking up a full page, wondered about the players in the XFL and them getting a shot at the NFL, noting that it was unlikely many would make the jump. Yet, few in the CFL and AFL annually get jobs in the NFL, but no one questions the level of play or the talent level of individual players. Who cares if the NFL raids the XFL for players at the end of the year? Yes, it would look good for the XFL, but it's not the barometer they were measuring success by. But it seems a lot of articles come full cricle to the NFL, or at least comparing the two leagues. No matter what, the XFL is always going to come out at the bottom of that discussion.

Sally Jenkins of the Washington Post wrote an article on February 18th, and it was nice to see someone "get" the XFL. She made the argument that stuffy media types were taking the XFL way too seriously when discussing what the implications on society and things of that nature would be in relation to the XFL. She dissected the differences between the XFL and NFL and noted that the XFL was meant to lampoon and be a satire of the NFL. It's true insofar as it's supposed to be different than the NFL. Jenkins wrote that "I find the princely masquerades of some NFL players far more frightening, and their hypocrisy far more corrosive than the lampoonery of the XFL." The XFL was just being honest about everything the NFL wanted to sweep under the rug, and columnists went along with it because they were the only game in town.

For the NY/NJ Hitmen, 0-2 is not where they planned to find themselves after the first two weeks of the season. The team held a closed-door meeting on Tuesday that was players only, and DT Christian Maumalanga did some trash talking and challenged the offense to step up. The offense was the main culprit for the collapse, causing Rusty Tillman to think about tinkering with the offensive personnel, even perhaps moving safety Butler B'ynote to the RB position. In the end, they stuck with Elias at RB. Neither the QB nor RB position had produced the results the Hitmen desired after two games. The Hitmen decided to stick with Charles Puleri for week three provided he outshined Wally Richardson (the Penn State product, who leaped over Corte McGuffey on the depth chart due to practice performance) in practice that week. Tillman, who was already feeling the pressure to produce, stated that he wouldn't hesitate to pull Puleri either if the QB started slow in week three. Tillman, whose background is in special teams, even vowed to have more of a hand in the play-calling on offense, certainly not a sign of confidence in offensive coordinator Greg Briner. The head coach complained to the league office about the sack of Bolts QB Casey Weldon that resulted in an apparent loose ball, yet the Hitmen didn't get credit for the touchdown or the safety on the play despite recovering the ball. Tillman even took a shot at the league, saying that rules seemed to change daily in the XFL. The Hitmen defense was the strength of the team but they had a tough test upcoming with handling the potent Orlando Rage offense.

The Demons got some bad news on the injury front, as TE Brian Roche was declared out for the season with a torn achilles tendon. Weber State grad Rich O'Donnell was to take over the TE position, while the Demons finally claimed a third QB in CFL vet Oteman Sampson. Sampson made his name collegiately at Florida A&M, where he passed for 52 touchdowns and almost 7,000 yards. Despite losing

Roche, the San Francisco offense became more electric for week three when WR Brian Roberson, the leading receiver in week one, returned to the lineup, and another CFL player was claimed in WR Travis Moore, a former all-Canadian pick in 1999. Moore's name was regularly atop the CFL receiving charts while playing up north. Coach Jim Skipper decided to limit the team's travel schedule, and they stayed on the East Coast betwen games in Orlando in week two and Memphis in week three, rather than heading home to the Bay Area. Heading into the Memphis game, the two areas that Skipper wanted to address was limiting turnovers and penalties, the latter something every XFL team probably wanted to improve in.

In Birmingham, the Bolts needed to find a way to better protect QB Casey Weldon, who was hit hard several times against New York. It didn't help that the wind-chill was a frosty six degrees, making the bone-crunching knocks all the more painful. Doug Segrest, covering the Bolts for the Birmingham News, identified the wrong Golic that was doing games for TNN in his story about Weldon. WR Kevin Drake, much like Rusty Tillman, took the time to voice his displeasure with the league, this time about the injured reserve rule. The rule states you must be on injured reserve a minimum of four weeks before you can be activated, but Drake complained that the hamstring injury that landed him on there took only a week and a half to heal. Coach Gerry DiNardo noted the four-week rule is to stop teams from hiding players on IR and thought it was a good rule. In the NFL, IR means you're out for the season, but they do have a larger roster where they can keep injured players there, even if they aren't able to play for several games.

Both the Los Angeles Xtreme and Las Vegas Outlaws were looking forward to their week three meeting, pitting perhaps the league's best offense in LA against the unquestioned best defense in Las Vegas. But the biggest worry for the Xtreme appeared to be special teams, as Jose Cortez missed two field goals in week two, while Noel Prefontaine had a punt blocked and returned for a TD. Al Luginbill was sharp-tongued to the media about the unit, saying "we were just horrible" and "our play the other night will not be tolerated" and threatened of personnel changes if it did. The only major injury the squad seemed to be nursing was starting CB Reggie "Dirty" Durden, who was doubtful against the Outlaws. Luginbill defended the level of play in the league, saying that "anybody who thinks those college teams could beat these teams is on drugs." He also said that many players from the #1 team in the nation wouldn't make it in the XFL. Much was made throughout the week of the rowdy behavior of many of the Xtreme fans, and the XFL garnered some negative press when a paraplegic suffered injuries during the game when a melee spilled over into his section and he became engulfed in it. Increasing security and cutting off beer sales after the third quarter were two policies implemented by the Xtreme and LA Coliseum after the incident.

The Chicago Enforcers were without two tackles going into week three, with one out for the year. Octavious Bishop, who had to be taken off the field in an ambulance Saturday night, was diagnosed with a fractured tibia and fibula and would miss the remainder of the season. Christopher Perez, their starting LT, was injured in the second quarter of the same game and was doubtful for week three. LB Brian Rogers would also miss the rest of the season when he tore his ACL. The Enforcers were finishing up a difficult three-game stretch to star the season, where each game was on the road.

Mike Cawley and Jim Ballard waged a war in practice to find out who would start against the Xtreme, with both Chuck Clements and Ryan Clement on the shelf for Las Vegas. They found their emergency third-string QB in RB Chrys Chukwuma, who worked there in practice during the week. Because of the injuries, the offensive line's pass-blocking became of utmost importance. The QB battle continued on the 14th and 15th of February, with the team finally settling on Mike Cawley as the starter. Local boy and UNLV product Jon Denton tried out for the Outlaws, who were still in search of some QB security. Rod Smart continued to be the center of attention after his breakthrough in week one, as after practice on the 16th, 17 journalists requested interviews with him. He even won two ESPN.com polls in one day, one being "What rift would you most like to see resolved this Valentine's Day?" He Hate Me got 31.1%, while the second place vote-getter,

Shaq & Kobe, got 23.2%. As far as injuries, both G Lamont Burns and WR Todd Flody were declared out with concussions.

Orlando got their second-straight defensive player of the week award, as S Omar Brown collected the honor, with LB Shawn Banks receiving the distinction the previous week. The big theme in practice leading up to the game with the Hitmen was the teams in the league and how no team was head-and-shoulders above another as far as talent. Defensive coordinator Charlie Bailey said that the team has to be prepared for a challenge every week no matter who they play, and RB Brian Shay was quoted as saying their 2-0 start meant nothing because any team could win any week. Brown addressed why the Rage don't feature nicknames on their jerseys like other teams—he said they like to have their actions do the talking.

Week three's NBC game was one of the most interesting to date: Los Angeles at Las Vegas. Al Luginbill preached the basics in his locker room speech, while coach Criner, in the Vegas locker room, told his team to just win the da'd gum game, in that Bobby Bowden-like gentlemanly Southern drawl. Juan Long and Shawn Stuckey, two Xtreme LB's, sported jerseys with the monikers "I HATE HE" AND "I HATE HE TOO." Clearly, the He Hate Me fever was continuing. The game also featured two of the biggest talkers going head-to-head, Outlaws DB Brandon Sanders and Xtreme WR Jermaine Copeland. Like any WWE crowd, the fans started a "bullshit" chant after two Las Vegas penalties on one play early in the game. The referees had their hands full then with not only the crowd on their case, but Outlaws DT Angel Rubio and Xtreme coach Al Luginbill, and the fans at home and in the crowd got to hear it all. At halftime, they aired an interview with injures Enforcers OT Octavious Bishop and his mother in the hospital in a package narrated by Mike Adamle. They still did the all-access halftime, but instead of airing it live when nothing might be happening, they showed clips before the third quarter of the important stuff that happened so you only saw the key stuff. Also at halftime, they aired a clip of Will Ferrell and Molly Shannon, at the time cast members of SNL, who were plugging the show afterward. Ferrell joked that he hoped everyone was enjoying the game between the Kansas City Shoplifters and the Anaheim Bloodthirsty Psychos, a reference to the rough-and-tumble nicknames the XFL teams had. Shannon begged the game to finish in time, because it was her last show. Dick Butkus once again joined the booth at halftime.

In the second half, Vegas recovered one of their own punts because of the 25 yard rule where the ball becomes free at that point, the first time it happened all year. With the game tied at nine in the fourth quarter, Outlaws QB Mike Cawley converted two important third downs. However, he couldn't find the end zone. Offensive Coordinator Vince Alcalde was clearly upset with him after taking a long sack, yelling at him in the helmet to "throw the ball away!" Cawley threw an interception with 1:20 left in the game, leading to Jose Cortez nailing a bare-footed 48-yard field goal with one second left. Another week, another set of images that defined the game, as Cawley had his head in his hands, while Al Luginbill was all smiles at the end of the broadcast. Cawley ended up 14-25 passing for 129 yards, but couldn't come through in crunch time. He Hate Me was held to under 2.0 yards per carry by LA's defense. LA couldn't run the ball either, and Tommy Maddox had just 166 yards passing, going 16-30. The sideline announcers seemed to be asking better questions and the players were doing a better job answering them, rather than giving a quick soundbite or just panting into the microphone. The play-by-play and color guys were still really heavily promoting the league and despite the XFL's policy for them to "tell it like it is," it was clear that they were also instructed to promote the virtues of the XFL, to the point that it was over-bearing. Not sure if this was the XFL's way of The alternate game saw the Demons beat Memphis, 13-6. New RB Terry Battle scored two touchdowns for San Francisco and Maniax backup QB Jim Druckenmiller relieved a struggling Marcus Crandell late in the game after Crandell suffered a foot injury.

Chicago visited Birmingham on the TNN broadcast. Like others around the league, Birmingham's attendance dropped by more than half in the second home game (though the temperature was cooler than usual). The storyline for this one was the Enforcers being away from home for 50 days and searching for their first win. Bolts RB James Bostic got the crowd into it early with a powerful stiff-arm on Enforcers DB Quincy Coleman that sent him to the ground flat on his back. Birmingham's offense seemed on target and had a good mix of run and pass early on. Defensively, Chris Shelling and Sedrick Curry each botched interceptions, and each did ten push-ups on the field as pennance for their gaffes. That's a sight you aren't likely to see in the NFL. Another story they seemed to focus on was the fact that the three top Bolts receivers, Stepfret Williams, Quincy Jackson and Kaipo McGuire, all live together. That could've made for some fun video packages during games. Speaking of video packages, one casualty of the speeding up of games was that the videos wouldn't get to be shown in their entirety. It would've been nice if they continued them after the play, or show it in a split-screen but too many times they didn't. It looked like another feud started as Bolts LB James Willis shoved Enforcers T Chris Perez to the ground after Perez bumped him following a play. The crowd got into that and Perez was dripping with sarcasm when interviewed about it on the sidelines, saying, "Oh, did you see him? He's such a huge man. He really scares me. I can't sleep at night, he's such a tough guy." This was just how Vince McMahon likely dreamed it up when he thought about reporters on the sidelines. Duane Butler sealed the game for the Bolts, who were up 7-3, when he returned a 97 yard interception for a touchdown with under 2:00 to go. Then, in trademark XFL style, he danced for the crowd to "Sweet Home Alabama."

Enforcers QB Tim Lester went 12-24 for 145 yards passing in this game, but couldn't get his team over the hump and to a victory. But to Lester, just playing pro football for the first time, was in and of itself the reward. In high-school, Lester led his team to the state title and won consecutive conference titles as well. The 24 year-old Lester thought his career was done after he set 17 passing records at Western Michigan as a four-year starter and finished fifth in NCAA history in passing yardage. He was the Mid-American Conference (MAC) Freshman of the Year in 1996 and second-team All-Conference in his junior and senior years. As a senior, Lester threw 34 touchdown passes for the Broncos. However, when the NFL Draft rolled around, Lester wasn't selected. He didn't even get an offer to latch on as a non-drafted free-agent, despite playing in a pro-style offense in college. He turned to coaching at that point, catching on as a high-school assistant at Wheaton-Warrenville South High School, his alma mater, in 2000. He also put his bachelor's degree in Math to good use, teaching the subject at West Aurora High School when the XFL came calling, with Chicago selecting him in the 6th round (41st overall) of the XFL P.A.S.S. He was a bit skeptical of the league at first, but like many players, his interest piqued when he heard of the coaches who would be involved, football men who wouldn't sully their reputation by getting into bed with a league that was going to be a joke. Lester also wanted to get an opportunity to show NFL scouts and general managers what they missed out on by not offering him a contract. And he wasn't the only one in the league wanting to prove doubters wrong. Lester told the Detroit News that many NFL personnel men had observed the Enforcers' practices, and he had even personally gotten advice from then-Lions QB Coach Jim Zorn, now the head coach of the Washington Redskins. Lester said that the wrinkles added to the game didn't really distract him or his teammates, for the most part: " Other than the camera guy that stood right next to our offensive huddle, I don't think it was much of a distraction." Four NFL teams even told him that if he wanted to get in the league, the XFL was "the best place to be." Lester never did get that NFL taste (though he did continue his pro football ride in the AFL and AF2)—he was replaced by Kevin McDougal for the Enforcers after four games and currently serves as the Head Coach for Elmhurst College, a position he has held since 2008. He also served in various capacities at other colleges (from QB coach to defensive coordinator), including Western Michigan, before Elmhurst came calling.

On UPN Sunday night, the Hitmen met the Rage. It was cold once again at Giants Stadium, whose crowd was 11,000 down from the first game. Rage coach Galen Hall even commented that metal cleats were dangerous for the players on the frozen field. Charles Puleri was once again met with cat calls from the home crowd, having to play through "Puleri sucks" chants. The league tried to access personalities of players by shooting videos of some players explaining the nicknames they wore on their jerseys. For example, LB Haven Fields explained that his moniker "Baby Boy" was given to him by teammates because he had a baby face and was the youngest player on the team. There were several big hits in the game, with Patrise Alexander of the Rage on special teams, Hitmen S Mark Tate drilling Skinny Culver on a punt return (violating the halo rule) and Rage LB James Burgess flatening RB Keith Elias on a screen pass. After another Puleri miscue before halftime, coach Tillman was heard to remark "that's it." And it was it, as Wally Richardson opened the second stanza for the Hitmen. He was received more favorably by the crowd, with "Wally, Wally" chants in the 3rd quarter. Puleri finished up 5 of 10 for 35 yards, while Richardson went 10-19 for 126 yards. With the game knotted at 12 with four minutes left (after the Hitmen had a 12-3 lead in the 4th), Richardson threw a pass to TE Marcus Hinton, which bounced off his helmet and into the hands of a Rage defender for an interception. Orlando's QB Jeff Brohm then scrambled for a 33-yard touchdown, thanks in part to missed tackles by DB's Damen Wheeler and Ty Talton. An exchange between Tillman and Hitmen special teams coach Paul Butcher took place that went as follows:

"That squib went right through the wedge (last time)."—Tillman

"Well, they're scared."—Butcher

"Oh, that's a good answer."—Tillman

"Well, they are."—Butcher

Good stuff. Not for the Hitmen though, as they dropped to 0-3, losing 18-12.

Terms like "worst team in the XFL" were thrown around in the media after the Hitmen fell to 0-3. Despite the QB play, Tillman refused to annoint either Puleri or Richardson as the starter before watching the film of the game. Puleri didn't seem happy about being pulled in a tie ballgame, pointing out that the team wasn't getting blown out at that point.

Orlando won despite the cold weather conditions in New York. QB Jeff Brohm acknowledged that the team wasn't used to it, but they adjusted and found a way to win. Brohm evoked memories of the man he used to back up with the 49ers, Steve Young, when talking about his 33-yard dash.

Doug Segrest, who misidentified Bob Golic the week prior, this time referred to the World Wrestling Federation as "World Wrestling Foundation" in his coverage of the Bolts game. Coach Gerry DiNardo was happy with the way the defense limited Chicago's John Avery; he ran for 87 yards, but his long was only 14 and he only made one reception for seven yards. James Willis headed the group as usual, with 11 tackles. In the locker room after the game though, talk turned to the tragedy in Daytona, where NASCAR legend Dale Earnhardt was killed in a crash on the final laps. Clearly, they were in the south. WR Damon Gourdine, who scored a touchdown in the first game of the season, was lost for the year with a broken ankle during the game.

A week after K Jose Cortez missed two field goals against Chicago, he made four, including the game-winner for the Xtreme in week three. Shutting down the running game and forcing the Outlaws to pass was the key to their defensive success in that game.

The Outlaws' offense once again cost them the game, and QB Mike Cawley took the blame. Cawley paid for the mistakes two days after the game, as he was placed on waivers by Las Vegas. The day before, they had claimed AFL stand-out (as in 62 TDs and 3 INTs in 2000) Mark Grieb to try to right the ship. Coach Jim Criner knew Grieb from his time in NFL Europe. Criner revealed that he had been trying to grab Grieb for two weeks. The team had determined that Cawley's strengths did not match the West Coast offense Vegas wanted to run. Grieb was scheduled to start in week four. The Outlaws also traded S Ron Carpenter, who was on the practice squad for all three games, to LA for an eighth-round draft-pick in 2001. Vegas also shored up their offensive line by activating OL Mark Nori from injured reserve.

The XFL was beginning to hit its stried after three weeks. While the play on the field improved, the scores didn't increase, a concern for the league considering the attraction of fans to offense. They seemed to be getting more and more comfortable with what they wanted to do on the broadcasts after the first and second week experiments. While the media was mostly negative still, the fervor began to die down with the novelty of the league wearing off to newspapers at TV journalists. The stars of the league were being identified and plugged by the league. The XFL continued to tweak its coverage and rules to appeal to a wider base of fans in order to keep attendance and ratings high, or at least, a level that would be considered respectable.

CHAPTER NINE

Ratings continued their tumble in week three. The NBC game lost another 1.5 rating points, down to 3.1 and below what NBC and the XFL promised advertisers. UPN dropped .6 to 1.5 and TNN fell to .9 from the previous week's 1.9. Many reasons could be given for the continued, not just fall, but free-fall: The poor performance of at least two teams from huge markets (0-3 Chicago and New York); the lack of offense (because of the sped-up clock, there were less plays being run than in the NFL or college, leaving less time for scoring); or perhaps because there were only eight teams in the league, leaving huge pockets of fans around the country that weren't near any of the teams and weren't emotionally interested in any franchises. One large sponsor, Honda, pulled out for week four, and the XFL gave more ad time to other sponsors to make up for the lower-than-promised ratings. Advertising Age reported that Vince McMahon was so furious with Honda after they left that he wanted to blow up one of its cars at halftime of one of the football games. Dick Ebersol had to talk him out of it, but it showed that McMahon didn't always cater to fans' wants, and rather, wasn't afraid to take his vengefulness out on someone/something on the air.

After only three weeks, there were rumors about NBC's unahppiness with the ratings and even whispers of them looking to pull out of the league. Basil DeVito told the Birmingham News that there was no truth to those rumors and that NBC would honor it's three-year contract with the league. The fact that these questions were even being asked after week three showed that the media was like a shark circling a small child on a raft, waiting for any sign they could tip over so they could dive in and dismantle the corpse.

On Monday Night Raw, WWE took advantage of the popularity of one of the XFL players, and tried to continue to increase his name recognition. Wrestler Chris Jericho did a promo backstage before he was to come out as a guest referee for a match, and he said that instead of wearing the traditional ref's uniform, since both wrestlers hated him, he borrowed the uniform of his friend "He Hate Me" Rod Smart to wear, and Jericho wore that instead. It was a relatively harmless plug and it sure beat the endless ads that ran during the broadcast for the XFL, but I'm sure non-XFL fans rolled their eyes at this clearly blatant publicity stunt.

Despite the league's tenuous footing on the sports landscape, The Pittsburgh Business Times reported that Vince McMahon claimed Pittsburgh was high on his list of potential expansion cities for the 2003 season. WWE's main lawyers were based in Pittsburgh, so they certainly had knowledge of the area. Despite the ardor of Pittsburgh fans, one would wonder if they would have the same difficulty New York and Chicago did in bringing fans to the stadium on chilly February evenings.

The Hitmen were ordaining a new starting RB, one who didn't even make it out of camp with the team, because he lacked the special teams skills the other backs had. Former Oakland Raider Joe Aska, who lost his right eye as a child, took over as starter in week three. Aska was brought aboard by Rusty Tillman in training camp, as Tillman coached Aska with the Raiders. He had been out of football since being cut by the Indianapolis Colts in 1999. In addition, QB Wally Richardson took the reigns of the QB job, a week after being inserted in the second half of the Hitmen's game against Orlando. GM Drew Pearson even went so far as to say Richardson had more pro potential than any other QB in the league. Richardson didn't start in the NFL, AFL, or NFL Europe, but he was good enough to start for the Hitmen at this point. Another position of interest was RT, as the Hitmen used three starters there in three weeks due to injuries. Week three starter Jeff Pilon was injured against the Rage, and his backup, Jason Sadler, was hurt in practice. With a new QB, protection would be key.

Greg Couch wrote a great piece for the Chicago Sun-Times on February 23rd, showing what these players we see on the field go throw and what they sacrificed to make it in the XFL. Enforcers K Andy Crosland and QB Paul Failla rented an apartment together during the season; Crosland had been a bartender in Miami before signing on for another football go-round and Failla ran a company in Pittsburgh that sold hats and t-shirts. Another QB, Tim Lester, was teaching Mat at West Aurora High-School. Coach Ron Meyer and other assistants were basically living out of Soldier Field when their deal for an apartment collapsed. It was an all-too-rare inside look at the players, ones football fans could relate to and that had interesting stories to share. A similar article in the Washington Times took a look at former Redskins in the league: DE Kelvin Kinney and LB Patrise Alexander both had injury concerns that scared NFL teams away. S Leomont Evans expected to use the XFL as a stepping stone to get another shot in the NFL. QB Casey Weldon didn't initially feel the league was for him until talking things over with former 'Skins GM Charley Casserly and St. Louis Rams coach Mike Martz. K Jeff Hall was fresh off a stint with the Rams and kept his job as a financial advisor while kicking for the Memphis Maniax. His biggest concern, and I'm sure this was true of others, is that Hall had to give it one last shot or fear looking back in a number of years down the road, questioning "what if?"

Pete Destefano, San Fran's starting safety, would be sidelined for week four with a concussion. But they did get a few other injured players back in the lineup, including LB Sam Manuel and C Curtice Macfarlane. On the offensive side of the ball, WR Brian Roberson was injured again, this time, his groin. That led to another start for Jimmy "The Jet" Cunningham, thanks in part to the AFL's lawsuit to keep Calvin Schexnayder off the field.

Bolts WR Damon Gouridne was shelved for the season after the son of famous singer Little Anthony broke his ankle against the Enforcers. Birmingham again got the wrong end of the broadcast schedule, as they were slated to be the Saturday night alternate game. The XFL seemed to be exploiting the bigger market teams with its coverage, featuring Chicago, Los Angeles and New York often on NBC. Of course, if the league really wanted to improve in the ratings, this was a smart thing to do—more viewers in those cities meant a better chance that more people would be watching.

Los Angeles was expected to do some scoreboard-watching in week four, as they played Memphis while Las Vegas and San Francisco, two 2-1 teams like the Xtreme, squared off. With only ten games, these two Western Conference battles were likely to have significant playoff implications. The keys for the Xtreme were to keep RB Rashaan Salaam in check, as they did to John Avery in week two. Also, they needed to keep 'Ax DE Shante Carver off of Tommy Maddox.

Speaking of Memphis, they too went with a new QB in week four, as Jim Druckenmiller stepped in for Marcus Crandell. Memphis' offense was sputtering and with Crandell hobbled by a foot injury, it seemed like the perfect time to try something new. The mental errors on offense is what Kippy Brown wanted to fix. Druck had a chip on his shoulder after not getting a great chance to prove his mettle in the NFL, released by the Dolphins after being traded by the 49ers.

Quarterback was the key in Las Vegas, where Mark Grieb took over for the recently-released Mike Cawley. He was going to be thrown into the fire the week that he was signed, but because he had played under coach Jim Criner before, the team felt he had a good grasp of the basics of the offense. Grieb was a smart, but not greatly physically talented QB, but after Cawley's mental mistakes, it was a trade-off the Outlaws would take. A master's student at Stanford as well as a graduate assistant on the football team, Grieb also had to get permission from his professors to play in the league, while also completing the semester. Only in the XFL. Ryan Clement, the starter at QB, did some throws during the week to test his shoulder and while it was sore as expected, it was a step in the right direction. He was even slated to be the emergency QB for week four.

More bad news for the XFL and NBC: NY at Chicago was the scheduled NBC broadcast and the weather, as you'd expect in February, was less-than-conducive to an offensive shootout. It looked to be another grind-it-out game, which could turn more viewers off. The other issue facing the game was that it was two 0-3 teams doing battle. To top it off, one of the most exciting players in the league, John Avery was out of action due to a quadriceps injury he suffered earlier in the week. It was noted by announcers that a pre-season scrimmage between the two squads had to be called before the game was over because there were too many brawls. They made sure to sneak this in, probably in the hopes fans would stick around hoping to see one themselves. The field was slippery, which became a problem from the start, as it cost Troy Saunders and the Enforcers the scramble of the ball. Chicago's QB, Tim Lester, began the game wearing gloves because of the cold weather. Jesse Ventura started the verbal onslaught toward Rusty Tillman again after trying it out a bit in the first game of the season—Ventura called him "Gutless Rusty" after not going for it on 4th-and-1 from the two yard-line and instead opting to kick the field goal. He probably thought he could get a rise out of the fiery Tillman. Fred Roggin asked Tillman about Jesse's comments, and Rusty seemed to want to play along at first: "Good for Jesse.I don't have anything to say about Jesse Ventura.he wouldn't know if a football was pumped or stuffed, how do you like that one?" After a sack, DE Israel Rabyon wanted a piece of Avery: "Put Avery in the game! We've been practicing (for him) all week!" As if the playing conditions weren't bad enough, the fog rolled in in the second quarter. Ventura was made to look afool after cheering the Enforcers for going for it on 1st-and-goal from the one yard-line with :01 left before halftime, but they didn't make it. They gave bonus coverage at halftime to the Birmingham vs. Orlando game, where Jerry Lawler made a remark about a player being "as dependable as a Honda automobile," no doubt fed to him from McMahon himself. After wearing #89 and playint TE in the first half, two-way player Tim Martin donned the #65 and returned in the second half as a DT. After losing two fumbles in the first half, perhaps due to the gloves, Lester threw an interception in the second that looked like the gloves could've had a hand in it—the ball slipped right out of his hands on a pass attempt, and right into the waiting arms of Hitmen S Tawambi Settles at the Enforcers one-yard line. A "Lester sucks" chant broke out late in the 4th, which probably made Charlie Puleri feel a little better about himself. Lester faced a lot of pressure from the Hitmen D, including from DT Christian Maumalanga, whom Enforcers coach Ron Meyer once called perhaps the best D-lineman in the league. With 1:51 left, and with the XFL needing something for viewers to take away from this broadcast, Jesse Ventura went down to the field to interview Rusty Tillman after the Hitmen's first win, by a score of 13-0 (another, predictably low-scoring affair). Jesse wanted to talk, but Rusty didn't, as the coach told Ventura, "I got nothing to say to you." Ventura even complained to Hitmen GM Drew Pearson, who was in his usual sideline spot for the game, about Tillman not talking and at one point said Rusty was afraid of him. The locker room had a cheerier mood to it, as the players sang "Hooray for Rusty" in honor of New York's first victory, and perhaps for lending some credibility to the league by not getting into a repartee with Ventura. Wally Richardson passed his test as the new starter for NY, though he only threw 13 passes, completing nine, but he most importantly, he got the Hitmen in the win column. The Enforcers struggled with the running game without John Avery, as Leshon Johnson netted just 48 yards on the ground. By the end of the game, both teams' uniforms were covered in mud and water, and you could see each player's breath in the cold. It was just how the XFL pictured it; but not necessarily how fans did. The alternate game ended with Orlando crushing the Bolts, 30-6. The Rage's three-headed monster running attack with Derrick Clark, Michael Black and Brian Shay ran for over 140 yards and nine different receivers caught passes. The Bolts, meanwhile, had no ground game to speak of; their lone offensive bright spot was WR Quincy Jackson, who made eight catches for 132 yards and a touchdown.

Quincy Jackson just wanted to play football. Indoors, outdoors, professional or semi-pro, it didn't matter. Jackson was a QB at Brundidge High School in Alabama, where he made all-state. He was recruited by Alabama as a defensive back, but not wanting to play that position, he decided on junior college. It was there that he transitioned into the WR position. After his JUCO stay, he did make it to Alabama and as a junior and senior, led the team in receiving. Despite playing at a big program, he found himself going undrafted in 1999, but latched on with the Cincinnati Bengals. That stay was short-lived, as he was cut during the summer after suffering an injury. In 2000, he went to play for the Albany Firebirds of the AFL. He set a team record for receptions in a game that season with 13. Once the XFL announced play, Jackson's agent suggested the league to his client, as some of the Western Conference teams (Las Vegas included) had heard good things about Jackson from the receivers coach of the Bengals. He got to stay at home with Birmingham though, once they claimed him as a territorial selection. "Q," as his friends called him, put up solid numbers for the Bolts as a 23 year-old, leading the team in touchdown grabs with six, and finishing second in receptions and receiving yards. But when no NFL team came calling after the XFL folded, Jackson kept the football dream alive. Instead, he traveled north to play in the Canadian Football League, then back to American for a stop in AF2. Every year he was getting older, and every year, further away from the big-time, but that didn't stop him. In 2006, he was driving truck, still looking to make it back into football. He attended a tryout camp for the All-American Football League (AAFL), another operation that went belly-up before it began. Because he was still in shape, he landed a gig in the American Indoor Football Association (AIFA), a league far removed from Jackson's few months in the NFL. In 2009, at age 32, he is still active in the league, listed on the roster of the Utah Valley Thunder. There aren't any names the casual football fan would recognize, but to Jackson, it's still football.

Las Vegas took on San Francisco in the Sunday afternoon contest. The story was Outlaws QB Mark Grieb getting the start with only five days of practice under his belt. It was really evident in this game that there were less field mics in the TNN game than in the NBC ones. The main event tussle for this one was Jimmy Cunningham of the Demons against the Outlaws' Kevin Scott, when Scott stood over Cunningham after making a tackle. The 165-pound Jet got right in Scott's face and they both grabbed each other's helmets and did some pushing and shoving. In another bout in the 2nd half, an unidentified Demons defender yanked G Lonnie Palelei's helmet off and threw it right back to him. The player then tore his own helmet off and appeared to want to throw down with the Samoan. LB Mike Crawford appeared to try an eye gouge on Demons QB Mike Pawlawski after he was down following a conversion—Crawford said Pawlawski tried to do the same to him and said it was all in good fun since the two were friends off the field. Jim Criner gave a speech to his offense after they scored late in the 2nd to tie up the game: "We go the damn points because we played our damn butts off." The Outlaws hung on to win, 16-9 and Jim Skipper (talking about turnovers and the QB situation, as Pat Barnes was brought in to provide a spark), Mark Grieb (praising his defense for their performance) and Brandon Sanders (confident about his defense and his new QB) provided good post-game interviews. He Hate Me had his best game of the season, running for 90 yards and a touchdown and though Grieb completed less than 50% of his passes, he managed the game well enough to earn the coaching staff's trust. The Demons dropped to 2-2 and while Pawlawski was able to pass against the Outlaws defense (25 completions, 223 yards), they struggled running the ball.

Memphis took on LA on UPN Sunday night. Another game with adverse conditions, as it had been raining in LA for two days, and it was a hard rain at that. The rain was sitting on the field in puddles at various yard lines around LA Coliseum. The stadium looked like there was barely anyone there, which did not make a great impression on viewers no doubt. Obviously not watching Tim Lester's performance the night before, Tommy Maddox opted for gloves on the second drive of the game. Jermaine Copeland blocked a punt and also showed viewers how to do his "X-Spot" TD celebration. Another player showed off a non-football talent of theirs, as Memphis S Rico Clark sang

"Amazing Grace" during an injury timeout in a pre-taped segment. At halftime, they profiled Jose Cortez and Paul Lacoste. They showed Lacoste going through his gameday procedures, from his hotel room (and talking to his girlfriend on the phone) to the stadium and all of his pre-game rituals. He even showed off a typewritten warning, aimed at those around to watch out for #52, written as if he were a dangerous criminal on the run from the law. He said reading them gets him pumped up for the game. Al Luginbill, as usual, gave a good halftime speech as again only clips were shown, so as to weed out the pointless (to fans anyway) halftime business that happens behind the scenes. The Xtreme leaned on RB Saladin McCullough to carry the load in the 2nd half. They also took advantage of a size mis-match on the outside where 5'9" CB John Williams had to guard 6'3" receiver Darnell McDonald. McDonald ended with six catches for 86 yards, so he didn't get as much out of that margin as he could've. The Maniax were down a safety late when Kevin Peoples had to be carted off the field in the fourth quarter. The announcers totally missed Kippy Brown saying, "get Beau Morgan ready for defense"—Morgan played multiple positions on offense, but it's pretty big news that they were planning on sending him out on the other side of the ball. Speaking of Brown, there were many more shots of him on the sidelines than Luginbill, a curious decision since Luginbill is usually the more up-tempo of the two; howerver, Al did have an occasion to spill a curse word now-and-again, which meant silence often becuase of the seven-second delay. Williams ended up getting revenge at the end of the game, breaking up the final pass to allow Memphis to hold on for the win, 18-12. In his first start, Druckenmiller went 13-22 for 215 yards. Asked by Chris Wragge whether he should be the starter next week, Druck responded "Yes, I do." Looked like even Memphis wasn't immune to QB issues.

With two of the three games being played in less-than-stellar conditions, making the play on the field look artificially worse than it could've been, the game recaps didn't fail to mention it. Much of the AP's recaps dealt with the weather conditions and even noted the cheerleaders had to dress reasonably. While 14,000 fans in Chicago braved the wind, rain and 30-degree temperatures, it was announced that each fan there would get to go to the next week's game for free as a thank-you for coming out in such frightful weather. As the season wore on, it was harder and harder to dig up coverage on the teams, even in area newspapers. In researching this book, my piles of information from each week dwindled as the weeks passed by. If it wasn't stuff on the back of the sports page, it wasn't there at all it seemed.

Perhaps that's why Jesse Ventura and the XFL decided to continue to fan the flames of the Rusty Tillman-Jesse Ventura feud that started in week one. They needed more play in the media, and this was guaranteed to get it. It didn't seem to matter that columnists would question Tillman's participation (or non-participation as it were) in this gimmicky scheme, but it also brought to light all those questions of moments being staged that the XFL fought so hard to answer before the league even started. They were adamant everything would be on the up-and-up and confrontations would be genuine and organic. Then this week, with Ventura unnecessarily all over Tillman, acting like a pro wrestling announcer or character would, it brought the media back out, but only to question the XFL's motives and legitimacy all over again. Was this a directive of the XFL for Ventura to do this, or did he see an opening and try to get himself into the headlines once again? Either way, it made all parties look bad at a time when bad press is something the XFL did not need. On March 6th, Pro Football Weekly's Andy Hanacek wrote a particularly scathing article slamming Ventura for his commentary, most notably his attacks on Tillman.

After the Xtreme/Maniax game, many players opined about the conditions they had to play in. Rashaan Salaam called it "the worst ever" that he had to play in, while Tommy Maddox referred to the surroundings as "the thoughest thing I've had to go through." Al Luginbill didn't use the weather as an excuse, citing his team's poor first-half performance as one big reason the team came out on the losing end. After the game, three teams were tied for second in the West at 2-2, with Las Vegas pacing the division.

The story of the Demons/Outlaws game was turnovers: The Demons turned it over, while new Vegas QB Mark Grieb did not, and that seemed to be the difference-maker in the game. Jim Criner, in heaping praise on his new QB, didn't seem to mind that he was taking shots at the departed Mike Cawley as well, saying they finally had a "legit quarterback" at the helm, which contritbuted in leading them to victory.

Those who questioned whether fans would come out in the traditional February and March conditions in cities like New York and Chicago got their answer in week four. Under 15,000 tickets were sold for Chicago's first home game, and the number was under 20,000 in LA during the rainstorm, with thousands less than that actually in the seats. The XFL, for the first few weeks, could always point to their attendance numbers when the TV ratings started collapsing in on themselves. With week five right around the corner, league officials had to even be questioning those figures.

CHAPTER TEN

NFL Commissioner Paul Tagliabue's decree that the XFL was a "non-issue," a quote the XFL used to its advantage to creat an us vs. them atmosphere for its fans and players, seemed to be truer as the weeks went on and as the ratings continued to fall. Week 4's NBC game, played in the rain and cold, registered a 2.6 rating, down from the week before's low of 3.1. NBC may not have been planning to abandon the XFL, but there was no doubt they were looking ahead to 2002, wondering what they'd do with this league that was quickly becoming an albatross in the ratings. By week five, the suggestion among some was that NBC would hold onto the XFL brand, but just not air it in primetime for season two. Instead, they'd find a Saturday afternoon timeslot for it. That seemed to make the most sense; then, the XFL's ratings wouldn't be scrutinized nearly as much. Plus, their target demographic would more likely be at home during these hours, instead of out partying on a weekend night. Trust me, I still fit into that category. The numbers on UPN and TNN weren't nearly as bad. UPN dropped only .1 in the fourth week, for a still-respectable 1.4 on the fledgling network. TNN's rating stayed the same at .9, while their number of viewers actually went up slightly.

The XFL made a rules adjustment to encourage more scoring. The bump-and-run rule was eliminated with the hope that passing games would take off. Receivers would be more apt to get open without defensive backs all over them downfield. It was one of those rules the XFL instituted to encourage more contact, to bring things back to the olden days of football. Instead, it contributed to low scoring games and the alarmingly low scoring games that permeated the schedule every week. At least the XFL acknowledged this problem and did something to fix it. Unfortunately, their goal was likely not better football, but better ratings. And thus was the problem with the XFL: It was a television product, not a sports product. And everyone could sense that, which is why many sports fans stayed away. They didn't necessarily gear the league enough toward the sports fan, despite all of the field cameras and microphones in the huddle.

Throughout the first four weeks of the season, finding statistics and information on the XFL was quite hard to find. The XFL had hoped they fixed that problem when, during week three, they brought STATS, Inc. aboard as their official provider and collector of statistics for the league. The official release didn't make it out until February 27th, however. STATS was also the provider of information for major sports leagues such as the NBA and NHL. When doing research for this book, it was frustrating trying to get statistics to match up, as some sources would say one thing and others would say another. Switching providers in mid-season can cause headaches (and it did), but at least they had a trusted name for the forseeable future in STATS. Too bad they didn't have them from the very beginning.

An ad hyping the Jesse Ventura/Rusty Tillman feud aired on Raw and Smackdown the week after the games, and clearly, WWE was trying to appeal to the scripted sports-entertainment part of their fan base with this one, even if the feud may have been genuine. The XFL continued to be mentioned on WWE broadcasts, as highlights of the week's games were generally shown and ticket info was sometimes given out. The theme song used when the XFL was talked about or shown was the same music WWE used for their "Brawl For All," a concept, like the XFL, which had some promise, but failed in execution. It was a gimmick where they pitted their wrestlers in shoot (real) matches where they wore boxing gloves, and take-downs were legal.

It was like the first grade of MMA. Too many guys got hurt though, and the guy they built the thing around to win ended up getting knocked out. The comparisons between the league and the "Brawl For All" were just too ironic to ignore.

In a story for the San Francisco Chronicle, David Steele extolled the virtues of the live XFL gameday experience, while decrying the below-par home viewing experience. It was nice to see someone rave about the in-stadium experience; but it would've been nicer if it weren't a columnist from the city that had no problem drawing 30,000 fans per game. Maybe in Birmingham or Chicago, the column could've been better-used. But to get any coverage at all at this point, and even one that was half-way positive, had to be considered a success.

The Orlando Rage made a flurry of transactions leading up to week five, selecting G Derrick Turner from the P.A.S.S pool, then flipping him and DE Sterling Palmer to Chicago for DT Corey Mayfield and future considerations. Interestingly, Chicago was the fourth team Palmer had been involved with, as he went to training camp with the Outlaws and was later claimed by the Enforcers, who traded him to the Rage. Orlando also brought back TE Vince Marrow, a former Buffalo Bill.

While the XFL claimed the Ventura vs. Tillman feud was not scripted, Tillman himself vouched for that, saying he had no interest getting invovled in the verbal jabs the Governor was sending his way. Rusty refused to be a party to whatever the XFL was trying to do here, and while it's fun to tease the guy easily exasperated and get a rise out of him, it isn't so fun when he calls your bluff and exposes things himself as getting too cartoonish and publicly says he won't be involved in that kind of entertainment that the league wants to offer. Suffice to say, it didn't make the league look good. But then, what had?

Turns out, putting Pat Barnes into the game for the Demons wasn't simiply to try to provide an offensive spark; it was revealed that Pawlawski was suffering from a neck injury that could keep him out up to three weeks. Coach Jim Skipper even had an inkling that something was wrong, which could've led to Barnes being inserted late. But Pawlawski wasn't the only injured Demon; against

Birmingham, they'd be missing WR James Hundon, LB Dave Thomas and TE Rich O'Donnell, all three of them starters. San Francisco, already without TE Brian Roche, was down to their third man at that position. However, they did acquire RB Kelvin Anderson, a five-year CFL veteran, to shore up their running game.

The Birmingham Bolts looked to improve their dwindling offensive prowess against the Demons on Saturday night. A combination of a struggling offensive line, poor field position thanks to sub-par kick and punt returns, and inconsistent running game were painted as the main reasons for the decline. Coach Gerry DiNardo simply posited that the team needed more red zone opportunities to be more effective. They also needed to fix their slow-starter status, as they had yet to score a first quarter point all season.

During the week leading up to week five, Enforcers coach Ron Meyer waffled on which one of his three QBs would starting, doing anything to get a leg-up on the Outlaws' pesky defense. Las Vegas was drawing comparisons to the Baltimore Ravens defense in the NFL for their aggressive, attacking nature. The Outlaws, sitting at 3-1, faced a potential trap game against the 0-4 Enforcers. Offensively, QB Ryan Clement returned to practice, but it was touch-and-go whether coach Jim Criner would give him the green light, or settle for Mark Grieb for one more week. Vegas also shored up their receiving corps by claiming WR Yo Murphy, a former member of the Tampa Bay Bucs and Minnesota Vikings. With a new QB, and one coming off an injury, they needed all the weapons they could get.

If there were any questions on the direction the XFL was headed, it was answered in the video packages leading up to the NBC game that week. New York was the featured game once again, against the high-powered Xtreme offense, and what did we get? Clips of the Rusty vs. Jesse "feud." "Real football" was becoming a "real farce." The one thing the XFL did add to the broadcast was Mike Adamle in the booth; as a former NFL player with the Chicago Bears, he could better translate to the fans some of the football-speak that went on on the sidelines between coordinators, coaches and players than either Ventura or Ross.

To replace Adamle on the sidelines, they promoted Chris Wragge from the UPN broadcast. Prior to the game, sideline reporter Fred Roggin flat-out asked Tillman if he was afraid of Jesse. Rusty just laughed in response. Early on in the game, after scoring a touchdown, Xtreme TE Josh Wilcox elbowdropped the football as his chosen TD celebration. Wilcox was no stranger to that sort of physicality; he was a pro wrestler and at one time, had a short stay as a WWE developmental wrestler and prior to that, made a few appearances in the original ECW as "All American Josh Wilcox." But he wasn't the only pro wrestlers/football player: Rage DE Bill Duff trained at the famed Monster Factory in New Jersey, and wrestled on the independent circuit as "The Urban Legend," and teammate FB Rich Young currently wrestles on WWE TV as Ricky Ortiz. But they weren't just wrestlers moonlighting as pro wrestlers: All three had experience in the NFL.

Adamle in the booth wasn't the only change to the XFL broadcast in week five. Dick Butkus replaced Jerry Lawler as the color man for the B broadcasts. Lawler had a falling-out with WWE after his girlfriend Stacy "The Kat" Carter was let go by the company. In protest, he left as well. This week's backup game was Birmingham at San Francisco. More rain there, but under the guidance of QB Pat Barnes, the Demons thrashed Birmingham, 39-10. The running game did most of the damage as Juan Johnson ran for 101 yards. Jermaine Copeland was popped by Damen Wheeler, but held onto the ball, furthering cementing his status as arguably the best receiver in the league. By the mid-2nd quarter, with LA leading 10-7, Xtreme WR Damon Gibson guaranteed a victory. Things got worse as Tillman nearly blew a gasket, shoving a cameraman out of the way following a Wally Richardson interception before the half. At halftime, we saw a day in the life of Rusty Tillman as the XFL did more pre-taped segments than earlier in the season. It was obvious as the game wore on that there were less field mics active to pick up the sounds of the game. One wonders if the budget got cut back once ratings started to slide. Also in the second half, Ron Merkerson and Tyrell Peters, two Hitmen LBs, suffered injuries, which helped cause New York's defense to fall apart. Jesse Ventura showed off "Coaching Football" and Football 101," books he had on hand to give to Tillman.

More big hits: S Leomont Evans planted WR Kirby Dar Dar of New York after a pass play, and Hitmen RB Joe Aska was ejected after throwing a punch that somehow, cameras didn't catch. Aska didn't agree with the call, but at least we got to hear his side immediately. Xtreme CB Terry Billups made a play late in the game, prompting the announcers to refer to his vast beanie baby collection. In a pre-taped, short video during a timeout, Billups even showed off some of his collectibles. Clearly, Billups wasn't worried about the inevitable questioning of his manhood that would come with showing off such a hobby. The way the ratings were going though, few probably heard about the manly pro football player collecting plush toys anyway. After finishing on the wrong end of a 22-7 score, all Tillman had to say was "we got our ass whipped on defense." They finished the broadcast off by showing some bonus coverage of the Demons/Bolts game. They showed about the last 4:40 of that one.

As if Rusty vs. Jesse wasn't enough, in what the XFL termed as "a desperate attempt to increase television ratings," a commercial for next week's game promised viewers they'd take them inside the locker room of the Orlando Rage cheerleaders when the Rage faces the Outlaws. At the half, Jonathan Coachman even did a pre-taped interview with said cheerleaders, in which the cheerleaders were given obviously scripted lines. While it was truly a desperate attempt to increase ratings, the XFL was also trying to be "in" on the joke that the league was quickly becoming. It appeared the league was trying to act cool by acknowledging the 1,000 pound gorilla in the room, that being the ratings. This stunt was bound to be panned by the purists, but at that point, they were either ignoring the league altogther or still writing about how reprehensible things were in the XFL, so they would only be staying the course. The XFL may have been hedging on the side of "there's no such thing as bad press." This would certainly get them back in the media's eye. But, if those coveted demographics, the male teens, returned in droves at the promise of seeing inside a place that was previously off-limits, the XFL would've considered it worth it, no matter how many critics piled back onto the league. The lack of sexual exploits the league had touted from the beginning, and that the media feared, was clearly what they thought was missing from the games. Shots of cheerleaders dancing in between plays and quick character profiles simply wasn't enough for that coveted population of fans the league was after.

Las Vegas visited Chicago on the Sunday afternoon TNN telecast, with Vegas trying to keep pace with the Western Conference counterparts the Xtreme and the Demons. Once again, the focus was on He Hate Me, and Enforcers DE Aaron Humphrey wasn't a fan of the attention he was getting. In pre-recorded comments, he said that the nickname was "embarrassing to me and the league" and said "it is catchy, if you're illiterate." He seemed more bemused than angry though. For the first time all year, the announcers stayed quiet during one drive during the second quarter and let the sounds on the field and the mics of the players and coaches take over in what they called "the sounds of the game." It was a good idea to really emphasize the wrinkles an XFL broadcast brought and a good way to separate the TNN contests from the other networks the broadcast the games, since they were really the only ones who did it. After Outlaws DT Angel Rubio laid the wood to RB John Avery, Avery said about the hit: "It was cute." Certainly not what a defender wants to hear about his work. The Outlaws got on the board twice in the first half to take a 13-0 lead into halftime. But the Enforcers turned things around in the second half. The Outlaws' main mouthpiece, S Brandon Sanders, was briefly quieted when he was sandwiched on a block by RB John Avery and a receiver. The Enforcers got their first offensive touchdown since week two mid-way through the second quarter when RB Charles Wiley scored from one-yard out. The Outlaws defense tried to protect a 13-9 lead with 1:59 to go, and on the sidelines, viewers got to hear new starting QB Kevin McDougal, head coach Ron Meyer and offensive coordinator Steve Endicott discussing the final drive. A big pass-interference penalty put Chicago in Vegas territory. With 1:00 to go, McDougal hit WR Luke Leverson down to the two-yard line, a 17-yard pass play. After a Leshon Johnson got down to the one-yard line, he punched it in from there with :19 to go in the game. It turned out to be the winning score, with Chicago on top for the first time all season.

The Orlando Rage tried to lengthen their undefeated season another week. One of the stories that led off the show: Memphis QB Jim Druckenmiller broke up with his Playboy Playmate girlfriend earlier in the week. Play-by-play man Chris Marlowe took the opportunity to make fun of The Boz, as earlier in the week, veteran Memphis OT Harry Boatswain got in Boz's face after practice for ridiculing teammate Kevin Prentiss for being too small on an earlier broadcast. Maniax DE Shante Carver continued to collect the heads of quarterbacks around the league, as he drilled Orlando's Jeff Brohm on a touchdown pass near the end of the first. Brohm was already nursing an elbow injury entering the game. The Rage QB laid on the ground, head twisted to the right side, not moving after the play. Brohm had to be loaded onto a stretch and taken into the locker room. The injury brought Wake Forest's Brian Kuklick into the game for the first time all year. Chris Wragge, pulling double-duty this week, updated Brohm's condition from the locker room a few minutes later. Brohm was being worked on as he layed on the stretcher and Wragge solemnly noted that one of the things Brohm wanted was for someone to calls his wife and let her know he was OK. Kuklick was a less-than-impressive 8-of-19 passing, but he did toss for 207 yards. Taking a 16-12 halftime score into halftime must've felt like 30-24 after all the low-scoring affairs in the previous four weeks. At halftime, LB Richard Hogans was profiled, both at home and on the job. Interestingly, both teams featured players who are ordained ministers: CB Stephen Fisher for Orlando and CB John Williams (who wore "Christian" on the back of his jersey) for Memphis. Humorously, a female fan in the stands, when the camera was on her (and who appeared a tad inebriated), tried to give viewers a look at her tattoo, which was a little south of the belt for the director, who cut away as soon as she began lowering the jeans in the stomach area. In a good sign for Rage fans, Jeff Brohm returned to the sidelines with a neckbrace on to watch the rest of the game late in the fourth quarter. They did show the x-rays and the ambulance heading to the local medical facility prior to his return, with Wragge saying Brohm likely suffered a concussion. A candidate for one of the best games of the year, this one was tight the entire way through, with the Rage holding on to win, 21-19.

Rashaan Salaam had his usual solid day of 90 yards and a touchdown, a theme that was becoming common in the XFL. Unfortunately, he also lost another fumble, his fourth on the year, and one of the problems that led to him being banished from the NFL. Salaam, at 26 years old, could boast that he was the only Heisman Trophy winner on an XFL roster to open the season, a season which he was very excited about starting and encountered numerous sleepless nights leading up to the game. Salaam's father and uncle both played major college football, and his cousin was WR Jason Shelley of the LA Xtreme. You could say football was in his blood. In high-school, Salaam had to play on a team that fielded only eight players at a time due to the low number of students enrolled. Still, he managed to be a highly-recruited player coming into college, and laned with the Colorado Buffaloes. His finest season was the one in which he won the Heisman, his junior year, where he also netted the Doak Walker Award for the nation's top RB and was named the player of the year by several outlets. He became only the fourth RB to reach the 2,000 yard rushing plateau in a season, averaged 6.9 yards per carry and rushed for 24 touchdowns. He came out of college as a junior and was taken in the 1st round of the NFL Draft by the Chicago Bears, a team that held the 21st pick. He set a Bears rookie record with 1,074 rushing yards in his maiden season and also found the end zone 10 times. He seemed to be on his way to a stellar career, but was derailed by injuries in the next two years, where he managed to play just 15 games. In 1998, his stock fell so far that he didn't even make the Oakland Raiders roster out of training camp. He bounced around with the Browns and Packers in 1999 but found himself out of work in 2000, though he continued to train in California for a spot to open up somewhere. Injuries, his alleged marijuana use (to which he entered rehab for in 1998) and a fumbling problem (14 in 31 games with Chicago) were three strikes against him and the "bust" label was already being thrown around to describe Salaam, at just 26 years old. He found himself a spot with the Memphis Maniax, headed by his position coach with the Packers, Kippy Brown, when he was drafted in the 26th round of the inaugural XFL Draft. He had a successful campaign with the team in 2001, rushing for 525 yards on 114 carries, but injuries struck again, forcing him to miss the final four games of the season. Still, he was able to finish fourth in the league in rushing. Though he was indifferent about using the XFL as a stepping stone to get back into the NFL, he tried out for the Detroit Lions following the XFL season, but was not picked up. He made another comeback in 2003, this time hooking on with the San Francisco 49ers. He was cut before the season began however. The Toronto Argonauts brought him aboard in 2004, but he was suspended by the team soon after. That was his last foray into pro football. His whereabouts today is unknown.

For the Hitmen, Joe Aska continued to profess his innocence on the punch he was ejected for. The Star-Ledger also revealed that, prior to the game, Jesse Ventura visited the Hitmen locker room, but didn't interact with Rusty Tillman. Ventura also said his shots at Tillman were not personal. The AP report on the game once again covered the feud extensively, which must've been considered a success for the league, since many news outlets poach the AP for their publications.

The San Francisco Chronicle got some of the cheerleaders' perspectives on the win over the Bolts. It was evident they paid varying degrees of attention to the game, but for the most part, seemed into the action and were at least aware of what was going on. Some even knew the names of a few of the players. It was an interesting take on the game by writer John Crumpacker, and it was an angle other cities should've followed up on. It would certainly get the fans to know a little more about the cheerleaders, who were little more than faces that you couldn't put a name with for most teams.

It was at this point of the season where the New York Times reported that the XFL was considering allowing high-schoolers, a year after graduating, to play in the league. At this point, the league's game-play was starting to improve, and there's no doubt that the few high-schoolers who would be good enough to play in the league would bring the level of play down a bit, having played against no competition at the college level or higher. It would've been questionable if the XFL would've been able to institute this policy; the Times also reported that the coaches' association was vehemently against the proposition. Of course, if Vince McMahon believed in the idea, it didn't matter who opposed him. He was used to getting what he wanted and probably, after a strong and public war of words, he would've gotten the XFL's way on this too.

Memphis was a team still searching for consistency, searching for an identity after another loss, this time to the undefeated Rage. Poor tackling on defense and turnovers on offense were culprits this week. Coach Kippy Brown was disheartened by being outplayed again and said that again, his team had chances they did not cash in on.

Chicago's attendance was up for their game against Las Vegas, even though it was so brisk that even coach Ron Meyer said after the game that he would've left early. The Enforcers got their first taste of the winning bonus money, and they needed more of it if they wanted to make a mid-season push for the playoffs. QB Kevin McDougal, in his first start, cemented his status as the team's new starting QB with a fine performance, especially against the much-regaled Las Vegas defense. Looking back, Tim Lester said being replaced happened simply because the team wasn't winning. He also noted how his replacement, McDougal, stood up for Lester to the local media. "My favorite part of this story was Kevin himself. The media had attempted to bash me after our first win, and Kevin didn't allow it. I really appreciated him pretty much telling the press about how I stacked up statistically in the league and how our team needed change and he was that change. Let me tell you, Kevin played great too. I had to sit the rest of the year, but totally understood why.After four games of tough losses, things were finally looking up for Chicago."

While the Outlaws suffered a tough defeat against the Enforcers, something that had been warned against earlier in the week, new receiver Yo Murphy made his mark. He turned two of his three catches into touchdowns. That wasn't enough to satisfy coach Jim Criner, who was still upset the Monday after the game, saying it was the worst he ever felt after a game. Two penalties really stuck in Criner's craw, and both of them had significant bearings on the end result. One penalty brought back a 45-yard pass play to Rod Smart; the other was a critical pass-interference call on the final Chicago drive, a penalty that advanced the ball 49 yards and put Chicago in a comfortable position on Las Vegas' end of the field. OT Tony Berti was acquired from the Hitmen in a three-way deal; Berti would only play for the Outlaws (he was a Vegas native) and refused to report to camp when New York selected him in the draft.

Week six meant taking a trip inside the Rage cheerleaders' locker room. More than the Rusty vs. Jesse feud, this was a hail-mary attempt to get a ratings bump and get the XFL back in the forefront of the viewers' minds. Unfortunately, for most people, it would take good football to make the XFL relavent. Perhaps the XFL wanted to tease fans, to bring them back with this ratings stunt so they could see how much the football had improved, and hope to keep them on after that. But as the ratings dipped, it would take a significant number of people to return and to keep returning each week, for it to be worthwhile.

CHAPTER ELEVEN

Week five ratings still dropped, but only to 2.4. At this point, even for a Saturday night, it was an alarming number. And, it was over two ratings points below what the XFL had promised advertisers. It appeared they had found the bottom, but there was no way NBC would keep them in prime-time with these numbers. TNN pulled in a 0.9 for the third straight week, and UPN dropped by 0.2, down to 1.2. This was beginning to be on the low-end of expectations for UPN as well. Even though the ratings were low, Ad Age reported that XFL was still drawing in the male 18-34 demographic, the one the league had been targeting from the start. But the overall picture, certainly, was bleak. All of a sudden, the one reason most people pointed to as a reason why the XFL would survive, that being their television partners, seemed in jeopardy for season two, if there even would be one. It must've felt like swimming upstream, trying to get people to tune in to the games as the media continued to ridicule or worse, ignore the league. The sponsors were staying with the XFL—for now—but at a discounted rate. Spots that originally went for $100,000 were being sold for $60,000. The XFL was even getting new advertisers at the lower rate, as Activision video games and Buena Vista motion pictures came aboard the previous week. And despite the low ratings, the Feb. 24-25 ratings were still good for second place that weekend, behind the NASCAR race. However, perception is reality, and the XFL brand was becoming like a leper—few wanted anything to do with it.

The XFL got some positive fan publicity, for the newswires that picked up on it, when Hitmen fans after a game assisted a police officer, who was being dragged out in traffic on the George Washington bridge, by another man. The fans tackled the man, who was later charged with attempted murder and numerous drug offenses. This would go against what most columnists would've had you believe at the beginning of the season, that fans of this league were crazed, blood-thirsty animals, the lowest common denominator of the vieweing audience. Unfortunately, by this time, reporters and media-types had moved on from the XFL to other sports stories as the calendar flipped into March.

Heading into week six, the XFL began to make the news for all the wrong reasons (save for the previous story that no one ran with). They tried to be "in on the joke" as far as the ratings were going and all week advertised that they'd go "inside the cheerleaders locker room" at halftime of the week six NBC game. They plugged it as a desperate attempt to hook viewers as the way to make fun of themselves. However, to those who had run out of venom for the XFL, they got more ammunition. By getting away from promoting the on-field action, the XFL was becoming everything they warned the media not to make them out to be: A league that WASN'T about football. But desperate times called for desperate measures, and the XFL needed to see something positive in the ratings. The curiosity factor may have brought people in, but realistically, what would they expect to see? You weren't going to get nudity (or really, anything close to it) on a broadcast network like NBC. So there was really no way to pay it off and leave viewers satisfied, but as long as their eyeballs were on the game, that's all that mattered.

In the week leading up to week six's games, the first-ever three-team trade was consummated. S Toby Wright was traded to San Francisco for OT Tony Berti, who the Demons received from the Hitmen for OL Robert Hunt and Harvey Goins. With all the QB injuries around the league, teams were still looking to shore up their offensive lines.

The Demons needed an extra D-Back to fill in for S Pete Destefano, who was still feeling the effects of a concussion suffered a few weeks earlier. Hunt was a starter for the Demons at right guard, while Goins was a backup. The Demons also parted ways with RB Vaughn Dunbar, their first round pick, who had struggled to return to the game of football. He got fewer and fewer opportunites each week as Juan Johnson saw his workload increase, plus they were getting Kelvin Anderson from the CFL too.

The Birmingham Bolts, following an injury to DT Eric Kerley, brought DL Kyle Schroeder aboard for the final half of the XFL regular season. Schroeder, a graduate of Dartmouth, was trading stocks in New York when he was called to put on the pads one more time. He was certainly making less money in the XFL, but he wanted to fulfill his dream of playing in the NFL, and wearing suits and working for Heartland Securities wasn't attention-getting enough for scouts. But Birmingham's real problems were on offense, and a 39-10 loss to an injury-riddled Demons team the week before was the wake-up call. They also suffered from turnovers against San Francisco, which hindered their progress on that side of the ball. Birmingham tightened their offensive line by acquiring OT Chase Raynock, a player they had targeted in the Supplemental Draft, from Chicago. Raynock was to immediately be inserted into the left tackle spot on a line that needed to do a better job of protecting their strong-armed QB, Casey Weldon.

DE Dave Richie was returning to action for the Xtreme in week six. Having never missed a game at any level of football, from high-school through the NFL, he had trouble dealing with the fact that he was on injured reserve. He was hurt on the first play of week one, but came back in better shape than before the injury. While the Xtreme's offense got most of the press, their defensive was doing a fine job as well. Starting G Bobby Singh also returned from injury and WR Todd Doxzon, who won LA's first scramble for the ball, was released to make room. Coach Al Luginbill, because of how tight the standings were in the Western Division, implored his team to treat every game as a playoff game, and ran practice as such leading up to the game against the Bolts.

While the Bolts were still debating on whether to start Weldon or Jay Barker at QB, the Las Vegas Outlaws were also trying to decide whether to go with Mark Grieb or Ryan Clement behind center. Clement was the third QB the week before, but the Outlaws didn't want to take any chances on another injury. They likely had to be convinced he was 100% healthy before he saw game action. However, they needed all the firepower they could get in the Western Division, where teams were doing all they could to stake a claim to a playoff spot.

I remember being at a friend's house for a birthday party on the Saturday night of the famed "inside the cheerleader's locker room" skit. I made sure to sneak in a couple peeks at the game as we were watching TV, but didn't see the actual halftime display until I got home and could watch it on tape. Saturday night in Orlando, there was another change at the broadcast position, with Matt Vasgersian back with the A-squad of Jesse Ventura and Mike Adamle, replacing Jim Ross, who went to work with Dick Butkus on the B-game. Vince McMahon is notoriously hard on his announcers in WWE and isn't afraid to switch things up if he deems something isn't working; it seemed evident in the XFL as well. However, the likely reason here was the XFL trying to get away from the WWE stigma, and having two men known for their work in that field hosting the show was not the way to do it. A video package on Jeff Brohm opened the show, who was starting on the night despite getting hit hard last week. When asked how he was starting, he answered Chris Wragge: "Well, let me answer that question by asking you two questions: One, ss this, or is this not, the XFL? Yes, it is. Two, do I, or do I not currently have a pulse? Yes I do. Let's play football." A soundbite Vince McMahon could be proud of. After the scramble, they finally went down to Fred Roggin with the Rage cheerleaders, and they discussed the "camera in the locker room" gimmick at halftime. I'm actually surprised it took them that long to get the first plug in. Vince McMahon walked up to them with a mic of his own, to the appreciation of the crowd. McMahon introduced the ladies to Bruno, the cameraman who would be going into the locker room. He was dressed as a guy on the field with a camera; helmet, black jacket, etc.

Ryan Clement was back under center for the Outlaws, which had to give coach Jim Criner some relief after seeing other QBs struggle to handle the offense in Clement's absence. During the broadcast, they profiled RB Rod Smart, who as "He Hate Me," had clearly become the star of the league. But it was Smart's backup, Ben Snell, who got the Outlaws on the board first with a TD catch from Ryan Clement. Orlando came back with two touchdowns in the second quarter, one on the ground and one through the air, as the Outlaws defense had a tough time matching up with the Rage's explosive offense. As expected, Adamle spent much of his time during the broadcast explaining the coach-to-QB communication fans at home heard, addressing the need for someone to translate that stuff into English for the casual viewers. That allowed Ventura to provide the meaningless soundbites that he excelled at. The announcers brought up the fact that Ryan Clement was saving the money he earned in the XFL to go to law school, an interesting second job for a football player. Every once in a while, they'd show Bruno, looking nervous about his halftime assignment. Wragge interviewed NFL DT Warren Sapp on the sidelines. Sapp, in particular, seemed to favor the hits allowable on the quarterbacks in the XFL. He played it politically correct by being neutral toward both the NFL and XFL. After a questionable pass interference call against "B.Mack" Brandon Sanders, Sanders, never one to mince words, asked the referee "how much they payin' you?" It was clear that Sanders was one of the league's favorites: Not afraid to speak his mind, and he could back it up with his play on the field. At halftime, with the Rage on top of the Outlaws and surprisingly out-physicating them, it was time to go inside the cheerleaders' locker room. If it was anything like the players' locker room at the half, people were bound to tune out. But the XFL made sure they wouldn't by providing a pre-taped skit for the occasion.

Vince McMahon was pacing back-and-forth in front of the cheerleaders' locker room as Bruno came running up to him. McMahon asked him if he understood how big of a deal this blatant attempt to increase television ratings was for the league. Vince asked him if he was nervous and Bruno said he was. McMahon turned kind, telling Bruno to sit down and take a load off. Vince told him to take the helmet off and said Bruno, a bald fellow in his late 20s-30s, was sweating like a pig. Vince offered him water to cool off for a few minutes, then walked away. After a break, they came back with some shots inside the team locker rooms, then back to Bruno. A better halftime spot was a profile of Maniax DE Shante Carver. Clement was interviewed for the piece and claimed "Shante is headhunting." That's the kind of controversy that creates intrigue—it wasn't forced like the cheerleader locker room skit and was just what the XFL wanted when they started: Letting the play on the field create the news and let the players speak their mind and be themselves. Clearly though, that alone wasn't getting it done, which explains the forced Rusty Tillman-Jesse Ventura feud and the hokey cheerleader skit. "There's no such thing as bad press" is something those in the XFL clearly believe in, because there was little in the way of good press relating to those two stunts. After a brief discussion of the first half, it was back to Bruno. He seemed a little more calm when McMahon, in that blustery way he has, walked up and made sure Bruno was ready to go. Vince told him that on the other side of the door was sheer paradise. He told him to go in there and get him some ratings. He pushed Bruno to the door, but the door didn't open, and Bruno slammed hard into it and fell to the ground. McMahon stood over him, slapping him in the face, calling him an idiot, trying to revive him. Things got all blurry and we got a dream sequence. Joe Cocker's "You are so beautiful" played as we went inside the mind of Bruno, where cheerleaders played Twister, walked around in towels washing a player in a Rage helmet (with "She Love Me" on his jersey), and hung out with dominatrixes and people in buny costumes, playing poker with Satan, you know, the regular cheerleader stuff. Out of the showers walked Rodney Dangerfield (seriously), who did his "no respect" schtick, towel wrapped around his waist. Bruno was finally awoken by the Rage cheerleaders, who were leaving the locker room to go to the field for the second half. Vince shooed them away and said he'd take care of it. He then went into his Mr. McMahon character, with the gravelly voice. He threw water on Bruno to wake him up and told him he ruined everything. He sent Bruno back onto the field, throwing his helmet at him as he ran away. You had to know they weren't REALLY going into the locker room. Then again, I'm not sure who that skit was supposed to appeal to. Would the teen crowd the XFL was supposed to be delivering on even know who Rodney Dangerfield was?

Conan O'Brien, who was hosting SNL after the game, did the same type of bit Will Ferrell and Molly Shannon did a few weeks back by making fun of the XFL teams' names. Once SNL started, Conan began his monologue with a very important announcement, then gave the score of the XFL game that aired. The fans went wild and O'Brien remarked that he loved fake enthusiasm. Nothing like taking shots at your own lead-in. I was hoping Ventura the next week would remark about how SNL hadn't been funny or since the 80s, but it didn't happen. Roger Clemens and his kids were interviewed on the sidelines as they were in attendance and each of the kids had Rage gear on. Vegas took a 15-14 lead in the fourth, but Orlando answered on the very next drive. On 3rd-and-6 at the Outlaws 50, Brohm found Dialleo Burks, who caught the ball for a first down and eluded tacklers down to the 18. With 5:00 to go, Brohm found WR Kevin Swayne in the corner of the end zone, 16 yards away for the touchdown. The Outlaws couldn't convert a fourth down on the next drive, sealing the game and Orlando's unbeaten season. Jim Criner let two f-bombs slip after Vegas failed offensively. With 1:02 left, they went to the Chicago vs. Memphis game for bonus coverage, but didn't stay long. Memphis was down by one after Leshon Johnson scored and proceeded to pretend to be a dog, urinating on the goal-post. It gets points for being unique. 23-22 was the score with 2:00 to go. With 1:10 to go, they wrapped things up from both venues. The Maniax came back to win, 29-22. A TD pass to Daryl Hobbs with 13 seconds to go sealed the victory and WR Charles Jordan chipped in with 10 catches for 240 yards. But it came with a price: The Maniax suffered injuries to their top two runners, Rashaan Salaam and Rafael Cooper. The Outlaws' bugaboo was injuries too, as they had three offensive linemen hobbled (David Diaz-Infante, who didn't play; Mark Nori, available only in an emergency; and Pat Kesi, suffering from the flu) and missed Smart, WR's Mike Furrey and Yo Murphy for parts of the game. After the game, Vegas coach Jim Criner headed off for a meeting of XFL head coaches to discuss possible rule changes to up fan interest and scoring, a meeting that was apparently called at the last minute. At the meeting, Criner said XFL officials assured the coaches of the league's viability at least through a second season.

The desperate Hitmen visited the Hell Hole in San Francisco to do battle with the Demons on TNN. Mike Pawlawski, still out with injury, served as an extra commentator on the sidelines. He wasn't foreign to the announcing job: He was the color man for the California college team. Lee Reherman talked to Hitmen GM Drew Pearson (who was mic'd on the sidelines as well) about opening up the offense, a sign of things to come. According to the public relations director from the Hitmen, TNN was quite happy with how it worked having those guys mic'd up. It was little touches like this that distinguishes each network others. On the game's opening kickoff, the Hitmen huddled around the man with the ball, and then broke out, with the Demons not sure who had it. But there was a penalty as the referees decided it constituted a forward pass of the ball. On the first play from scrimmage, they went for a long bomb, but Wally Richardson's throw was incomplete for Kirby Dar Dar. Jimmy Cunningham returned the punt after the first Hitmen drive for a touchdown. New York responded on their second drive with a score on the first play, a backward pass to WR Zola Davis, who threw to a wide-open Kirby Dar Dar for a 74 yard touchdown. But the Hitmen were just getting started. Obviously feeling like they had nothing to lose, they again went for a long bomb on the first play of their third drive; it too was incomplete. On the same drive, RB Dino Philyaw tried a halfback pass, and while he didn't complete it to Dar Dar, it did draw an illegal chuck penalty on the play. The very next play up Rusty Tillman's sleeve was a reverse to Dar Dar. On fourth down, they attempted a fake field goal, up 7-6, but the pass by holder Corte McGuffey was dropped by Michael Blair inside the five. Certainly a mixed bag, but it kept the Demons off-balance. The Hell Hole fans started a "New York Sucks" chant in the first quarter as well. Pawlawski, thoughout the game, provided insight on the field conditions, the Demons offense and the Hitmen defense. The Hitmen had a rare lead at halftime, and against one of the XFL's better clubs, 14-6. The field really began to get torn up in the second half, as playing on a field that a baseball team also calls home clearly had its disadvantages. The Demons made a game of it, making it 14-12 early in the fourth. But after a pass-interference call put the ball at the two, RB Joe Aska scored to give the team some breathing room. After a late turnover by San Fran, New York held on to win, 20-12. Once the game was in hand for the Hitmen, some Demons fans got on top of the dugouts and danced sans shirts and others ran onto the field. Well, it is the area of Oakland Raiders fans as well and their craziness has been much talked about. Speaking of the crowd, the Demons continued to draw the biggest gate, as 33,522 fans paid to see the game. Things like that amaze me as to how the XFL didn't make it to a second season, when in the middle of a firestorm that the XFL was facing from the media and other sports fans, 33,000 people still showed up to watch a game. That blows my mind.

The Los Angele Xtreme traveled to Birmingham to face the Thunderbolts. The crowd was sparse (a hair over 11,000), but vocal. The Bolts revamped their offensive line and wanted to open up their offense against LA. Their offense got a lift when Xtreme CB Terry Billups, the beanie baby guy, was forced into the locker room with a hamstring injury. In a funny moment, they showed highlights of WR Jermaine Copeland's college days on the Titan-tron. Copeland was in the huddle and told his teammates, "that's when I KILLED Alabama!" I'm sure the Birmingham fans didn't appreciate that. It was 23-19 Bolts at halftime, and either the lack of bump-and-run was doing wonders, or the offenses were finally figuring things out. The halftime show was more behind-the-scenes stuff with players, which did a lot more to give the fans a view of a player's personalities than the bland inside-the-locker room stuff did. Like TNN the week before, UPN did a "listen-in" for one series, where the announcers sat out and let the sounds of the game do the talking. Bolts QB Casey Weldon, who had been taking vicious hits all year, finally didn't get up from one. Following a sack by LB Shawn Stuckey, who came from the blind side, and a hit by DE Dave Richie on the following play, Weldon slowly walked off the field, saying "I'm done." He identified the problem as his left wrist, which opened the door for Jay Barker, who got a big pop from a crowd that had been waiting for him to get a chance since day one. Weldon was checked on by team medical personnel in the locker room, which the viewers got to see. It accounted for Barker's first playing time of the year, but he couldn't lead Birmingham to any points, and LA came away victorious, 35-26. RB Saladin McCullough did most of the damage, running over the Bolts defense for 124 yards and two scores.

McCullough, whose brother was also a RB in the NFL and CFL (Sultan McCullough), born in Monterrey Park, California, a neighborhood with a high concentration of Asian-Americans. When in high-school, McCullough set prep school records in rushing yards and touchdowns. He had always dreamed of going to USC, but his test scores weren't high enough to get him in, so he went to junior college. Interestingly, his XFL head coach Al Luginbill recruited McCullough when Luginbill was at San Diego State, and Saladin fell asleep on the recruiting trip. Luginbill remembered this and on McCullough's first day with the Xtreme, Luginbill jokingly asked him if he was going to be able to stay awake. While at El Camino Junior College, his sophomore season saw him break out for an astonishing 8.4 yards per carry rushing in ten games. He got into trouble while at JUCO, which McCullough described as him being in the "wrong place at the wrong time," when police arrested him for being in what they suspected was a stolen car. In the end, USC shunned him a second time. Upset at the California school, he decided to enroll at rival University of Oregon, where he wanted to get even with the Trojans. He started both years at Oregon and became the first back in school history to notch 2,000 rushing yards in just two years. Bad luck struck again when McCullough broke his ribs in the East-West Shrine Game, a post-season all-star game to showcase seniors for the NFL Draft. In addition, according to McCullough himself, almost every NFL team he interviewed with prior to the draft asked him if he was a gangbanger. Things failed to fall into place for McCullough, who couldn't catch on with an NFL team. He was working in California as a trainer of young athletes when Los Angeles selected him in the 58th round of the XFL P.A.S.S, only one round higher than the last. The odds were stacked against him once again in camp, and he found himself behind former Kansas City Chief Rashaan Shehee on the depth chart. When the former 3rd round pick proved ineffective, McCullough took over as the feature back in week six. He finished the only XFL season with 383 yards and 5 touchdowns, as well as 14 catches for an additional six points. After the league folded, the NFL finally came calling for McCullough. He signed with the San Francisco 49ers, but produced only 15 yards on 12 carries in the exhibition season. It wasn't enough to stick and he was cut. Saladin stayed with football and went north of the border to play a few seasons in the CFL.

Joe Aska, a former Raider and one of the keys to the Hitmen win over the Demons, mentioned that some in the crowd were throwing things at him; but having played in the area, it didn't surprise him. Rusty Tillman noted his team's desperation when discussing the myriad of trick plays he pulled out of his bag for the game. WR Kirby Dar Dar, the Syarcuse product who was the beneficiary of most of those plays, said the team had only installed many of those plays in game-week preparation for San Fran. Tillman hinted the plays would stay in the playbook.

The communication between teams and the media weren't the best. It was easy to blame the media for mistakes on reporting the XFL, but sometimes, you had to perhaps look deeper into the situation and think maybe lines were crossed somewhere. The Demons waived RB Vaughn Dunbar on March 5th, the same day they made a three-way trade with the Hitmen and Outlaws. But on March 12, in a game recap for the S.F. Chronicle, it was noted Dunbar was out with a knee injury, explaining why he didn't play. While the writer could've dug deeper to find out why he really wasn't playing, I also think it's on the teams to provide the media with up-to-date rosters and transactions so they can better cover the league. Demons coach Jim Skipper acknowledged that the trick plays kept the Demons' D off-balance, but said there was a lot of season left. Skipper did assure fans that Mike Pawlawski's job was safe and he would have it when he would be healthy enough to return from his neck injury.

The Las Vegas Outlaws blamed big plays given up in the final three minutes of the game for their loss to the unbeaten Rage. The Rage pass rush went after QB Ryan Clement, returning from injury, and the passing game failed to take off. The loss dropped Las Vegas to .500 on the season, but the bumps-and-bruises the team suffered in the game wasn't expected to effect their week seven match-up against the Bolts. The Outlaws also had the battle of field position won during the game, until the final few drives.

Orlando made a rare come-from-behind victory over the defensive-minded Outlaws; WR Kevin Swayne pointed to the confidence the Rage had in each other to get the job done. Galen Hall acknowledged the Vegas defense as one of the best, despite Orlando being able to step up to win in the fourth quarter. Hall also said his offense and defense both played well, but they could get better.

With week six in the books, the XFL regular season was entering the homestretch. It was also an important time for the XFL itself. Did the ratings stunt work? Or did they already reach bottom? Plus, it was time to start looking toward next season and what could be done to fix the problems in the league. But first, they had to finish out the season, a season where looking at the ratings every week must've been like Chinese water torture; I'm sure execs from the XFL and NBC were just waiting for the season to end so they could just turn the page, move out of primetime (at least on NBC) and start things back up running further under the radar.

CHAPTER TWELVE

The "inside the Rage cheerleaders locker room" had managed to stop the bleeding as far as the ratings went. Week six pulled in a 2.4, identical to the rating from the previous week, though in terms of millions of viewers, week six actually saw a slight increase. It wasn't cause for celebration, but it had to be a relief for the XFL brass to not have to open their newspapers up (or their internet browsers, as it were) to see the sports media discussing how rating had gone down yet again. Still, it was 89th out of 89 television shows that aired on the four major networks of the week, beating only shows on the WB and UPN. For the first time in three weeks, the TNN rating dipped, but only 0.1, as it dropped to 0.8. Still, for Sunday afternoon programming, it wasn't bad. UPN's rating took a hit of 0.1 down to 1.1. When the media was covering the league, it was usually pointing out the numbers and were more than happy to point out how they were right and, as it turns out, no one wants to watch poorly played football mixed with attempted sex appeal. The league needed to find a balance in its presentation, and it needed to find it fast. They needed to find a way to get those people who tuned out after week one back into the product. Unfortunately, due to the less-than-great first impression they made, combined with the media piling on the league, that would be a tall order.

Many XFL fans pointed to other sports leagues and noted that NHL, MLB and NBA regular season games have ratings that rivaled the XFL or were even lower. The problem in pointing this out is that those are not aired in prime-time on a major network. If they were, you can bet they'd be facing the same kind of scrutiny, even more perhaps because they are established leagues. The XFL talked so much at the start about how they were going to revolutionize the game, it wasn't a surprise that columnists wanted to remind them of that and throw the ratings in their proverbial faces. If the XFL were on in the afternoons, or at leasted started out there, I don't think there would've been nearly the problems they encountered in the first season. No one pays attention to afternoon ratings, and money from sponsors would be less, therefore you wouldn't have that many dropping out and there would be another negative story gone.

While many news outlets had stopped covering the XFL altogether, some did pay them fair attention. Pro Football Weekly featured a commentary from Andy Hanacek after ever week's games, providing more coverage online than many hometown newspapers were at this point. Perhaps my favorite website, which also featured a message board, was XFLBoard.com, run by Mark Nelson. Each team had a "reporter" that was designated to cover the team and some even provided interviews with the general managers of the teams. That likely wouldn't happen in any other league. XFL information wasn't that difficult to find on the internet, but on TV and in newspapers, it was becoming extinct. Some information, like weekly injury reports, still took time to find, whereas in the NFL it was virtually one click away. XFL.com left a lot to be desired in terms of providing information about the league. Each team's website was designed similarly, leaving the creativity available to each team, out in the dark. With XFL fans even struggling to find certain news, it must've been difficult to reel in new fans as the weeks progressed, as the average fan probably didn't run into much XFL news (unless it was about the ratings) on a daily basis. On March 13th, a press release was sent out by the league, touting the XFL's online presence. All eight team websites and the XFL.com site itself had ranked in the top 30 of the most-searched sports websites.

During the first week of the season, XFL.com had more viewers than the NFL, NHL and MLB's websites. It would be more interesting to see the updated rankings and to see if activity had fallen off. The Demons website had the most viewers of any other XFL website, not a surprise since they were also pacing the league in ticket sales.

The media was particularly hard on commentator/governor Jesse Ventura, who didn't add a whole lot to the NBC broadcast except bravado, which the league itself was not short on. In his radio show during the week, Ventura assured fans that he wouldn't quit and that he made a committment to the XFL that he'd fulfill. While having a big name in Ventura may have gotten the XFL some press early on and drew in some curious fans, it was negated by the fact that he just wasn't very good. His pro wrestling announcing in the late 80s and early 90s for WWE was very good, but it just didn't translate to football. He didn't have the same feel for the game that he showed for the wrestling business. Too often, especially early on, he would simply cheerlead for the league, and add little of substance to color commentary.

Jim Rome continued to look afool when talking about the league, denying there was a conspiracy against the league and McMahon (who had even suggested this?), then said he thought the media's coverage of the XFL was fair in the beginning. Really? Which beginning? When the XFL was officially announced, and media types scoffed at Vince McMahon, the guy who runs the fake wrestling business, trying his hand at pro football. Jokes abounded about mixing WWE and the XFL, wondering whether games would be scripted. Or was Rome talking about after the first week of the season, when ESPN Sportscenter showed the lowlights from the game in their video package rather than treating it seriously and countless columnists around the country did their best to discredit the league and thereby, also, the players in it. Rome used to be cutting edge, but in this case, he must've felt he had to fall in line with everyone else.

But that wasn't the worst of it from the media; in fact, the worst was brought on by Vince McMahon himself on the March 14th episode of HBO's "On The Record," hosted by Bob Costas. McMahon, clearly frustrated by the media's treatment of the league and his wrestling company, did more damage to himself and his credibility than any single column ever could. Vince acted more like his Mr. McMahon character from WWE television in the interview, trying to intimidate Costas, brow-beating him for interrupting him and everything else under the sun. The term McMahon threw out when referring to the XFL was "brand building," as in, they were building a brand and it would take time to get to where they were satisfied with things. He still hoped NBC would stick with them for a second season, and all but guaranteed a second season of the league. He even said, "we're in it for the long run." He insisted it wasn't too late to get viewers back that were lost in week one and talked about how the level of play had improved. "This is a start-up league, Bob, you've got to gives us a little bit of a break here," McMahon said, and for that, he was right. "We're going to have to convince the media, quite frankly, to cover this for the event that it is, not the perception that you, as an elitist in my point of view or others, would have." Vince went on to say. Again, he was right. But the way he conveyed it was wrong and it didn't get many fans feeling sympathy for how he or his league had been treated. McMahon got agitated again when Costas asked if he would fix games if it meant an increase in ratings, an absolutely ridiculous question from a guy who is better than that, who shouldn't have to lower himself to asking a game fixing question to a man who is clearly swimming against the stream to try to get his league accepted in the eyes of the media and the public. The interview got a lot of coverage, but it was more circus-like, as in, "take a look at the blustry McMahon, acting all crazy," rather than, "McMahon made some salient points about the XFL." McMahon, whose ego size not even he has doubted, could not set it aside in this interview to put the focus on the XFL: He had to be the story. Or maybe it was more "there is no such thing as bad press," whereby McMahon thought the media wouldn't cover the interview if he did it straight, so he argued with McMahon, guaranteeing the press would cover the interview and perhaps mention the XFL in passing, putting it back in the public's eye for a few days at least. Former wrestling announcer, sports columnist and radio host in Pittsburgh, Mark Madden, told Pro Wrestling Torch's Jason Powell that while

McMahon didn't do himself any favors in the interview with Costas, the host himself deserved some blame because he was not prepared, and that "the attitude to which Costas handled the interview was the most disrespectful thing of all."

Jim Ross, on WWE Monday Night Raw, took time out to implore viewers to give the XFL another shot, and to contact their local media in an effort to get the XFL covered more fairly. No doubt this was a directive from McMahon himself, and the desperation really showed with this move. Clearly begging fans to give the league a chance wasn't going to work, and they weren't playing up the underdog angle in a way that would make people want them to succeed. It just seemed so pathetic to have to resort to getting fans to write to their local media about XFL coverage.a true grassroots campaign taken in by the fans themselves to start this up would've likely meant more, but the fact that it didn't start should say something to the XFL about its fans, either in their numbers or their dedication.

With the XFL clearly getting into hole as far as ad revenue went, some wondered how long the players' paychecks would come in on time. This was one thing the league had to do correctly, because if word got out that paychecks were being withheld or given out late, no players would want to attach their name to a product that can't pay its players. While scheduled pay was on time, the Pro Wrestling Torch reported that at least one XFL player told a friend that the game-winning bonus checks usually take a while to be given out.

The Hitmen again spent time working on trick plays during practices leading up to their week seven game against Memphis. Tillman cited having a quarterback with the ability to scramble as a reason for installing some of the plays. NBC decied to air the B-game in those team's markets for the first time all season, meaning fans in New York and Memphis would get to see that game. The decision was likely made due to the high ratings the Memphis area was bringing in for the XFL. Airing the B-game as a regional broadcast, like the NFL does, would've been a good idea from the start, and it would perhaps get those team's area fans more into their hometown team and be able to identify with them more. As all eight teams were expansion teams, the fans had no identity to latch on to. Being forced to watch an out-of-market game on Saturday nights instead of their team may have taken the wind out of some fans' sails as far as supporting the team went.

A story in the San Jose Business Journal was written on the success of the San Francisco Demons in a relatively unsuccessful league. The writer cited the Demons high attendance numbers as a sign that fans in the Bay Area had bought into the team. To show the stigma the XFL was carrying around at that time, Andrew F. Hamm, the author, wrote that the Demons had only one local sponsor on board, even though General Manager Mike Preacher said it wasn't a priority to collect local sponsorship. Still, with over 30,000 at every game, you'd think that a lot of local sponsors, especially in that area of California, would love to jump on board. But so many looked down on the XFL that for some companies who really needed the press, it wasn't worth it. Even then, the Demons had surpassed their income goals by 25%. Their team apparel was selling well and according to GM Mike Preacher, three games worth of merchandise sold out in one game. Hamm expressed the idea that with so many distractions at the stadium (the Titan-tron, the mics on the field, the cheerleaders), that the game was almost secondary to everything else going on. I doubt one single fan in the stadium would have football far down the list of reasons they came to support the Demons. Those characteristics of the XFL game helped enhance the game, they weren't the reason people went, and they didn't overshadow the play on the field. But the media sometimes got distracted by all the shiny things the XFL was providing for fans and because the football wasn't on the level of the NFL, surmised that the play on the field must not be important. They still didn't get it. The same week, Birmingham's Business Journal reported that the city's UPN affiliate for was the top-rated affiliate in the nation for the previous week, thanks to the Birmingham game airing on that network. Birmingham was also the home to the highest TNN ratings for the first six weeks of the season. Even then, it was difficult to get local advertisers because of their affiliation with Vince McMahon. The radio home of the Bolts sold out all of its advertising before the season, another sign of interest in the market.

Meanwhile, the Demons were tied with two other Western Division teams at 3-3, trailing the leaders, the Xtreme, as week seven approached. Consistency was the theme preached by Preacher and coach Jim Skipper. The Demons would have a brand new backfield against Chicago, as Juan Johnson and Terry Battle were injured, leaving Kelvin Anderson and Brandin Young as the 1-2 combo for the week. But in the good injury news, QB Mike Pawlawski and WR James Hundon would both return after missing two weeks of action.

The Birmingham Bolts, whose QB situation was an issue in training camp, began to revisit those troubles when Casey Weldon failed to finish the week six game. They ended up claiming Mark Washington, who was with the team in training camp, to serve as their third quarterback. Two days before they claimed him, it was announced that Weldon was out for the year with a torn rotator cuff. That moved local legend Jay Barker into the starting QB spot, with Graham Leigh stepping into the backup role. Weldon, in second place in passing in the league at the time of injury, wouldn't even be able to throw for at least six months, hurting an already average Bolts offense that would be facing the now-famous Outlaws defense on the nationally televised NBC game. Interestingly, coverage of the Bolts seemed to increase in the area newspapers as the injury hit—not really a surprise with Barker now getting playing time; unfortunate it had to be under such circumstances that they finally started paying attention again. Barker would have no problem stepping into the leadership role required of the QB position, as he had take a similar position off the field for many of his teammates. The Bolts were down a TE as well, when Nicky Savoie, who had been with the team since training camp, left the team rather than be assigned to the practice squad.

Las Vegas, which had also struggled offensively, was counting on RB He Hate Me to provide some burst against the Bolts, but he was questionable heading into the game. The passing game was aided by the addition of WR Yo Murphy two weeks prior. Murphy was using the league to get noticed by the NFL, and his agent suggested he go the

XFL route. Even Vegas' defense was showing cracks, having lost to Chicago and then having given up 21 points to the Rage. Luckily, they were going against a Bolts team that was breaking in a new QB.

Birmingham got their first taste of NBC Saturday night action as they visited Las Vegas. Bolts DE Charles Preston got in Ryan Clement's face after a sack and told him, "Oh boy, it's gonna be a long day, baby." Vegas was propelled by two defensive scores, a 99-yard fumble return by S Jamel Williams, and a 45-yard intereception return by S Chris Bayne. Comedy was the name of the game it appeared, as Clement asked his receiver Yo Murphy in the huddle, "Hey, are you Irish, Murphy?" "Black Irish" replied the African-American Murphy. After punter Brad Palazzo ran down Kevin Scott from behind to make a punt return TD-saving tackle, Scott told Fred Roggin, "uh.yeah.that guy must've run a 4.3 (40 yard dash time), I only run like a 5.0 flat." Vegas' 13 points in the third quarter increased their lead, and they went on to a 34-12 victory to stay in the playoff hunt in the West. On his third quarter touchdown that put the Outlaws up by seven, TE Rickey Brady plowed over S Chris Shelling as he crossed the goal line. It was suspected to be a recepit for a shot Shelling got in on You Murphy earlier in the game. Rod Smart didn't play, probably making NBC unhappy that their big star was out, but Ben Snell had 59 yards in his absence. Las Vegas held Birmingham to just 113 total offensive yards and sacked Jay Barker seven times. Even as the ratings continued to slide, it really seemed like the announcers were having fun, loosened up and not held to the same standards stoic NFL announcers are. It was a breath of fresh air really.

The Outlaws defense continued to be the strength of the club, and it was thanks in part to two men in particular who took different routes in getting to the XFL. LB Kurt Gouveia brought a championship pedigree to the Las Vegas defense, and at 36 when he played in the XFL, he was considered over-the-hill for an NFL player. He was even older than six of the nine Outlaws coaches. He began his football odyssey as a high-schooler in Hawaii, where he played QB and CB, leading his team to three state championships. He was also the first player in Hawaii history to earn Player-of-the-Year honors on offense and defense. Gouveia traveled to the mainland to attend Brigham Young University, where as a junior, he was a part of the 1984 National Championship Team, and was an All-Western Athletic Conference (WAC) selection as a senior. Drafted by the Washington Redskins in the 8th round in 1986, he saw his first NFL action a year later, playing in 12 regular season games and three playoff games. In 1988 and '89, he earned his stripes as a special-teams stalwart for the perennially contending 'skins. Gouveia captured his first starting job in 1990, at middle-linebacker for the final seven regular season games. It was back to a reserve spot in 1991, then in '92, he started 14 games and led the team in tackles. For the first time, he started all 16 games in 1993 and again led the team in tackles, this time with a career-high 174. 1994 saw a return to bench, but he was used frequently as a situational pass rusher. He went to the Philadelphia Eagles in 1995 and started most of the games that year and in '96. Gouveia was starter again with San Diego in 1997, until he suffered his first serious injury in the business and finished the season on injures reserve. He was a bit player in 1998 and 1999 for the Chargers and then finally the Redskins again. In all, he played in 151 regular season NFL games, won two NFL Championships in 1987 and 1991, and even made an interception in the Super Bowl in '91. The reason he decided to strap on the helmet one more time in the XFL? His pure love of the game. There's no doubt he made enough money in the NFL to retire a happy and contented man, but it wasn't about that. He missed the camraderie, being around the game, being around his fellow players, teaching younger guys his craft and also competing on the field. Gouveia officially joined the Outlaws on December 19th when he was claimed with one of the team's territorial selections. He impressed the coaching staff in camp, showing that he hadn't lost much of a step and was adept at knowing where he needed to be on the field. He unofficially had 31 tackles for Vegas in his final pro football season. After coaching linebackers in NFL Europe, these days, he's still around football; only this time, as a parent and spectator, watching his son who currently plays at Virginia Tech.

Gouveia's partner-in-crime on the linebacking crew was Joe Tuipala, a low-key person off the field, but a hard-hitter on it. Tuipala played at Burroughs High School in California and played FB and ILB. He led his squad in tackles in both his junior and senior seasons, then parlayed that success into a career at San Diego State college. While there, he started nine of 12 games as a freshman, earning All-WAC honorable mention. He started a handfull of games each season in college at multiple linebacker positions, culminating with a fantastic season year in which he was named the MVP of the Las Vegas Bowl. Tuipala went undrafted, but hooked on with the Detroit Lions. He was released before the season began, but laned with the New Orleans Saints. They allocated him to NFL Europe and eventually made it from the Saints practice squad to the active roster, but didn't get into any games. When the XFL came along, he tried out for the league and was protected by the LA Xtreme with a territorial selection prior to the draft, but was then traded to the Outlaws in exchange for LB Mike Croel. Tuipala flourished with Las Vegas, where he led the team in tackles with 51 and made the All-Pro team. Outlaws coaches heaped praise upon him, talking up his quickness, instincts and his ability to simply make plays. Those traits caught the attention of the Jacksonville Jaguars, who signed him after the XFL folded. He made the team and became an impact player on special teams, leading the team in special teams tackles in 2001 and 2002, and even making a dozen tackles on defense in his second year. After suffering a shoulder injury, he was released in 2003 and spent 2004 out of the game. He got back in the league when the Washington Redskins signed him in 2005 and he went back to NFL Europe to freshen up his skills. It didn't work out though, and the Redskins cut him. Tuipala learned a lot from Gouveia in his season with the Outlaws, as both shared a lot of similarities: they were both Mormon, both from Hawaii, and both linebackers. Both men fed off each other, made each other better, and developed a relationship that evolved off the field as well as on.

The NBC alternate game, the first one actually shown in some markets, saw the Hitmen eek by the Maniax, 16-15. QB Wally Richardson played well, going 22-35 and WR Zola Davis caught two TD passes. Without Rashaan Salaam in the lineup, Wisconsin product

RB Brent Moss carried for 95 yards, but wasn't the breakaway threat Salaam was. The other problem was QB Jim Druckenmiller passing for just 89 yards. Despite these stats, the Maniax held a 15-3 halftime lead, but Davis erased it in the fourth with his two TDs, the final one coming with just over 12 seconds to go in the game. Moss was inches short of a first down that would've all but sealed the game for the 'Ax, but they had to punt and the Hitmen ended up recovering for the win.

Orlando at LA, a battle of two offensive fire-powers and two of the elite teams in the league (both in first place—Rage were undefeated), was the Sunday afternoon game on TNN. The Orlando Rage got in trouble with penalties early, and nine hankies were thrown their way in the first half. In the final seconds of the first quarter, with LA up 9-0, Leomont Evans made a statement tackle on Rage WR Dialleo Burks, stripping his helmet as he made the hard tackle. On the first play of the second quarter, Orlando QB Jeff Brohm was sacked by LB Juan Long. Brohm had to be helped off the field and it was later discovered that he separated his shoulder. Another week, another QB down and this time, Brohm with his second injury of the year. Brian Kuklick took over for the Rage, down 12-0 in the 2nd quarter. Not a position you want to put the backup with little experience in. It wasn't what they wanted, but they had to put the game on Kuklick's shoulders as the lead increased to 25-0 at halftime. Kip Lewis caught up with NFL Pro Bowler Jonathan Ogden on the sidelines, and he praised the players on the field for their effort. Any time the XFL could get an NFL player to put over the XFL experience, you knew it made them happy and also gave them credibility for the casual fans. Unofrtunately, the casual fans probably weren't paying that close attention by this time in the season. The Xtreme continued their dominance on the scoreboard and their physical dominance on the field, when CB Ricky Parker laid out WR Mario Bailey with a shoulder-first strike. Parker wasn't playing the ball, which was in the vicinity, so he was penalized for it. Luginbill, as usual, was almost out to mid-field arguing the call. During the season, he was on the field about as much as his players. The crowd agreed with their coach, chanting "bullishit" and later, "Orlando sucks." The announcers made mention of Al Luginbill saying he never had a better coaching experience than this year with the Xtreme. Once the score reached 31-6, Scott Milanovich took over for Tommy Maddox at quarterback. During the fourth quarter, they showed dinner at a local restaurant in LA from one of the previous nights, where announcer "Big" Bob Golic and 350 pound Xtreme OT Jerry Crafts had a battle of the bulge as they showed how much the men ate. In addition to Ogden, they showed Keyshawn Johnson on the sidelines as well and Milanovich was talking about a house he bought in upstate New York.interestingly enough, that house that he was referring to was likely the one he had in Hornell, NY, just a town or two over from where I live in Wayland, NY. Kuklick ended up going 17-24 for 202 yards, but couldn't bring the team more than six points. In the post-game interviews, WR Jermaine Copeland was confident enough to say, "this is a team that's going to blow somebody out at the championship, trust me." That's actually what happened too. Not sure if anyone went to Copeland for lottery numbers after that.

San Francisco was at Chicago for the Sunday night UPN game. Chicago was in a must-win situation, but for the Demons, if they ran the table, they'd have home-field advantage in the first round. On a cold March evening in Illinois, the Enforcers kept the ball on the ground on their first drive, rushing eight times and passing just once. Brian Bosworth was a fan of RB John Avery, saying "he's got moves Michael Jackson would be envious of." Later, Dr. Boz made the right call on a funny-bone injury that Avery suffered. He acknowledged, "he (the defender) hit me in the funny bone, but it wasn't funny." The Chicago fans were clearly falling in love with their star RB, chanting "Avery, Avery" during the game. Chicago rushed 40 times during the game and had over 100 yards at halftime, and stayed with the strength of their team, riding it to a 25-19 win; RB Leshon Johnson scored twice and Charles Wiley scored once on rushes. During a break in the action in the fourth quarter, they showed a segment called "XFL Raw," where they aired audio and video of verbal exchange highlights on the night. They've also previously done this with big hits. The cold weather also seemed to induce a lot of injuries from both sides, the Demons in particular, who couldn't really afford any more losses on their team.

The Xtreme win, covered in the LA Times by first mentioning the low ratings, then noting how few people were in the stands despite the tickets sold number, was the first in which all three phases really came together, according to coach Luginbill. The Times did get a quote from Keyshawn Johnson, at the game visiting his college roommate and Xtreme LB Errick Herrin—he said he was impressed by the quality of play on the field.

Before their Saturday night game, veteran Kurt Gouveia held a team meeting imploring the team to have more fun on the field, trying to get the players motivated to break out of a tightly packed Western Division. The Outlaws did their damage with Smart and C David Diaz-Infante, but did have QB Ryan Clement at the helm, which piqued the offense's confidence according to coach Jim Criner.

Part of the reason Chicago was able to upset San Francisco had to do with defensive alignment; CB Ray Austin was moved around the field by Chicago, and even played up near the line of scrimmage. Coach Ron Meyer was disappointed that his team couldn't put the game away in the first half, then damned the penalties that kept his team from clinching things early in the second half. The Enforcers had their own good luck happen int he 2nd quarter though, when Demons P Mike Panasuk nailed one of his blockers with a punt, sending it backward. Chicago was able to capitalize and score a touchdown on the ensuing drive.

With week eight approaching, the XFL and NBC likely had a good idea of where their relationship would be in 2002, if there was to be one. And the league was no doubt looking over its rules and television production, looking for ways to improve and tweak things for the second season. Still, the first season was yet to finish and no matter how bad the ratings got, the XFL had to trudge through the final week in search of the two teams that would participate in the championship game, still without a name: It was still, at this point, referred to as "The Big Game At The End," a cute ironic name, but not one for a league that was still fighting to be taken seriously by media and fans alike.

CHAPTER THIRTEEN

More bad news on the ratings front for week seven: The NBC rating nose-dived to a 1.6, a monumental drop from the week before and moving the number from "laughable" to "just plain sad." The rating was the lowest in Nielsen Ratings history for any of the big three networks: ABC, CBS and NBC. It was a .8 drop from the previous week, meaning perhaps the viewers that were left were turned off by the pro wrestling-like skit taking fans inside the cheerleaders locker room. In the end, it appeared to do more harm than good. However, March Madness was also in progress than evening and could've taken a good chunk of the sports fans away from the XFL game. With every week that passed, the XFL brass hoped that they finally hit "rock bottom." Was this the true "rock bottom"? Or could it get worse? Because it was on national prime-time network television, it became a joke not only in the sports media, but in the entertainment genre as well. Unfortunately, it was two areas the XFL hoped to cash in on, turning the sport of football and giving it more of an "entertainment" feel. The UPN game dropped again to 1.0. The network hadn't seen the extreme drop between weeks two and seven that NBC did. Neither did TNN, which actually increased a titch to 0.9, up from 0.8 the week before. Since the third week, the TNN rating had basically stayed the same. The main difference you could say is that this was a cable channel, whereas the other two were on network TV. TNN was also the home of Raw, and those fans were likely the ones tuning in on TNN, and since the XFL was promoted on WWE Raw, the fans likely just tuned in on Sunday afternoons to the same station they watched Raw on. It is interesting, nevertheless, that the rating had pretty much not seen the constant drop that the other two had.

The XFL tweaked another rule heading into week eight. Previously, no one was allowed to leave the line of scrimmage before the ball was kicked on a punt. However, the XFL allowed the gunners to leave once the ball is snapped, while everyone else still had to wait. This may be one of the switches that came out of the coach's meetings a few weeks back, and could be explained by simply making things simpler for the coverage teams. But with increased scoring being the order of the day, one would think the league would want to give the returner as much room as possible to bring the ball back. This was a good sign that the XFL was listening to the coaches even though the thing that would make the most sense for the league, at least in the short term, was to keep things as they were.

On March 22nd, the XFL Expansion Committee announced it would be visiting Washington, D.C. on March 27th. Former Enforcers GM Rich Rose was in charge of the committee and had a checklist of needs a city would be in charge of supplying for any XFL team. RFK Stadium was the site most likely to feature an XFL team had the expansion process been seen all the way through. A decision was expected by June as to whether any other teams would be added for 2002.

During the week leading up to the eighth game of the season, XFL Director of Football Operations did an interview with Fran Stuchbury. Keller characterized the media's coverage of the XFL as "brutal," but did not whine about it; instead, he said that Vince McMahon and Dick Ebersol can be easy targets because of their brashness. He also made note that having to overcome the stigma that the league has attached to it was the biggest challenge the league faced. Another point Keller made toward the XFL was the amount of minority coaches, where 27-30% of the coaches in the league were minority coaches. He also clarified NBC's contract, saying it stipulates two years of XFL airing in prime-time. He talked about long-range development of the league, but I would think that even the XFL brass would agree that prime-time for season two wouldn't be a good idea, and NBC would jump at the chance to remove it from the schedule and hide it in a weekend afternoon slot. As for expansion, he said if they were to expand, they'd want to add 2-4 teams in season two and also conduct a college draft. In addition to Washington, Keller also gave the cities Portland and Detroit when discussing expansion.

One day before the week eight games, WWE consummated a deal to purchase its main competitor, World Championship Wrestling (WCW), in one of the biggest pro wrestling news stories in history. WWE and WCW waged a high-profile war since the early 90s, when WCW was bought by Ted Turner. It intensified when WCW was given a Monday night TV timeslot on TNT, opposite WWE's USA show, Monday Night Raw. The feud was often bitter and very public. But WCW, due to mis-management at the creative and monetary level, had fallen on hard times and its top show, Monday Nitro, was about to be taken off the Monday night schedule. McMahon then swooped in and purchased the company. Because of this, many logistics had to be worked out, from whose contracts to purchase and whose to let go, and how exactly to integrate the WCW brand with WWE creatively and otherwise. This had to have taken a lot of McMahon's attention, and I think much of McMahon's time went into this project, leaving the XFL on the back-burner. How it ultimately affected the XFL and its future was unknown.

If the Orlando Rage were to win the Big Game At The End, they were going to have to do it without their offensive captain, QB Jeff Brohm, who the team announced would undergo season-ending surgery the Monday after week eight. This was to repair the separated right shoulder he suffered in week seven against Los Angeles. His replacement, Brian Kuklick, didn't bring the big arm or experience to the table that Brohm did, and he threw three interceptions in relief of Brohm against the Xtreme. But he did complete a good percentage of his passes, and there was really no option for the team. Plus, they had already clinched a playoff berth. Veteran NFL LB Joe Cummings was also released by the Rage before week eight. On the Wednesday before their game against New York/New Jersey, Orlando hosted a party for their season ticket holders on the field of the Citrus Bowl, where fans could meet the team's players and cheerleaders, as well as participate in activities, enjoy refreshments and tour the locker rooms. I can't imagine the multi-million dollar NFL players hob-knobbing with fans like this, but that's what made the XFL great. It would've been a great photo op and media story, but by this point, few were paying attention.

The Hitmen would be trying to stop the Rage and trying to claw their way into the playoffs. On the injury front, DT Israel Raybon would be in the lineup after being listed on the injury report as "questionable." That would help the Hitmen try to stop the Rage's triple running back attack. They also liked what they saw in Joe Aska, who would be getting the start over Dino Philyaw, who opened the season as the lead RB.

San Francisco continued to fight the injury bug when they placed their fifth player on injured reserve, that being big DT Emile Palmer. DT Pene Talamaivao, cut during training camp but 15 pounds lighter, was signed to replace Palmer. Also brought aboard to shore up their pass defense was seven-year CFL veteran CB Marvin Coleman. They set to play Memphis on Saturday night, looking to break a two-game skid and to get back to .500. Demons fans could look forward to give-aways on their last home date to thank them for their support throughout the year, packing Pac Bell Park with over 30,000 a game.

The Birmingham Bolts pretty much had to run the table to make the playoffs, thanks to a four-game losing streak they were mired in. Most of the games weren't even close, leaving little hope they'd be able to turn things around, especially with backup QB Jay Barker now at the helm rather than starter Casey Weldon. Barker's short time with the team combined with the rather difficult offense to pick up equaled a bad combination if Birmingham wanted to end the season with three wins in a row. After being sacked seven times in the previous game against Las Vegas, Barker needed to work on getting the ball away quicker; his O-Line simply needed to do a better job protecting him.

For Xtreme S Ron Carpenter, all he wanted was payback when LA faced Las Vegas. He was stuck on the Outlaws practice squad for the first few weeks of the season before he was traded to LA. In an article in the LA Times, he called the bash in LA, set for coverage on NBC, "a vendetta game" and said "I guess they didn't think I was good enough to play. It was a slap in the face." After the third week of being on the practice squad, he said he was set to demand a trade or go home and wait for the AFL season to begin. In the end, Al Luginbill said they offered a 10th rounder for Carpenter while the Outlaws countered with a 3rd rounder. LA said they'd go as low as the 8th round and the teams were able to come to an agreement. The Outlaws defense against the Xtreme offense was a major storyline for the game. It was the same when the teams met earlier in the year, with LA coming out on top 12-9.

As for the Outlaws, they too needed a win to stay in the playoff hunt. A win would tie them with LA at the top of the Western Division; a loss would leave Vegas fighting with the other two teams in the division for a playoff berth. With Ryan Clement healthy and added offensive weapons since the last time the two teams met, there was reason for optimism in Nevada. The defense continued to dominate, with the Outlaws having three players sitting atop the league leaders in sacks and S Brandon Sanders leading the XFL in picks.

Las Vegas at Los Angeles, the marquee match-up in week eight, aired on NBC. Interestingly, Honda was back in the line-up of commercials, perhaps because the XFL was almost giving away ad time. For the first time, the scramble for the ball wasn't shown—instead, the announcers talked over it, perhaps as a way to cut down on time once again. The last time the Xtreme took on Vegas, Juan Long and Shawn Stuckey expressed their distaste with Rod Smart by way of the nicknames on their uniforms. They had fun with it once again this week, with "Still Hate He" and "Still Hate He 2" on their jerseys. The Outlaws stumbled right out of the gate, as Chrys Chukwuma fumbled the opening kickoff, which was recovered by LA. The announcers mentioned that QB Ryan Clement was playing with a broken finger and eight stitches in his chin, in addition to still getting over a separated shoulder. They focused on his toughness and it would be doubtful that $50 million NFL quarterbacks would play with those injuries. In fact, at halftime, there was a video package profiling the toughness of the XFL's quarterbacks. When Clement was in trouble on 3rd-and-long in the 2nd quarter, he threw the ball to the closest person to him: Unfortunately, that person was ineligible receiver and OL Lonnie Palelei. Palelei, who caught an extra point in the first game of the season, didn't miss a beat and ran with the ball about ten yards. When the refs called a penalty, he tried to convince them it was a fumble. He told an Xtreme player before the next play, "Damn.that was sweet though, you gotta admit." Tommy Maddox tried to play peace-maker for the Xtreme when G Bobby Singh got into a row with DT Adriano Belli after a missed extra point. "Bobby, Bobby, we need ya," Maddox told him, indicating he didn't want Singh to get tossed for being involved in a fight. While some coaches got angry in past weeks with cameras being in their face on the sidelines, the XFL altered things a bit by having the cameras lower to the ground, looking up at the coaches so as not to be in their face. Maddox commented that the Xtreme receiving corps was the best he had ever played with at any level. High praise, but coming from inside the league, it wouldn't mean much to fans the XFL needed to get back into the action. In addition to the QB profiles at halftime, they showed the Xtreme cheerleader routines too. Less and less time was spent every week, it seemed, inside the locker rooms at halftime. The game was expected to be really hot, but there were 14 flags against the Xtreme in the game and 13 against Vegas, slowing the play on the field down and making the teams look sloppy, even eight weeks into the season. The announcers acknowledged this, with Matt Vasgersian getting exasperated and uttering the term, "He Flag Me." Late in the game, they showed the playoff seedings for the first time, and of course, even this the XFL had to change-up from the norm: It would be the #1 seed from the East against the #2 of the West and vice-versa. Despite the flaggage, it was a high-scoring affair, as the Outlaws showed cracks in their defense, recently nicknamed "The Dealers of Doom," for the first time, losing 35-26. Scoring was mostly done through the air, with Clement throwing three TD passes to his

TE, Rickey Brady, and Tommy Maddox tossing the ball for 279 yards and four touchdowns.

Memphis vs. San Francisco was the "B" game, and the Demons broke their two-game losing streak and got a foot-up on the Maniax and Outlaws in the playoff race, winning 21-12. Without Rashaan Salaam, who was out for the year, the Maniax struggled to get things going and had to rely on their passing game too much. WR Charles Jordan's 111 receiving yards was not enough to earn the victory. Demons RB Kelvin Anderson had his second 70+ yards rushing game and QB Mike Pawlawski threw for 215 yards.

The Hitmen looked to keep their playoff hopes alive against the first-place Rage. The injured Jeff Brohm wasn't even in the stadium for this one. His replacement, Brian Kuklick, got good field position right off the bat to ease any jitters he might've head, when the diminutive Brian Shay returned the opening kick to the one-yard line. Hitmen GM Drew Pearson was again mic'd on the sidelines for TNN, able to talk to the announcers, and he displayed a lot of passion (and yelling), but spiced up the broadcast a bit, not that it needed it; Minnervini and Golic weren't Jesse Ventura or The Boz in terms of personality, but that was the great thing that made the broadcast different. The cameras and mics on the sidelines caught Rusty Tillman calling for a fake field-goal, but they were forced to call time-out when Rusty didn't like the looks of the defense. In the second quarter, Rage C Cal Dixon was profiled; more specifically, they showed video of him at his second job, manning the Dairy Queen he owned in Melbourne, Florida. At halftime, two rather large men with Rage helmets on did a scramble for the ball in mid-field to entertain (disgust?) the fans in attendance. In the second half, Hitmen WR Kirby Dar Dar had a tough succession of plays: On the first, he was drilled on a PR by Kelly Malveaux. Then, on offense, he was hit hard in the back by Ricky Bell as he went up for a ball. Later in the game, the referees must've been confused about which league they were officiating in when they called Hitmen CB Donnie Caldwell for an unsportsmanlike conduct penalty for spiking the ball in front of the Rage sidelines after an interception. Pearson wasn't happy about THAT. Big Dwayne Sabb later de-helmeted G Dan

Collins for Orlando in the middle of a play, and tossed it across the field. No penalty there. New York had plenty of chances, including causing four turnovers, blocking a punt and recovering a botched snap on a field goal attempt, yet they trailed 17-12 with 2:00 to go. Their game-winning drive stalled once they crossed mid-field, and Wally Richardson suffered a hit that took them out of the game. Much-maligned Charles Puleri came in, but couldn't lead the Hitmen to victory. Like in training camps, NFL scouts were keeping tabs on the XFL games from close-up: Representatives from the Jaguars, Buccaneers and Dolphins all made the short trip to Orlando for the game; and the Montreal Alouettes and Calgary Stampeders sent scouts to the game as well, according to Slam! Sports.

Brian Shay returned kicks for the Rage in 2001, but he was also one of three running backs the Rage utilized during the season. Shay had two things working against him getting a real shot in the NFL: One, he was from tiny Emporia State, an NCAA Division II school; and two, perhaps most damning for his chances, was that he stood just 5'8". Small backs tend not to be able to take a full-season bruising in the 16-game NFL schedule, which is why most teams shy away from them. This despite Shay's overwhelming credentials during his time at Emporia. At high-school near Kansas City, Shay re-wrote the school record book, leaping to number one in yardage and touchdowns in a season, with 1,800 and 27 respectively. His team also won the Class 4A State Championship while he was in the backfield. Despite his football credentials, Shay was just as polished in wrestling, where he receieved numerous scholarships to play that sport in college. After four years of football at Emporia State, all Shay did to cement the idea that he made the right choice in staying with football was to end his career as the all-time leading rusher. In College Football. History. He averaged over 2,000 yards rushing his final three years and won the 1998 Harlon Hill trophy, given to the best Division II player in the nation. Three times Shay made the Division II All-America team. After his college career, and after going undrafted, he signed with the Kansas City Chiefs in the NFL. He was released in the final cut-down, but spent five weeks on the team's practice squad. NFL Europe was his next destination, where he finished third in the league in rushing during his one season with the Berlin Thunder. He went back to the Chiefs in 2000, but still couldn't crack their RB rotation. That's when he went into the XFL draft and was drafted in the 30th round by the Orlando Rage. Shay wasn't one to embrace the XFL's lenient rules on celebrations, but he appreciated the fact that he gave players the opportunity to express themselves. Football was in his blood, and he told the Topeka Capital-Journal that he'd like to play the sport as long as his body would hold up, an attitude held by many XFL players. Shay got the least carries of any of the three Rage RBs, but averaged 5.6 yards per carry on 36 rushes. Shay never got another chance in the NFL, but he'll always have the NCAA records to hang his hat on.

The city of Chicago appeared to have found a new sports star in route to the Enforcers 13-0 win over Birmingham on another frigid evening at Soldier Field. RB John Avery continued his bid for league MVP honors, as he ran for 170 yards and the only two scores of the game, including a 73-yarder on the first play of the game. Fans chanted "Avery, Avery" once again and a fan (not one of the few who went shirtless) even held up a sign, reading: "Avery has a touch of 'Sweetnes,'" in reference to famed Chicago Bears RB Walter Payton. In the last game between the two, a long interception return iced the game for the Bolts and James Willis and Christopher Perez had a confronation. That was revisited before kickoff, with both men being interviewed. The production staff had a tough night; Gerry DiNardo's name was spelled "Jerry" on the chyron. Injured Bolts QB Casey Weldon provided perspective from the sidelines, much like Mike Pawlawski did a few weeks bac, and Drew Pearson did on the TNN game. However, Weldon was caught saying, "Should I look right into the camera when they're talking to me?" when he thought his mic was closed. But when there are so many mics in play on the field, that kind of stuff is bound to happen, even though it does make things look sort-of bush league. The announcers talked about Chicago starting the season lining up in the 3-4 defense, but moving to 4-3 as the year progressed. Midway through the second quarter, the Bolts' second-string QB, Jay Barker, was the recipient of a helmet-to-helmet hit on a scramble that knocked a few screws loose upstairs. He suffered a minor concussion and New Mexico's Graham Leigh had to take over, the third QB the Bolts were forced into using. He was just 9-of-27 for 102 yards. In one of the more poignant XFL moments on the year, Barker, a few minutes after getting the concussion, asked the team doctor, "what happened, I have no idea?" The doctor told him he got hit and fumbled and had a slight concussion. Barker replied: "I mean, I'm having trouble remembering things.could you please just stay with me?" The doctor seemed to comfort him and even felt the need to remind Barker who he was when it appeared Jay didn't know. This scene felt like it was out of a chick flick, and I'm sure, for some ladies watching at home, it brought a tear to their eye. In truth, it was a telling look at what a concussion can actually do to a person for all the viewers at home who always hear about injuries like that but don't know the toll they can take on someone. At halftime, they showed footage of the cheerleaders' week that was, and all that they do leading up to the game. They did the "listen in" feature twice during the game, once in the third, and once in the fourth. Like the Rage trio of running backs, we learned that Avery and LeShon Johnson sub themselves in and out of games as well.

With their win, the Rage clinched a division title. Head Coach Galen Hall gave credit to his defense and said they had been underrated all year. It also had to be a positive for the team, in rallying around Brian Kuklick, who was forced to replace one of the XFL's most prolific passers in Jeff Brohm. The ability of the running game to put the team on their collective backs no doubt eased the transition. Kuklick wasn't happy with his performance after the game, despite leading the team to the victory. Coach Hall said he was concerned about the number of interceptions his backup QB threw.

With the loss, the Hitmen were forced into having to win their final two games to be eligible for a playoff spot. They were likely down to battling the Enforcers for a spot, as the Bolts were all but eliminated with their latest loss. Luckily for the Hitmen, they could control their own destiny with a week nine showdown coming up against Chicago.

It was do or die time for the Demons, and they "did" in their win over Memphis. The coaches and players were elated with the play of Mike Pawlawski, especially coming off an injury a few weeks back. Like most teams, a prescription of wins the rest of the way out was the way the Demons could recover from playoff fever and actually clinch a spot. In a game recap for the San Francisco Examiner, writer Doc Drake derided the league and even the live experience, despite a crowd of over 35,000. The debauchery in the crowd, including garbage being thrown and flashers; seemed to disgust him. Yet in the NFL, the same thing likely happens on a weekly basis. It was a hack job disguised as a game write-up, continuing to pile-on the Demons despite the success the league had in the San Francisco area. Apparently, some columnists saw this and thought perhaps fans and the league needed to be taken down a notch. He called the live experience "an unabashed celebration of vulgarity." Hey, 35,000 people can't be wrong.

XFL President Basil DeVito talked to the media before the Birmingham/Chicago game, and he reminded writers that while the NBC ratings haven't been good, UPN and TNN were both satsified with the numbers they were getting from the league. After RB John Avery ran for an XFL record number of rushing yards, DeVito credited the Enforcers as being one of the better stories of the year, in coming back from an 0-4 start to be on the verge of a playoff spot.

The story of the Xtreme vs. Outlaws game in the papers, but not mentioned much on TV, was the relationship between Jim Criner and Al Luginbill, who had also coached against each other in NFL Europe. They had been friends for 26 years, but neither coach wanted to give an inch in that week eight battle. The Xtreme clinched a playoff spot with the win, and the Outlaws fell to 4-4, tied with the Demons in the West. Criner preached making the corrections necessary to come up big in the next two games.

For whatever it was worth, the XFL Playoff Picture was clearing up as the weeks went by, and the XFL continued to adjust the rules to make things more fan and player friendly. It seemed, in doing this, they were already preparing for season two, and all the quotes from guys like Basil DeVito and Michael Keller, high-ranking XFL officials, seemed to indicate a second season. From the expansion committee to the interviews with curious columnists, who had come out of the wordwork as the season ended to question if a season two would even happen, it was clear and there seemed to be no question: Season two would be a go, no matter how low the ratings went. And really, that was it: Attendance was good, merchandise was hot, website hits were plentiful. The only ingredient missing in the league was decent TV ratings. Unfortunately, for a made-for-TV football product, that was bad news no matter how many promises of continued leage play were made.

CHAPTER FOURTEEN

The NBC rating went up to a 1.8, a rise of .2. At this point, anytime the ratings rose would be cause for celebration by the league, even if it was miniscule. Las Vegas vs. LA was a pretty strong match-up to air on NBC, with the defense of Vegas as well as He Hate Me, now a universally known product, taking on one of the best offenses in the league in the Xtreme. That may have drawn some curious viewers to see what they missed in the weeks prior where they didn't tune in. The rating dipped a bit for the TNN game, but since it had held steady for so many weeks beforehand, it was likely not a big concern. UPN's rating fell below 1.0 for the first time, down to 0.7. With the ratings in the tank, many news people were contemplating whether there would even be a season two. Since this was most of the coverage given to the league in the latter weeks, readers of these stories likely said to themselves, "well, if these columnists think it won't be around next year, why should I spend my time watching it?" This even though people like Mike Keller and Basil DeVito did their best to convince media types and fans that there was no doubt they'd have a season two. Fans may have felt it pointless to get invested in the games if they thought the league wouldn't be around in the future.

XFL President Basil DeVito did an interview with Pro Football Weekly talking about a number of things. As for expansion, he said cities are calling him quite often, and even said he fielded four calls the day before. He seemed frustrated that the bulk of the reporting done on the XFL concentrated solely on the NBC ratings. DeVito put a lot of pressure on weeks 10-12 in the XFL season as far as ratings went, saying it might be the ratings NBC looks at when it decides whether to continue airing the league or not. He also said that if he could do one thing over again, it would be to put the game and broadcast that aired in week five or six on during week one. This is an obvious one, since week one's game and broadcast turned so many viewers off. He also mentioned the switching of announcers to give fans some understanding of what is going on on the field. He also hinted at changes in the salary structure, saying that if they offered QB Joe Hamilton more money, perhaps he would've come to the XFL instead of sitting on the bench in Tampa Bay. This would be an effort to draw better players to the league, but I wouldn't really want to screw with the pay structure, unless you were to raise them all at a level that would keep them in the same hierarchy they were at that point. As for press, DeVito characterized it as "downright vicious, as though we're overthrowing the government." He did note that the XFL should've taken more initiative in meeting with the media and fully explaining what the league was to be about. DeVito insisted in another interview that losing the NBC wouldn't make or break the XFL since they originally started off as being owned 100% by WWE and they'd revert back to that business plan if NBC was to leave.

The NFL continued to play into the XFL's hands, but the XFL didn't really take advantage of it. The NFL decided in the off-season during meetings of the competition committee this week that they would ban bandanas worn under helmets, they would more strictly enforce taunting and unsportsmanlike conduct and also focus more on protecting the QB. New York Giants VP John Mara told the New York Giants website that the bandanas made players "look sloppy" and that they made the ban "for their own good." Yes, because when I thnk of NFL players, I think the NFL needs to be a babysitter. This isn't a fashion show: It's football. As long as it doesn't effect the play on the field, who cares what they look like? Too think bandanas send the wrong message is just stereotyping the people and players who wear them.

Detroit was the next city in line for a visit from the XFL Expansion committee. They also met with the mayor. After turning down Detroit for season one, the XFL this time looked at Tiger Stadium as a potential playing area. Before the first season, the Pontiac Silverdome was offered, but the XFL declined as they wanted all outdoor stadiums in the league. Some other cities considered for expansion, or at least rumored to be, were Denver (a city that supported the USFL team in that city quite well), another New York team, Miami (like NY, concerned with having a glut of teams in that area), Portland, San Antonio (like Denver, drew well in other pro football leagues, but only had an indoor stadium to offer), San Jose, and Toronto (which was rumored as a possible city among the first eight).

The San Francisco Demons were amped up for a re-match with the Las Vegas Outlaws in week nine, after suffering defeat at the hands of team made famous by He Hate Me, earlier in the year, 16-9. The playoffs provided extra motivation for the Demons: Win and they're in, lose and they're out. Both clubs' records were 4-4 and the winner would own the tie-breaker even if they ended the season with the same record. On the injury front, the Demons were returning RB Terry Battle and CB Dwayne Harper to the lineup. While the Outlaws run D had remained stout, their pass defense was exposed last week against the Xtreme, and with the Demons strength being their passing game, they looked to have a favorable match-up against Vegas.

Early on in the week, it appeared the Birmingham Bolts would at least have QB Jay Barker available to play. He was even scheduled to start as of Tuesday, as long as he was free of any lingering problems during the week, and was cleared by the Bolts medical staff after suffering a concussion via a hit by Enforcers DB Ray Austin the previous week. Then, just before the weekend, it was announced that Graham Leigh, the team's third-string QB, would start instead against Orlando. A win would mean the Bolts would still have a chance, however small, to make the playoffs. It was week nine and no one was eliminated from the playoffs yet. The XFL had already, in its first season, achieved parity. Leigh, a paltry 9-of-27 the week before, did have some incentive in playing against the Rage, as they were coached by the man that once cut him in NFL Europe, Galen Hall. Barker, meanwhile, still felt dizzy as of Thursday and was experiencing soreness in his upper body as a result of the hit and had not, in fact, been cleared to play. What was thought at the time to be a minor concussion at the time turned out to be a bit more severe than expected. The defense continued to get bad news, as DT Johnny Mitchell and S David Knott, who both suffered injuries in week eight, were announced as being out for the year. The Bolts, in anticipation perhaps for the Rage's through-the-air offense, claimed two safeties during the week: Kevin Sigler and one-time starter Fred White, who was released by the team earlier in the year.

The game against the Rage wasn't the only concern for Birminghm fans during week nine. The Bolts were near the bottom of the league in attendance and their team on the field was struggling to get a few more wins to avoid having the worst record in the league. Some rumors were swirling that the NBC deal would be off the table, with the Birmingham News sayin that NBC leaving the league would be "imminent." Other rumors made it seem like the XFL would relocate the Birmingham franchise because of its low attendance numbers. President Basil DeVito denied the rumors.

For the Memphis Maniax, in their final home game, against the Los Angeles Xtreme, they had a raffle to give away the same $2,500 player bonus to a fan if the Maniax came out on top. Memphis' playoff outlook was dim: They needed to win their last two games and have the Demons lose their final two. Like most teams in the league, the Maniax head coach, Kippy Brown, had a call-in radio show at a local watering hole, where fans were invited to gather. It was a good way for fans to get a close-up view of their head coach.

The Las Vegas Outlaws were in a must-win situation against the Demons in week nine. It was hard to believe this was the same team that crushed the Hitmen in week one and dominated on defense in the first half of the year. DL Kelvin Kinney opined that this was the best defensive line he had ever played with, and they needed to prove it against San Francisco. The team did charity work throughout the year, including the cheerleaders and players serving as guest waiters and waitresses at a cafe in Vegas to help raise money for an organization that works with children who have cancer. Instead of a nice write-up about it though, there was a once sentence blurb about it in the Las Vegas Review-Journal. I guess those headlines aren't as attention-grabbing as the ones that portrayed the league in a negative light.

In New York, the Hitmen tried to defend their turf against the Chicago Enforcers on the NBC game in a game billed as "You win, you're in; you lose, you're out" of the playoffs. The Hitmen were behind the eight-ball off the bat, as they were forced to start Corte McGuffey at QB as Wally Richardson had suffered a leg injury during the week and did not play. The scramble for the ball was shown on tape for the first time. Enforcers RB John Avery had strong words for the Hitmen defense when interviewed: "I'll be like Al Pacino in New York: I kill for fun." Because Avery tweaked a hamstring in the waning seconds of last week's game, he didn't carry the load as much this week. Even with McGuffey at the helm, New York got out to an 8-0 first quarter lead. In the second quarter, a young lady named Rachel, working the sidelines for NBC doing the sound, was nailed by Avery as he ran out of bounds. There was a big cheer from the crowd when she got right back up though. "Scary, very scary" is all she said about the incident when interviewed. Matt Vasgersian tried out his comedy by saying, "For those of you still missing 'Golden Girls' int his timeslot, we'll have Rue McClanahan in full pads, right after this," before going to commercial. Chicago took the lead and went up 16-11 at the half. Things started turning back toward the Hitmen in the 2nd half, when Joey Eloms returned an interception for a TD to take an 18-16 lead. In addition, Enforcers QB Kevin McDougal suffered a hit that took him out of the game. He was replaced briefly by former Maniax QB Craig Whelihan. Neither team did itself any favors with both exhibiting sloppy play to the tune of three turnovers each. The Hitmen were up by two in the fourth with 2:34 left, and they were in "run out the clock" mode.

Unfortunately, RB Joe Aska fumbled on the New York 43, and it was recovered by Chicago DB Quincy Coleman, giving the Enforcers new life. With 1:41 to go, and McDougal returning to the game for this drive, he found TE Willy Tate, who had bounced around the NFL for several years, caught a 19-yard TD pass. The Hitmen got the ball back and actually got down to the Enforcers six yard-line, but penalties drove them back to the 20. On 4th-and-15 with :06 to go, a last gasp shot at the end zone was intercepted. Enforcers 23, Hitmen 18. McGuffey ended up a respectable 13-of-22 for 144 yards. John Avery had just six carries for the Enforcers. In a nice touch, the Hitmen, in their final home game, honored the fans who came to the aid of the police officer who was being attacked after the first New York home game. They were awarded all-access locker room and sideline passes, and were acknowledged by the team at halftime.

In the alternate game, Orlando squeaked by Birmingham, 29-24. QB Brian Kuklick seemed more comfortable leading the offense, as he passed for 257 yards, but he did have three interceptions, all picked by CB Eric Sloan. WR Kevin Swayne continued his late-season surge, catching six passes for 56 yards. The Bolts held an eight-point lead in the fourth quarter, but their defense couldn't hold on. With the loss, they became the first team eliminated from playoff contention. RB Derrick Clark found the end zone on the score that allowed the Rage to take the lead. The game was certainly closer than the one between the two earlier in the season, which Orlando won 30-6.

Los Angeles and Memphis squared off and once again, the Xtreme didn't have a remedy for the 'Ax, with Memphis winning 27-12. Memphis was led by QB Jim Druckenmiller, who beat the LA defense for three touchdown passes. Somehow, one of the league's best teams couldn't find out how to beat an under .500 team, losing to them for the second time of the season. The Maniax once held a 20-6 lead and in the first quarter, CB Corey Sawyer, who had 11 career NFL interceptions, handed the football he intercepted to a fan in the front row. QB Tommy Maddox struggled for LA, completing less than 50% of his passes and throwing two picks to go along with zero touchdowns.

In place of the injured Rashaan Salaam, Ketric Sanford, a University Houston product, ran for 82 yards.

The San Franicisco Demons clinched a playoff berth by beating the Las Vegas Oulaws, 14-9 on the UPN game. The game was tied at six in the third quarter when wily veteran Dwayne Harper picked off an errant pass, leading to a 25-yard TD pass from Mike Pawlawski to Terry Battle. The first score was straight out of the XFL's new rules, when Outlaws PR Jamel Williams couldn't corral a punt, but Demons' Lee Cole could, and it was in the end zone. In the fourth, Rod Smart had the ball stripped of him on the Demons one-yard line, and the ball rolled through the end zone for a touchback, another mistake on the Outlaws part. Ryan Clement was injured once again for the Outlaws, and Demons LB Jon Haskins was tossed out of the game for the hit.

Some players played in the XFL to try to get back into the NFL. Some played for the paycheck. Others played simply for the love of the game. Demons OT Scott Adams fell into that last group. The hulking 6'5", 310 pound starting lineman for San Francisco, one of the many veterans on the Demons at 34 years old, began as a two-way player in high-school. He earned a shot to play college in Division I at Georgia, and was a stalwart at guard for three years, lining up at tackle as a senior. Adams was an honorable mention All-American and second-team All-SEC player following his senior season. After graduating in 1988, Adams found himself on the outside looking in after time in camp with the Dallas Cowboys and Atlanta Falcons. He brought experience starting up a league to the XFL, as he was a member of the first-season World League of American Football (WLAF) with the Barcelona Dragons. During his stint playing overseas, he caught the eye of the Minnesota Vikings, who brought him onto their practice squad in 1991. He finally got a chance to be on an active roster for an extended period of time in 1992, getting into 15 games as a swingman on the Vikes' offensive line. The next year, he advanced up another step, nailing down a starting job at right guard for ten games in Minnesota. However, because he had accrued three seasons, he was due to be paid more than what the Vikings wanted to pay him; they could've saved money by getting a younger guy to fill his spot, and that's exactly what they did, releasing Adams before the season in 1994. He hooked on with the New Orleans Saints where he played 11 games and earned a game ball, a rarity for a lineman, for his blocking asssitance on the kick return team for that particular game. In 1995 and 1996, he played for Chicago and Tampa Bay respectively, getting into only a handful of games each year. After being cut in training camp by the Broncos in 1997, he landed with the Falcons in mid-September to back-up the guard and tackle spots as Adams' football odyssey continued. By now, most athletes would've conceded that maybe the NFL was not for them, but Scott's love for the game kept him chugging along, no matter how many teams decided they no longer had a use for him. He spent the next two season out of football before signing with the XFL, bringing his 69 games of pro football experience (playing with seven different teams) with him. The Demons made Scott their second round pick, 11th overall, in the XFL P.A.S.S. Adams, who owns a national supplement franchise, started for the Demons all-season and at home games, wore the nickname "Hell Hole" on the back of his jersey, in honor of the fans who filled Pac Bell Park to cheer him and their team on. He didn't seem to mind that he had to ice himself for 30 minutes after every practice as, at 34, his body wasn't what it used to be. Adams was also very active in charity, organizing a yearly motorcycle rally to benefit the American Cancer Society, in honor of his father, who perished from the disease. During the football games, he also wore around his wrist a lace from his late father's workboots in tribute to him. While his football career ended after coming up short in the Million Dollar Game, Adams was a player who, it would seem, absolutely cherished every day he got to put on a uniform.

To show how little coverage the XFL was getting at this point, the only recaps of the week nine games I could find in doing research were AP articles, which were becoming smaller and smaller earch week. It seems that even the hometown newspapers of the teams were giving up on the league. The Las Vegas Review Journal, though, seemed to have the most consistent coverage. "I think we covered the league the same from start to finish. I went to practice every day and wrote on the league after it concluded as if it were coming back until the infamous conference call in which they killed it," said beat writer Kevin Iole. It's debatable whether "bad news is better than no news," but if people aren't reading about the league, or seeing coverage of it on TV, it's not in the front of their sports mind, they'd forget all about it. Most fans had already sampled the league and passed, but they may have been willing to give the league another try if that kind of coverage was out there. But as ratings went down, so did coverage. With the MLB season on the verge of starting, the end of NCAA March Madness, and the NBA and NHL seasons winding down, there wasn't much room left for the XFL. NBC was closing in on a decision on whether to keep the XFL for season two, so it was a bad time for fans to forget about the league, contributing to the continuing downfall of the ratings.

CHAPTER FIFTEEN

While ratings on NBC continued to drop to red-alert levels, the TNN ratings also hit a bit of a rough patch late. Week nine dropped to 0.5 after it had been holding steady in the 0.8-0.9 range. UPN settled with another week of 0.7 ratings. In an effort to raise ratings by any means necessary, the XFL flipped the schedule for week 10 around a bit. Orlando vs. Chicago was supposed to be the week 10 game on NBC, but that was switched to San Fran at LA. That game was a battle for the Western Division lead and featured two of the more potent offenses in the league, with the thought that a higher scoring game and more at stake would draw more viewers. Orlando had a good offense too, but Chicago was all John Avery. The Rage already clinched the East and Chicago was pretty much in: A win here or a Hitmen loss against Birmingham would buy them an extra week. Memphis at Las Vegas stayed the "B" game, as both teams had already been eliminated from contention, and the Sunday TNN game stayed in its spot as well. The Orlando vs. Chicago game was to be played on UPN where the LA vs. SF game was originally scheduled.

In addition, the XFL finally found a name for the Big Game At The End, as it had previously been called: The Million Dollar Game. Not exactly brimming with creativity, but it was something. This was in concert with an amped-up marketing campaign the XFL planned to utilitze for their playoff push. Another rule change would come into play during the playoffs, that being the extra point rule. It had been modified so that teams could choose to go for one point (from the one yard line), two points (from the five) or three points (from the ten), instead of having to go for one point from the two-yard line. If the defense created a turnover and ran it back for a touchdown during the extra point attempt, they'd be awarded the same number of points the offensive team was trying for. It was just another way to bring the overall scoring up a bit. Once again though, it made the XFL seem minor league in what from the outside looked to be desperation and haphazard rule changes to simply get more eyeballs to the TV set. If these changes had been made in the offseason, perhaps they would've been more widely accepted.

Because of the QB situation in Orlando, they made a deal to bring in Patrick Bonner to back up Brian Kuklick and Jim Arellanes with Jeff Brohm out for the season. Bonner's pro experience was with the CFL and NFL Europe prior to joining the Rage. In college, he played one season in the area for Florida A&M before transferring to Temple University.

Making the playoffs was out of the NY/NJ Hitmen's hands; while they needed to win at Birmingham, they also needed a loss by Chicago to coincide with it. The Hitmen players acknowledged before the week 10 game that they put themselves in the hole they were in, but could only do as much as to beat the Bolts and let the cards fall where they may. They would have to do it without QB Wally Richardson, who was doubtful for the game. While they were on their second-string QB, the Bolts were on their third, as Graham Leigh was slated to get the nod again for Birmingham due to injuries.

The Demons were heading into Los Angeles winners of two in a row, and they aimed to make it three in winning the Western Division. The Demons did have a conflict on the date of the Championship Game though—the Milwaukee Brewers would be in town to face the San Francisco Giants at Pac Bell Park, so if the Demons did win their next two, the XFL would be in a bit of a quandary about what to do there. It wouldn't seem fair to have the game at the other team's home if the Demons truly did earn it.

The XFL and the Demons got some more negative press and this was for doing something positive. The team had offered to build new locker rooms and offices for Diablo Valley College, the place where they practiced, as a sort of thank-you for putting them up. Yet, the school worried they'd be out of compliance with Title IX. However, San Francisco also contributed $25,000 to a scholarship for female athletes, in addition to the $50,000 they put toward the construction. One person at the college, a Faculty Senate Vice President, wasn't happy with her college getting into bed with the XFL and Vince McMahon, even if the XFL was showing her, by doing this, that they aren't all bad. She was worried about the prestige of the college in working with the XFL. It was really sad that people couldn't acknowledge that the XFL wasn't, in fact, run by Satan and that those who watched the league or did business with them wouldn't spend their afterlife burning in the fiery pits of Hell for doing so. It was just ridiculous some of the mis-conceptions people had about the league. Most of it, unfortunately, was due to the coverage of it by the press, and not from actually watching it.

Home field advantage was of utmost importance to Xtreme coach Al Luginbill. After another loss to the down-and-out Memphis Maniax, the Xtreme were likely looking to beat up on someone in week 10, and the Demons just happened to be the ones standing in the way. An injury would sideline one-half of the best WR tandem in the XFL, as Darnell McDonald was listed as doubtful due to a calf injury. Also on the shelf was WR Larry Ryans, who was a two-year starter at Clemson. Luckily, the strength of the Xtreme were their wideouts, and Damon Gibson (selected by the Cleveland Browns in their expansion draft in 1999) and Damon Dunn (at the time, Stanford's all-time leader in kick return yardage) were ready to fill the void. LA fans had to wonder though how Tommy Maddox would respond, coming off arguably his worst game of the season.

The Las Vegas Review-Journal ran a story on TE Rickey Brady heading into the final week, focusing on some of the players and their stories since the Outlaws weren't going to get into the playoffs. Brady, who graded out better than any Vegas linemen in blocking, was coming off a three touchdown game against the Xtreme two weeks prior. His pass catching skills were unquestioned, but his numbers for the season were down a bit due to injuries he suffered while preparing for mini-camps and the season the previous fall. He had grown a bit bitter about his time in the NFL, having been a part of eight different teams or training camps. He said he'd prefer to stick with the Outlaws in the XFL. I bet there were quite a few players with that same attitude, and I think that would've surprised a lot of people in the sports media.

The Chicago Enforcers were hitting their stride at just the right time, and they needed it to continue against Orlando. The Enforcers were on a three-game winning streak and seemed to be mixing good offense (led by Avery and Kevin McDougal) and good defense (headed by LB Jamie Baisley and DE Aaron Humphrey). Avery was questionable, thought, with a bothersome hamstring and McDougal was coming off a concussion.

The importance of the SF at LA game on NBC was evident when they once again showed the scramble for the ball live. Unfortunately for the XFL, it didn't look like it would be a close game off the bat, as the Xtreme charged out to a 14-0 lead in the first quarter, behind touchdown runs by Saladin McCullough and punter Noel Prefontaine (on a fake field-goal). That score in particular fired up coach Al Luginbill on the sidelines. During the first cut-in to the Memphis at Las Vegas game, Jim Ross and Dick Butkus as usual handled things. But for the second update, it was JR and Dan Hampton, a former Chicago Bear DT who had worked NFL games for NBC when they had the rights to the games in the 1990s. Not sure why they had both Butkus and Hampton there (unless it was a three-man booth), but if Hampton was to be added to the broadcast in season two, it would've been a good get for the league. Butkus had more important things to do than color commentate the B game and I always assumed he was just a fill-in until they got someone to replace Jerry Lawler. After Rashaan Shehee caught a pass for minimal gain, Al Luginbill, his mic open for all viewers to hear, said to an assistant coach on the headset: "He can't make a play with the ball in his hands.it's like watching fuckin' paint dry." While it was a classic quote, not sure if it was about Shehee though (bad timing it would've been—the LA Times had a story about Shehee earlier in the week with Luginbill having kind words for his RB), but the announcers clearly didn't know how to react to Luginbill bashing a player and landing the f-bomb on the broadcast. After a few moments of silence, Mike Adamle chimed in with, ".or watching grass grow." That's not the kind of insight fans were probably looking for. Speaking of Adamle, he was guilty of several times referring to the LA squad as the "Express." The Los Angles Express was a USFL team from 1983-1985. As much as Adamle brought to the booth in the second half of the year, it kind of hurts the credibility of the announcers when they keep mixing up a team's nickname.

At halftime of the game, the announcers presented the XFL.com Fan Picks of the Year, in which fans could vote for their favorite in several categories online. One was the Lugz Hit of the Year (Lugz was a sponsor of the XFL): Chicago's Ray Austin knocking out Jay Barker; Shante Carver knocking out Jeff Brohm; Shante Carver separating Ryan Clement's shoulder (I'm sensing a pattern here.); Jamie Baisley crushing Memphis PR Damien Dodson on a punt return attempt; and Corey Ivy lighting up Damon Dunn in the back of the end zone in the OT thriller from week two. Adamle's pick was Ivy's hit, and it would've been mine too. The Burger King Player of the Year for Offense: John Avery, Jeff Brohm (Mike's pick), Jermaine Copeland, Tommy Maddox (Jesse's pick), and Mike Pawlawski. The Burger King Player of the Year for Defense: Shante Carver (Mike's Pick), Kelvin Kinney, Ron Merkerson, Joe Tuipala (Jesse's pick) and James Willis. Hard to argue with either of Jesse's picks, which makes me worry for my sanity a bit. And the All-Access Moment of the year—"Jim Criner's Fourth Down Decision," where they captured Criner, a few players and coaches deciding on whether to go for a fourth down; "Jay Barker—Post Concussion," where Barker spoke to the trainer after getting knocked loopy; "Charles Puleri vs. New York," Puleri's promo on the fans, telling them to keep booing; "Tommy Maddox—Tommy's Tirade," imploring

Luginbill to go for it rather than rely on kicker Jose Cortez early in the season when he was slumping; and "Mike Pawlawski—Pre-Game Passion," a speech he gave to his teammates in the locker room before a game.

Things didn't get better for the Demons in the second half. They found themselves down 24-0 at the end of three quarters, which caused head coach Jim Skipper to tell a group of players on the sidelines: "They're embarrassin' the hell outta you guys on national television." Another NFL player was found roaming the sidelines, in New York Giants CB Jason Sehorn. He told Fred Roggin that the league was entertaining and said the game gives guys another shot at the NFL. Another endorsement from an NFL player, but maybe too little too late. Another girl working sound for NBC was hit on a play that went out-of-bounds, making that two weeks straight now. She too was uninjured in the collision. With the game firmly in hand, Xtreme fun-loving WR Jermaine Copeland danced with the cheerleaders on their perch and also signed autographs near the end of the game for fans. That's all-access right there, and good that they caught it on camera. Maybe in the pre-season you'd see NFL players doing this, but not during a regular season game. LA players missed a Gatorade bath on Luginbill, as he was able to get out of the way (NFL players likely wouldn't have missed!). Roggin and Luginbill though were doused with water on a second try. Mike Pawlawski was 17-of-29 passing for San Francisco, but tossed two interceptions. Tommy Maddox had a relatively easy day, finishing 15-of-24 for 164 yards and a touchdown to Copeland, who reeled in nine passes for 99 yards. The Xtreme defense, at the time ranking seventh in the eight team league, picked a good time to play their best game of the season. Just south of 20,000 people paid to see this game, which made the cavernous LA Coliseum appear nearly empty, which was a problem the XFL had at a few stadiums around the league. It just didn't look good on TV and gave even more of an impression that no one cared about the league, even though attendance figures were higher than what the league had targeted.

A bonus side-effect of the extra $2,500 given to winning teams is that even if two squads are battling in a game in which neither team has a chance at the playoffs, they're at least playing for something (oh, and pride). That was the story when Memphis visited Las Vegas. The Maniax got the money and the win, 16-3, as the Outlaws offense ended the season the same way they played during it: struggling. The Maniax stats were not gaudy (no one rushed for over 39 yards and Jim Druckenmiller passed for just 152), but they were the recipient of two Vegas turnovers. All the scoring in the game was done in the first half. He Hate Me finished the year on a low note, carrying only 10 times for a paltry 19 yards. The Las Vegas Outlaws lamented their last-place Western Division finish, with players still saying they thought they were a playoff team. But they admitted that the offense was behind the defense for too much of the season. They failed to reach the 200 total yard plateau in their final game for the fifth time in ten games. Coach Jim Criner seemed incredulous at how the season could've turned for the worse after such a good start.

Memphis didn't get a lot of TV coverage on the year, but if they had gotten more, one player the TV crews should've focused on was a man making history. Shin Yamada became the first Japanese to play professional football in America when he suited up for the Maniax. The nickname on his jersey was "Samurai," as a visiting Japanese television station covering his trek suggested. Yamada, at 215 pounds, was a little light for a linebacker, but it made him perfect for special teams duty. According to the Nichi Bei Times, as a child, Yamada spent some of his school years in Memphis, as his father, a businessman, traveled extensively. To make friends, Yamada joined the football team. After moving back to Japan, he continued playing football, a sport he fell in love with in America. He was on the team that won a Japanese Amateur League Championship in 1993. Even after growing up and getting a job in Japan, he stuck with football, playing in a semi-pro league, even earning divison MVP on the team in 2000. While he continued playing and excelling in Japan, there was a part of Yamada that earned to try his hand at pro football in America, to see if he could make it with the best of the best. After watching a Kansas City Chiefs practice in 2000 as a guest of his former coach in Japan, Yamada became mesmerized by the American way of professional football, which was very different from Japan's version. In an effort to expedite the process, Yamada sent tapes to his coach to spread around the United States in the hopes some team, somewhere, would give him a shot. His coach called Yamada with the news that Memphis was interested in bringing him in. A coach from the Maniax called Yamada to invite him to the team's training camp in early 2001. He not only went to camp, but made the team on his first pro football try. Yamada was on the active roster for five of the first six games of the season and played well. His goals were lofty though: To become the first Japanese player to play in the NFL. His parents attended the final Maniax game of the season, to see their barrier-breaking son play. Yamada never made it to the NFL, but his goal of getting Japan interested in American football succeeded the first time he set foot on an XFL field.

Sunday was the day fans would find out the final team to make the playoffs. The afternoon game on TNN pitted New York against Birmingham; The Hitmen had lost to the Bolts in week two in their previous meeting during the season. Hitmen S Joey Eloms (who had two INT's on the afternoon—one of which was latereled to fellow DB Donnie Caldwell for a TD) gave another sterling quote in a pre-taped segment when asked about returning to play football in the southeast: "As long as they keep the cows off the field, we'll have a good game." Both back-ups, McGuffey and Leigh, played pretty poorly early on. McGuffey was even replaced by Charles Puleri, who did an admirable job in relief, going 5-of-7 for 158 yards (one a 77-yard bomb to Kirby Dar Dar) and one TD. Casey Weldon was again mic'd on the sidelines to provide an X's and O's analysis of the Bolts offense and play-calling. Interestingly, the cameras seemed to be focused on Bolts head coach Gerry DiNardo rather than his counterpart on the Hitmen, Rusty Tillman. It's notable if only because Tillman was an early "star" of the league in his feud with Jesse Ventura. Perhaps him not wanting to play ball and match Jesse blow-for-blow was the reason the league decided to take the focus off of him. At one point, they actually used a small split-screen to show Weldon talking during a play; if only they had done that when video packages were still going on and they had to get back for a play, or if something was happening on the sidelines and they were forced to cut away for a play. For as much as the XFL talked about how revolutionary their broadcasts were, they probably should've made sure they had the basics like that down before going to the X-Cam (which disappeared after the first few weeks—it would've been nice for replays and the like, but it wasn't great for every-down coverage) and mics on the field. The Hitmen took care of their business, winning 22-0 in convince fashion; they now had to wait for the result of the Enforcers vs. Rage game. Five Bolts turnovers helped the Hitmen get the win and be able to drench Tillman in Gatorade in celebration. He even said after the game that the first year of the XFL had been fun. I'd say, considering all he went through, that's pretty high praise.

The last XFL regular season game was not short on drama. Win and Chicago was in, lose and the Hitmen would get the final playoff spot. Chicago coach Ron Meyer tried to give his team a pep talk in the locker room, shouting in his trademark raspy voice, "You're the best team in the XFL!" If the Enforcers were to win, they'd have to do it with RB and league MVP candidate John Avery at limited capacity. He was getting his hamstring worked on in the locker room, and Leshon Johnson got the start. They received 10 carries each in the game. Chicago started off with a lot of emotion early on, no doubt feeding off the home crowd. DT Don Sasa, a third-round pick of the San Diego Chargers in 1995, got a sack during the game and the announcers relayed the story of how he quit the team early in the season, then later called coach Meyer and asked to come back to the team. Throwing the ball into the crowd once again seemed to be the "in" thing to do, as WR Aaron Bailey did it after scoring a touchdown, then TE Willy Tate did the same after catching the subsequent conversion pass. Orlando had only two passing yards at halftime, and finished the game with 108. Orlando was stymied by three turnovers, not a good sign heading into a playoff meeting with the Demons. In the second half, after a holding call went against him, Enforcers G Rob Murphy complained to the Bubba Cam that "The only time we get on camera is when we get called for holding." That, and false starts! The Rage saw themselves down 20-6 in the fourth quarter, but the announcers noted that the Rage had four fourth quarter comebacks on the season to date. Chicago scored in each quarter of the game and reigned supreme 23-6, much to the dismay of the Hitmen and their fans. Ron Meyer got a water bath (luckily, it was 55 degrees in Chicago at the time) after the win and the crowd chanted "MVP" for Avery. The players even high-fived fans in the front row as the game came to a close. Speaking of fans, unlike most NFL teams, the Enforcers attendance spiked to their highest total of the year, with 17,195 on hand. It probably had to do with a combination of (a) their first home game being so late in the season; (b) the playoff implications and (c) the nice weather in Chicago for once. Also in attendance were Chicago Bears WR Marcus Robinson and CB Thomas Smith, according to the Chicago Tribune. But due to the renovations slated to occur at Soldier Field after the NFL season in 2001, the Enforcers may have been without a home, though GM Connie Kowal said the team was looking into playing at Wrigley Field (home of the Cubs) or Comiskey Park (where the White Sox play) if the repairs were not done in time for the 2002 season opening. Enforcers RB John Avery was happy with the win, but knew they may have to beat the Rage again down the line if they were to become XFL Champions. As for the Rage, Brian Kuklick said the team simply didn't make enough plays to win the game. The players seemed content to put this one behind them and focus on the Demons coming up in the playoffs. An odd note: The Rage scored the first AND last touchdowns in the XFL regular season; and they both covered 51 yards.

With the playoffs on the horizon, would the all-important ratings see an uptick? If the ratings continued to slide for the post-season, including the newly titled Million Dollar Game, that would not bode well for the league in its attempt to secure a second season. The two games, San Francisco at Orlando and Chicago at Los Angeles, featured three of the strongest offensive teams in the league. High-scoring was likely to bring some fans back, but would fans be aware that games had been more offensive-oriented as the season waned? Or would they be abreast of the point-after rule changes that encouraged higher-scoring games and more excitement? Unlikely that the average fan would've come across these two nuggets of information in their daily trolling for sports news. Seemingly everyone had given up on the XFL and despite the playoffs kicking off, it was doubtful that the media coverage would increase by a substantial enough margin that the league would see the results in the ratings.

CHAPTER SIXTEEN

Week 10's ratings stayed stable at 1.5, not dropping off from week nine. While it was a good sign, it wasn't good that the number was still three ratings points below what the XFL had promised advertisers. TNN's rating was about the same as the week before as well, and UPN's dipped 0.1 to 0.6. The NBC number had dropped a full eight ratings points since week one; TNN's was down about 1.4 and UPN had fallen 2.5 since the first broadcast. Those last two might seem like small drops, but when the numbers you are pulling in are less than 1.0, it makes the decrease seem even steeper. The XFL's media blitz for the playoffs included more ad time in various markets for TV and radio as well as newspaper ads in prominent periodicals such as USA Today and Sports Illustrated (including playoff game recaps, short team capsules and players to watch in the Million Dollar Game—all on one page). But would viewers be enticed to give the league a second look?

Bruce Lowitt of the St. Petersburg Times, took a look at the XFL's season heading into the playoffs. In it, he carried a quote by AFL founder and Kansas City Chiefs owner Lamar Hunt, who said that after watching the first few games, he thought the league was trying to promote its games as a "wrestling show." Yeah, except without, you know, the wrestling. It was football being presented DIFFERENTLY, and because it was run by a wrestling czar, they assumed it was like wrestling.

When do you think the last time Lamar Hunt watched wrestling was? Do you think he'd know what wrestling was like, really like, if he saw it? It wasn't a traditional NFL broadcast, so it was looked down upon. Simple as that. Sports agent Leigh Steinberg said in the article that the league over-promoted itself, building itself up so much that there was no way what took place on the field could meet the hype they put into it. That was probably true. And I think the league realized that early on and scaled back on the hype. But it was too late to reel in those fans who had already been turned off by the initial showing. Lowitt seemed to rely heavily on quotes of others, making few proclamations about the league of his own, which was OK; the quotes took the league down enough on their own.

The San Francisco Demons would once again be without the services of starting QB Mike Pawlawski for the most important game in the franchise's history. This time, it was a shoulder injury keeping Pawlawski idle and forcing Pat Barnes back into the lineup. Coach Jim Skipper didn't put a lot of pressure on Barnes, saying he just needed to limit the mistakes and take advantage when opportunities present themselves. Despite completing less than 50% of his passes in the regular season, Barnes was at the helm when the Demons scored their most points of the season, 39, in a win over the Thunderbolts. But the Rage would certainly be a tougher test than Birmingham. Skipper also wanted to put the week 10 stinker against LA behind them, saying he was disappointed but they couldn't focus on that game; it was in the past. The Demons had already played one game in Orlando in 2001; they lost 26-14 in the second week of the season.

The Rage too were going with a backup QB in Brian Kuklick. He was susceptible to interceptions, having thrown 10 in limited playing time in the regular season. Orlando's defense was simply "OK," but it might have been enough to hold Pat Barnes and newly-minted starting RB Kelvin Anderson at bay. They did have one thing going for them— DE James Roberson, who tallied six sacks in his NFL career, was among league leaders in the XFL with 5.5 sacks.

A rematch of perhaps the most exciting game in the XFL in 2001 was on tap in Los Angeles when Chicago made their second visit to the City of Angels. But two key players, Chicago QB Kevin McDougal and LA RB Saladin McCullough, didn't play in that game. Both Meyer and Luginbill said that, if they could do it again, they would've begun the season with both men in the starting lineup. Los Angeles was armed with a QB not afraid to throw it to one of several receivers downfield in Tommy Maddox, and a running back who really came on in the second half of the season in McCullough. McCullough, though, was suffering through a hamstring problem and WRs Darnell McDonald and Damon Gibson were also among the walking wounded. Coach Al Luginbill wanted the Xtreme defense to really pin their ears back against the Enforcers, who were becoming more and more of a two-dimensional threat as the season progressed as well. He especially wanted to limit the big play for the Enforcers.

Kevin McDougal had stabilized the QB position with the Enforcers, after first round pick Paul Failla failed to win the job in training camp and was later released, and Tim Lester played only so-so during his early-season opportunities. While he was still looking for an NFL opening, McDougal did sense that at 28, his time was running out to make an impact. Despite McDougal's emergence, the Enforcers lived-and-died with John Avery, who was expected to be almost fully healthy when the Xtreme lined up against him and the Enforcers. Pounding the ball on the ground not only played to Chicago's strength, but it also would keep LA's ferocious offense off the field.

How did the Enforcers do it? How did they go from 0-4 and the worst team in the XFL to making the playoffs? According to their ST coach Kris Haines, it was a combination of things. "Players finally bought into Ron (Meyer) and Steve Endicott's (Offensive coordinator) system and way of doing things," he said. Probably of equal importance was the inserting of.QB Kevin McDougal. He was like a mini-Montana with his leadership and control of the players and game. Tim Lester, the QB he replaced, was a good smart player who had some bad breaks during games but the team rallied around Kevin and as we won more games, Kevin got more and more confidence."

San Francisco and Orlando was the NBC game on Saturday night. Curiously, the scramble again wasn't shown live. They seemed to go back-and-forth on that, probably depending on what kind of talking points and video packages they had to lead off the game with. It was announced that this was the warmest game-time temperature all year in the XFL, which makes sense being in Orlando in mid-April. Things were going Orlando's way in the first half. After a Jay Taylor field goal, DT Ben Huff, a graduate of the NCAA powerhouse Michigan Wolverines, intercepted a Pat Barnes pass and ran it in for 17 yards and a touchdown. However, he failed the celebration test—he went to spike the ball, but it fell out of his hand as he was bringing it down, so his empty hand spiked nothing but air. Huff then jumped stomach-first on the ball when he realized it was on the ground. By the end of the first, the Rage had raced out to a 16-3 lead. It looked like another blowout at a crucial time in the XFL's existance. But fans who tuned out in the first missed quite the comeback. Pat Barnes scored on two 1-yard dives, evening the score at 16 all mid-way through the third. It sounded like there were fewer players mic'd on the field than usual for the playoffs. By the end of the third quarter, the Rage had dropped four passes, but it seemed like more than that. Rage LB Patrise Alexander showed some rage on a 3rd down stop, ripping his helmet off and slamming it to the ground after the play. Matt Vasgersian said, "he runs the grill when the Orlando defense has a cook-out." I couldn't tell if that was a metaphor for him being a leader on the defense or if it was to be taken at face value. Mike Panasuk nailed a 40-yard field goal early in the fourth to put the Demons on top for the first time, 19-16. Orlando coach Galen Hall took Brian Kuklick out of the game at this time, replacing him with Jim Arellanes, who was seeing his first game action for the Rage all year. Kuklick was 5-of-16 with one interception, but it was his receivers who had mostly let him down. Arellanes was promptly picked off by the elder statesmen of the Demons, CB Dwayne Harper, who returned it 40 yards for a touchdown, padding the Demons' lead. Both teams turned the ball over four times on the evening, not exactly stellar numbers for two playoff clubs. Orlando fired back when

Arellanes threw a 55-yard TD to Dialleo Burks, and with the three-point conversion, the score was 26-25. But there were under four minutes to go in the game and the Demons simply ran out the clock. Interestingly, Vince McMahon was at the game, but he was not shown on camera. He did attend at least one game a week throughout the season, and he was only on camera during the first week and for the "inside the cheerleaders' locker room" skit. But I thought they'd show him on TV here if they bothered to acknowledge him. Perhaps NBC and the XFL wanted to really make separate the wrestling world of WWE and the football world of the XFL, and were actually serious about it this time.

Dwayne Harper had one of the most extensive NFL resumes of anyone in the XFL. And at age 35, he got to hear all the nicknames from his teammates, from "old man" to "uncle" and everything in between. Harper attended South Carolina State college after high-school at Orangeburg-Wilkinson High in Oragenburg, South Carolina. At S.C. State, he tied a conference recrod with eight interceptions as a senior, and was All-League all four years. He finished his career with 11 picks and was selected in the 11th round (back when there were 12 rounds) of the NFL Draft by the Seattle Seahawks in 1988. Harper spent his first six years in Seattle, playing in all 16 games every year but one. He was a full-time starter in five of those years. He moved on to San Diego, where he spent five more years, again, all as a starter. In 1995, he even reached All-Pro Status according to Sports Illustrated and got to play in Super Bowl XXIX against San Francisco. But in 1998, he played in only one game, due to a neck fracture suffered in the season opener, the same game in which he snagged three interceptions. He returned to the league in 1999 with Detroit, but played in only three games. In his illustrious 12-year career, Harper played in 148 NFL games, starting 128 of them, and he intercepted a total of 24 passes. Harper made himself eligible for the XFL P.A.S.S. in 2000, partly because he enjoyed playing and had kept himself in top physical condition, but also because his young son had never seen him play football, and he wanted to change that. Some people assumed he was broke because he was looking to play football again. Harper wasn't selected until the 26th round of the XFL Draft, but mostly because personnel directors and coaches were leery that someone with that much mileage in the NFL may change their mind about "lowering" themselves to playing in another league. But that wasn't an issue with Harper. He provided experience and leadership right off the bat for San Francisco. He even stood up in front of the team prior to the first game, imparting his knowledge in a group of players who were about to play the highest level of pro football they ever had. But he wasn't just an aging veteran hanging on; Harper insisted he still had something to offer on the field as well. In addition to his playoff touchdown scored in this game, he also was credited with the first QB sack in Demons history, as well as the first forced fumble. Harper made 21 tackles in the regular season (unofficially), as well as two interceptions. Playing in the big game at the end meant a little more to Harper: In all of his playing days, from age eight through the pros, he had never won a championship of any kind. There's no statistic to show how much Harper's veteran savvy contributed to them reaching the Million Dollar Game, but if you asked his teammates, they'd likely say he brought as much to the table as anyone else on the team.

Those who tuned into the UPN game between Chicago and LA the next night on Easter Sunday got a bit of a surprise: Craig Minnervini and Bob Golic, the TNN team, were doing the game. This had to be a good sign for them, probably with the XFL recognizing how good the pairing was and wanted them doing their other playoff game. Chris Marlowe and Brian Bosworth were tolerable, but the XFL was clearly looking for more substance at this point, and with the Boz's bluster, that duo brought them more style than traditional football analysis. On the sidelines, it was Chris Wragge from the UPN team and Kip Lewis from TNN. The Xtreme led first, up 9-0 on a touchdown pass to Jermaine Copeland and a Jose Cortez field goal. After Andy Crosland matched Cortez with a three-pointer of his own, the Enforcers grabbed the lead when Kivuusama Mays, a former NFL special teams standout, blocked a Noel Prefontaine punt (the second blocked punt in two games against Chicago) and Chike Egbuniwe returned it for a TD. Leshon Johnson converted the extra point to make it 10-9 Chicago. Like the week before, the cameras paid more attention to the less fiery coach, as Ron Meyer got more face-time on the broadcast than Al Luginbill. Perhaps it was Luginbill's penchant for cursing (an f-bomb of his made the air the previous week) that made the NBC crew decide instead to focus on Meyer. The Xtreme re-claimed the lead heading into halftime, up 17-10 on another Maddox TD pass. They revealed another XFL.com Fan Pick of the Year category at the half, Finish of the Year. Nominees were Week 1—LA at SF, where Panasuk hit the game-winning field goal with no time left; Week 2, Chicago at LA, the double-overtime thriller; Week 5, Las Vegas at Chicago, where the Enforcers picked up their first win in the waning seconds of that one; Week 6, Chicago at Memphis, where Daryl Hobbs hauled in a 26-yard TD from Jim Druckenmiller with 20 seconds left; and Week 7, Memphis at New York, where the Hitmen prevailed late. Throughout the second half, the Enforcers stayed within striking distance, but could never really catch up to the Xtreme's potent offense. LA wrapped things up in the fourth behind a Saladin McCullough TD run and a Clifton Abraham interception return for a TD, getting the win, 33-16. Luginbill was absolutely drenched with Gatorade this week and players signed autographs for fans in the stands after the game. John Avery was held in check, running for 59 yards on 14 carries. Kevin McDougal had a poor game, going 15-of-31 with three interceptions. McCullough ran for 164 yards on the ground in leading the offensive attack for the Xtreme.

After the loss, Rage coach Galen Hall lamented the fact that his team let the game slip away after getting a big lead early on. Rage players laid blame on both sides of the ball for the loss. Many Rage players told the Daytona Beach News-Journal that they were even looking forward to season two, and none had regrets about playing in the league and getting a second chance to play the game they love. Demons head man Jim Skipper gave the usual "it ain't over 'til it's over" type of comments. Despite the lead, the Rage offense had gifts handed to them by the Demons, and hadn't really put a lot of yardage up on the board against them, a fact that Demons Defensive Coordinator

Michael Church used to rally his guys after the team got down on the scoreboard.

Xtreme coach Al Luginbill saw the championship game as the final of a best two-out-of-three tournament, as they had faced each other two times in the regular season, with each team securing a win. Whoever won got bragging rights and, oh yeah, $1 million. Chicago coach Ron Meyer cited the score before haltime as what really turned the game in LA's favor.

If ratings had fallen for the playoffs, it would've made the XFL look even weaker, if that was possible. But on NBC, they stayed the same at a 1.5. On UPN, they were up to a 0.7, a 0.1 increase from the previous week. The XFL continued to push hard their playoff hype, buying ad time everywhere they could. With a rebound in the ratings for the finale, the XFL would have at least some leverage and momentum heading into season two. But it would have to be significant for anyone to truly get excited. Another drop would seal their fate on NBC, if it hadn't been already, and could even leave the league out in the cold for a season two altogether. The problem with the championship games was that the Demons vs. Xtreme had already played twice before, and once just two weeks ago in the final week of the season, a game in which LA won handily. The week one win by San Francisco was a distant memory to fans.knowing this, would they have any interest in these teams facing each other again?

The XFL Player of the Year Award was handed out in the middle of the week prior to the Million Dollar Game. It went to LA's QB Tommy Maddox. Maddox completed 57.3% of his passes and perhaps most importantly, was the only QB in the league to start every game for his team. He tossed 18 TDs and nine interceptions on the year and threw for almost 2,200 yards. Coaches, league GMs and the media collaborated in choosing the award.

The coverage by the media was nothing if not predictable heading into the final week. The Associated Press' report on the upcoming game started by pointing out the number of empty seats likely to be at the Coliseum (well, it could hold almost 100,000 so yes, even if 50,00 filled the stands, it may look empty, but I digress) as well as the collapsing television ratings. Later on, author Ken Peters touched on the same subjects again and wrote about what "critics" had problems with during the league's first season. I thought this was about the game? The last quarter of the article was actually spent previewing the game. No wonder people couldn't get into the league—articles like this were one of the reason, more of the same criticisms masquerading as actual information. The horse that was the TV ratings, by this point, had been beaten to death, revived, and beaten again.

The day of the game, the Minneapolis Star-Tribune ran a story about Jesse Ventura's involvement in the league. After Vince McMahon had earlier in the season seemed to sour on the idea of bringing Jesse back for a second season, he seemed to think Ventura was re-energized by being paired with Vasgersian AND Mike Adamle in the booth. McMahon also acknowledged that it wasn't likely NBC would air games in 2002, that UPN would be the main outlet for the league in year two. But NBC declined to add fuel to that fire, saying they'd evaluate everything after the season. Despite McMahon's claims that NBC wouldn't air the games, he was hesitant to say they'd completely back out of the monetary investment they had in the league. But if NBC did back out of the deal, they'd likely have to pay a fee to get out of it, and the money they'd have to pay may have been enough to keep the XFL train on the tracks.

There was no East Coast Bias in the Million Dollar Game, as two Left Coast squads squared off on April 21st for the One Million Dollar Prize and the right to call themselves "champion." For the Demons, the latter was more important than the former. It wasn't about the money for most of them, a purse which would be split among among the 38 active players on the roster and one share going to those on injured reserve and the practice squad, which meant a cool $25,600 for active players. The losing team would pocket 1/4 of that, $5,000 each. Veterans Scott Adams, James Hundon, Dwayne Harper and Mike Pawlawski all spoke out in favor of the championship being most important, money coming second. The good news for the Demons is that they'd have starting QB Mike Pawlawski back for the game, despite backup Pat Barnes leading them past Orlando the week prior.

In La-La Land, Al Luginbill pointed out that, with his running game finally producing, defenses would have to choose which aspect of the offense to focus on defending. That is when they could strike with the other phase. The Xtreme ran up almost 180 yards on the ground the last time the two teams met. Would it be more of the same this time?

It would be if OT Jerry Crafts had anything to say about it. Crafts, with the nickname "Big Daddy" stitched on the back of his oversized jersey, was hard to miss: He stood 6'5" and weighed 350 pounds. He had the distinction of being one of the few (if only) players to have played in all five major pro leagues at the time. Crafts started out at the University of Oklahoma, but transferred to Louisville where he started his final two seasons. The Indianapolis Colts drafted him in the 11th round of the NFL Draft in 1991. He didn't make the team however, and played with the Orlando Thunder in the WLAF that year. In 1992, Crafts, a noted prankster, joined the Buffalo Bills, where he played as a backup guard/tackle for three season and in a Super Bowl. After getting in all 16 games with the team in 1994, he sat out of football in 1995. He joined the NFLE in 1996, which lead to him catching on with the Philadelphia Eagles, where he played 15 games in 1997 and one in 1998. In 2000, he became famous for being an iron-man of sorts, playing football for 42 straight weeks in the AFL and CFL, and played even longer in 2001 due to his stop-over in the XFL. At times, when all the football work seemed like too much, he considered switching careers: to professional wrestling, where he sought advice from former Atlanta Falcon and WCW World Heavyweight Champion Bill Goldberg. He even sent in a photo to the TV show *Walker, Texas Ranger* in the hopes of landing a role as a biker. In the end, Crafts decided to stick with what he knew. When the XFL came along, of course, Crafts had to sample that league as well as if the pro football world were a buffet and he was filling his plate with all kinds of different treats. He and his 54 games of NFL experience were drafted by LA with a second-round pick in the Supplemental Draft. Playing with LA was his ticket back to the NFL, where he spent the 2001 training camp with the Oakland Raiders. He didn't make the cut there, but that didn't stop Crafts from continuing his journey, playing three more years in the CFL and AFL. As a football player, he also spoke with young folks about the dangers of alcohol and drug abuse, demons Crafts battled throughout his career that were bigger and badder than the ones he'd line up against on the football field for $1 million. When his football days were over, he moved into the coaching realm, heading up the Erie Freeze of the American Indoor Football League in 2006. Crafts is currently an assistant offensive line coach at Jacksonville State College. If anyone can teach college kids about the ins-and-outs of professional football from the smallest league to the biggest, it would be Crafts.

Saturday night had arrived, and so too had the Million Dollar Game. In the weeks leading up to the MDG, some of the games opened with a woe-is-me video package, talking about how the media had been overly critical of the league, while showing highlights from the first season. If it were me, I would think it best not to acknowledge that stuff, as tempting as it may be to do so in order to get your side of the story out. Before the game, the announcers used a telestrator to show how effective LA's offense had been in past games; they also used the device throughout the game on replays. It can't be a good sign from a technological stand-point when you're finally breaking out the telestrator, something that had been used for decades on other broadcasts, yet your bread-and-butter is supposed to be the "television presentation" of the league. It was 3-0 after one, with Jose Cortez nailing a field goal for the Xtreme. In the second quarter, that lead increased to 9-0 on a 1-yard touchdown catch by Josh Wilcox, who once again celebrated by elbowdropping the ball. Among those he thanked on the sidelines after the play when being interviewed by Fred Roggin (Roggin had to playfully pull the mic away because he was taking so long thanking everyone) were "the guys in ECW," where he had wrestled professionally a few times. In a nice touch, every team's cheerleaders were at the game doing their thing. Even the Demons special teams were having a rough day, when Reggie "Dirty" Durden returned a punt 71 yards for another score, putting LA up 15-0. Cortez hit two more field goals within 20 seconds, sending the Xtreme into the locker room at the half up 21-0. Not a good way to get viewers to stick around, but that wasn't the players' jobs. At halftime, they showed highlights of the season, with several players giving their favorite moments. The final fight of the year wasn't much of a fight, but there was a major verbal confrontation between Xtreme G Chris Brymer and Demons DE Eric England. Brymer especially was pissed, and he let everyone hear about it in between plays. LA continued to pour it on in the third, Maddox finding Jermaine Copeland for a TD, and with the extra point, it was 28-0. That's when Jim Skipper decided to pull Pawlawski (8-of-20, 2 interceptions on the day), but not before telling him on the sidelines that he needed a spark and it wasn't just him that was the problem out there. They ended by saying "I love you" to each other, which is probably why so many Demons loved playing for Skipper. The announcers again seemed much looser than earlier in the season, perhaps sensing they had nothing to lose. Vasgersian even thanked Jackie Singer, the delay switch girl, for being on call all season in a league that necessitated it. Maddox was pulled with 11:00 to go in the game, and up 31-0. It looked like Skipper had tears in his eyes on the sidelines as he continued to try to do his job despite the overwhelming disappointment and sadness he must've been feeling. On fourth-and-goal, with 3:48 to go, Rashaan Shehee threw a halfback pass to WR Latario Rachal for a touchdown, adding on to an already bulbous score, making it 38-0 after the conversion. When questioned about this play on the sidelines, Luginbill said the Demons called time-out prior to the play, which made trying to score fair game. Pat Barnes was hurt late, so third-stringer Oteman Sampson got his first game play, and helped ease some of the disappointment by scampering for a 21-yard touchdown with under a minute to go. The final score was 38-6, a thorough thrashing. McMahon was present again, even signing autographs for fans, but never made it on camera, even for a trophy presentation or to lead off the game. In the S.F Chronicle the next day, San Francisco players and coaches weren't afraid to label the Xtreme the better team, with England saying as much and Skipper telling the media that the Xtreme were simply the more talented team. When you put a season-low 149 total offensive yards ont he board and committ four turnovers, that's not exactly going out on a limb. Vince McMahon was complimented by Xtreme players and coaches after the big game, with Maddox giving Vince credit for giving players another place to play, and Luginbill saying he appreciated what Vince did and called him "a man's man." Of course, there was also plenty of scrutinization of the ratings and what the league did wrong too.

The end of the season meant it was time to see which players would be good enough to get a shot in the NFL. A general manager in the NFL spoke to the LA Times on the condition of anonymity and said that "a whole bunch" of XFL players would get a shot in camps. Greg Garber of ESPN wrote that, off the record, NFL personnel men love the NFL: It just gives them more tape on guys and another chance to see players in action and find that "diamond in the rough" that could be the difference. That goes against a column by Len Pasquarelli, which stated that most of the players wouldn't interest NFL teams, with some personnel directors and GM's providing quotes that not only denied interest in players, but also put them down as well; strange, considering I would think the NFL front offices would applaud another league giving players a chance to play football and giving them that experience. The XFL was certainly more like the NFL than the AFL, which would make it easier for them to translate over. Bills GM Tom Donahoe said it was unlikely any XFL players would be at their camp, since they didn't even bother scouting the league. I can't believe that in the league closes to the NFL in quality of players and play on the field, that a team wouldn't even scout them. Oh, and Donahoe was wrong: Bolts backup RB Curtis Alexander and Rage K Jay Taylor made it to Bills camp. The XFL's Mike Keller expected about 200 of the 360-400 players to opt out of their contracts to try and hook on with the NFL, while ESPN.com's Greg Garber said the number was over 214. The only reason players may want to stay under contract, especially those older ones who know the NFL would have no interest, would be to continue to receive health benefits. Surprisingly, just ten Outlaws opted out of their contracts: CB Hurley Tarver (the first to sign, agreeing to a deal with the Packers), DE Ty Parten (battled injuries during the season; already had 62 games of NFL experience), DT Adriano Belli, DT Angel Rubio, LB Joe Tuipala (who, according to Jim Criner, had been drawing interest from almost 10 teams), S Jamel Williams, OT Jon Blackman, WR Mike Furrey, WR Corey Nelson, RB Rod Smart and TE Rickey Brady.

Columnist Dean Juipe in Las Vegas was ready to cheer for the demise of the XFL if it came to that. He called the product "dreadful," and even chided those in attendance for contributing to the "drunken, sex-crazed atmosphere" of the live crowd. "I'll handle the news with unfettered glee," he proclaimed. OK, if you don't like it, don't watch! It's as simple as that, and it's the route many fans had taken by the end of the year. That's fine, it's their right. But I think they were tuning out the week one product in week 10, and I think that those two products offered were wholly different. But it's pretty sad that someone like Juipe would dance on the grave of the XFL if he had the chance; it's an opportunity for players to make money and a living doing what they love. Just because you don't like the games doesn't mean the league needs to go away. I know though, it's for the betterment of society that the XFL wouldn't have a second season. But I say again, he's talking more about the week one games than the final few weeks, which had as little to do with sex as any NFL broadcast. But when you can so easily sit and look down on the XFL from your mighty perch, why change the view? Demons QB Mike Pawlawski said it well when talking about critics of the league to the S.F. Chronicle: "Just like anything else.people.want to get in somebody else's business and hate something (just) to hate it.A lot of people were set to hate this thing before it ever started."

With the season over, the XFL put their own spin on the numbers that had been put out by many media outlets in their 2001 Season Review Pamphlet (more in the ratings section below). Low-scoring games were the bane of the league and fans early on, and while they improved in that facet as the season marched along, the XFL met the NFL even in points per play at .34; the XFL ran about 20 fewer plays per game thanks to the clock rules, and the points per game reflected that. As for advertisers dropping out, not all were disappointed with their partnership with the XFL: U.S. Army's website saw traffic jump by 53% and their ads on XFL.com saw viewers click on the Army ads at a rate that was higher than most industry standards. Discover Card had 40,000 people apply for credit cards thanks to their appearance at games. Over 24,000 computer users registered for a Buell Motorcycles promotion thanks in part to XFL.com's coverage of said promotion. Spalding became the #2 selling football, seeing their market share increase in that department by 14%. For a first year league, those numbers were very promising despite the low ratings on television. They even carried a quote from renegade Dallas Mavericks owner Mark Cuban, who said about the league, "I absolutely, positively love it.if I ever decided to buy another team, I'd get an XFL franchise." Of course, somebody forgot to tell Cuban the XFL owned all the teams, but that wasn't the point. The point was, Cuban, a shameless self-promoter himself, was a fan of what the league was doing.

The final ratings came in at 1.8, better than the 1.5 the week before, but still not saying much. It was still nowhere near the modest goal set out at the beginning of the season for ratings. On the other hand, even though NBC's ratings got all the press, by the end of the regular season, the XFL on TNN ratings still beat the NBA on TNT, NHL on ESPN and NCAA men's basketball on ESPN in key demographics (18-49 males). UPN saw their yearly ratings increase by more than four percent, and more than 78% in men 18-34. In nine of the 12 weeks of the season, at least one XFL game ranked in the top ten of the highest-rated sports programs of the week. NBC, the XFL and the WWF had some major decisions to make if year two was to be a reality. And most would have to be made within the next month or so.

CHAPTER SEVENTEEN

Things were relatively quiet on the XFL news front after the Million Dollar Game. The All-Pro Teams were announced, and Galen Hall won the Coach of the Year Award. Tommy Maddox was Player of the Year (with John Avery coming in second). Despite the head honchos of the league all but promising a second season, I didn't believe it. So every day, I made sure to scour the top sports websites, as well as peruse XFLBoard.com's message board to see if there was any news about a network dropping out, or new rules being put in place, anything that would give a hint one way or another. And then it happened: One day, as I was on the board, someone made a post saying the league would announce it was closing its doors later in the week. Everyone brushed him aside as a rumor-monger, but I just had this bad feeling, and I was hoping to just get past that day with no news. Then, on May 10th, it happened just as that poster prophetized. I read it on the message board, and had to go to CBS' Sportsline.com just to see for my own eyes. And there it was, in the headlines. Not only was I disappointed that there was going to be a second season, I knew the onslaught of jokes and "I-told-you-so's" from the media would ensue like a landslide. And it did.

An unannounced conference call with league GMs was set up for 2:45; some didn't even know about the call until 2pm and even then, had no idea what it was about. It only took a few minutes; XFL President Basil DeVito broke the news about the league folding. Later in the day, they broke the news to reporters via conference call. It took everyone by complete surprise. In fact, the coaches spent two days in Stamford, Connecticut at the XFL/WWE headquarters going over plans for season two only a few days prior to the big announcement. One of the things decided upon there were ways to improve the quarterback play in season two. Jim Criner said it was the most productive meeting he'd attended about the XFL and Demons player personnel chief Greg Mohns categorized the meetings as "very positive." Another issue addressed was money, and according to Enforcers defensive coordinator Pete Adrian, coaches would've gotten a raise and players would've seen their salaries rise by $5,000, and the playoff pot increase as well. In another week, the league was scheduled to meet to discuss plans for a second season. At other meetings, the structure behind-the-scenes for each team was addressed, as Bob Ackles, in his autobiography "The Waterboy," said that on April 24th, this was discussed, mostly the chain-of-command between coaches and GMs and how the GMs would handle personnel and business decisions. He revealed that Vince McMahon regretted giving teams only six months to prepare and said if he were to do it again, he'd wait another year.

According to Bill Baker, the league held general manager meetings at the end of the season first. He said that the GMs were asked to review the season and each was given an evaluation. A week after that, the league did the same thing with head coaches and personnel directors. Baker said that after the coaches meetings, many of them had tickets behind home plate for the New York Yankees ballgame; 24 in total. Everyone was to be driven to the game, then they'd return to Stamford where the meetings were held. At 4:15, it was announced to the media that the XFL was ceasing operations. Many of the coaches and personnel directors, having just lost their jobs, decided to go home. Baker said only five or six stayed for the Yankee game, and those who did got the entire row to themselves.

The press release WWE sent out in announcing the end of the league contained quotes from Vince McMahon, in part saying that he had a responsibility to his shareholders and partners to shut down the league. And another piece of the puzzle was put in place. WWE was losing money thanks to the stock tanking every time another low was hit in the ratings or another column came out bashing the league. This was costing the company and its shareholders tons of money. And it was, in my opinion, a big reason the XFL didn't survive past year one. If WWE was not a publicly traded company, perhaps they would've let the XFL twist in the wind for a little while longer in an attempt to find a new broadcast partner, and maybe they'd be able to settle for a spot on cable TV. Both McMahon and Dick Ebersol both espoused pride in the project, however, in the press release. Vince said it was the most fan-friendly league in sports history. Ebersol noted he had some of the most fun times of his life during the league's existence. McMahon would later say that there were, according to a quote that appeared in the Toronto Sun, "some challenges in our own core prodcut that needed attention." And a second piece of the puzzle fit—WWE being the main concern of Vince McMahon, both financially and in terms of time spent on it, even moreso with the purchase of WCW, which he was looking to spin off as a separate entity. I wonder if the league ever came to Cuban, who professed his affinity for what the XFL was about, before they closed up shop, to see if he'd infuse some of his billions into the league. Cuban is now in bed with the new UFL, a football league scheduled to start up in October of 2009.

DeVito said the league couldn't survive without a network TV spot, and NBC obviously dropped out. That left them with UPN but once they found out NBC was backing out, UPN made the relatively surprising decision to leave the league high-and-dry as well early that Thursday—it wasn't long after that that the XFL ceased operations. In his book, Ackles said UPN was still upset about taking a backseat to NBC after UPN was on board with the XFL from the start, and NBC later came aboard the bandwagon. UPN's nearest competitor, the WB, also passed. TNN was still happy with the ratings and was a go for season two, but some of that might've had to do with keeping WWE happy, which provided the network with their highest-rated show in Monday Night Raw, but the XFL needed network TV to survive. With no other options left and little time to procure any, the XFL via conference call that it could no longer continue from a financial standpoint. McMahon conceded that Sunday afternoon was the best time for football rather than Sunday or Saturday nights. Rage GM Tom Veit, who said he had no idea until the conference call came that the league was folding, held out hope that the XFL would continue in some fashion after sitting a year out. Demons GM Mike Preacher was looking for future practice facilities when he was told of the conference call. Many coaches had bought homes in the area they were coaching them, leaving some of them in a bad situation as far as that was concerned. Enforcers GM Connie Kowal said each team was making plans for the next season.

Because it was Vince McMahon's baby, and McMahon would never NOT make money off something he came up with, it was pretty much useless to think of the XFL being resurrected under new management, though Michael Keller did mention looking into the viability of keeping the league going. Nothing of substance surfaced though. McMahon would have to hand over the rights, something he likely wouldn't do. He could always stay on in some capactiy, but that would again cause columnists to go up in arms over things and besides, Vince doesn't play well with others; if he's not in charge, he's not interested. That's what made the XFL operating sans WWE a tough sell.

Players and coaches all had their reasons why they thought the XFL failed. Vegas LB Toran James said the league shouldn't have been taking shots at the NFL in the beginning. Defensive Coordinator Mark Criner said the announcers and the focus on wrestling and cheerleaders hur the product. His father, Jim, went a step further and said Jesse Ventura hurt the league immensley on commentary. Ackles, in his book, said the league and teams simply didn't have enough time to prepare for the first kickoff. Gerry DiNardo thought the first broadcast wasn't very good. Ventura stuck to his anti-media stats, criticizing the press for not covering the XFL during the season, then putting their death on the front page. Sideline reporter Michael Barkann was one of the few to blast the league, telling the Philadelphia News his time there was "miserable" thanks to the often freezing conditions he had to work in, and that the XFL hyped the league up too much to start, so much so that there was no way they'd be able to deliver. He liked the new rules, but said the play on the field was "awful." In an online chat, Matt Vasgersian said the XFL's problem was challenging the NFL (even though they didn't really do it, since they played in two different times of the year and didn't compete for players) and that the announcers weren't given the ability to joke around on commentary as much as the fans were led to believe (McMahon and Ebersol both said they wanted the announcers to be honest) and said they were instructed to "sell" the league too often (this was obvious when listenting to games). He said he thought he got demoted to the second team for making fun of the league on air too often, but again, he probably thought he had the latitutde to do so. He did compliment Vince McMahon though, saying he was a "good dude." According to Enforcers ST coach Kris Haines, McMahon himself was too brash in the way he handled himself. "I'm not a fan of his act. He was successful with his wrestling but I think he got his ego handed to him when he thought he was bigger than the NFL and its owners. They ran him out of town with his tail between his legs. I think it would have worked if he would not have alienated the NFL. I played in the USFL for three years and personally experienced mistakes that doomed that league. I thought this concept was perfect and would alleviate those mistakes, at least financially." Haines said he talked to Mike Adamle on the day the league shut down, and Adamle pretty much agreed with Haines as to why the XFL failed. Outlaws beat writer Kevin Iole, who described McMahon as "no different than any other promoter with something to sell," acknowledged that McMahon was ready to change things up: "I think he really believed in the product. I think he realized early that he miscalculated in trying to promote the league like he would the WWE and he adjusted." Iole also offered up his opinions on what went wrong, starting with marketing it as "WWE meets football" and trying to create a feud between Rusty Tillman and Jesse Ventura. "I think they needed to find a way to work with the NFL to increase the level of quarterbacking in the league and I think they needed to promote it more aggressively as legitimate professional football." Tim Lester said that while some had it out for McMahon, he was more concerned about how the league was marketing itself as some sort of tougher and rougher version of the NFL. He also took issue with the coverage Chicago gave their hometown team, saying "I know many of the Chicago sports guys treated us like a joke. We were just guys trying to make it."

The league didn't just cost the XFL money, but the companies they had marketing deals with as well. Topps, the trading card supplier of the league, expected to come out on the negative side. An XFL spokesman said most of the league's equipment would likely be given away to high-school teams. Retailers weren't sure how long to hold onto products, such as mini-helmets by Bike, or team pennants. Some held on to them longer than others, hoping fans would seem them as a collector's item. And some, thinking they wouldn't be able to sell after the league folded, simply got rid of them.

After the league disbanded, all players were let out of their contracts and were free to test the NFL waters. By my own count, 72 players from the XFL were in NFL camps in 2001, and 20 of them were on a team's active roster, injured reserve or practice squad as of the mid-way point of the 2001 season, both numbers a whole lot more than most NFL people or columnists would like to admit. Those who didn't make it further than camp, from Memphis: LB Richard Hogans (Jacksonville), K Jeff Hall (New Orleans, S.F), TE Mark Thomas (Kansas City), OT Mike Sheldon (Chicago), LB Paris Lenon (Green Bay, Seattle), G Glenn Roundtree (Green Bay) and RB Rafael Cooper (Tennessee); From Las Vegas: WR Corey Nelson (Seattle), OT Jon Blackman (Carolina), RB Chrys Chukwuma (Tennessee), G Lamont Burns (New York Jets), TE Rickey Brady (Dallas), DT Adriano Belli (New York Giants), CB Kelly Herndon (Giants), CB Kory Blackwell (Jacksonville), S Jason Kaiser (Washington) and CB Hurley Tarver (Green Bay); from San Francisco: DE Jermaine Miles (New Orleans), S Pete Destefano (Baltimore); from Los Angeles: OT Jerry Crafts (Oakland), WR Damon Dunn (Dallas), WR Jermaine Copeland (Dallas), RB Saladin McCullough (S.F), P Noel Prefontaine (Baltimore), DT Matt Keneley (Green Bay); from Orlando: K Jay Taylor

(Buffalo), TE Terrance Huston (Oakland), C Jason Gamble (Dallas), G Dan Collins (Dallas), LB Sedric Clark (Philly), WR Dialleo Burks (Carolina), CB Stephen Fisher (S.F.); from Chicago: S Kerry Cooks (Jacksonville), G Rob Murphy (Indy), K Andy Crosland (Carolina, Minnesota), DE Larry Fitzpatrick (N.O; S.F), LB Aaron Humphrey (NYJ), RB John Avery (Dallas), DE Hubert Thompson (N.O.), CB Quincy Coleman (NYG) and WR Junior Lord (Det.); from New York/ New Jersey: CB Donnie Caldwell (Seattle), S Tawambi Settles (Seattle), LB Ron Merkerson (Carolina), S Brad Trout (K.C), CB Mark Tate (Oakland), TE Ryan Collins (Dallas) and WR Zola Davis (Cleveland); from Birmingham: OT Chase Raynock (Indy), WR Kevin Drake (Dallas), DE Quinton Reese (San Diego) and DE Cedric Pittman (NYG). QB Jim Druckenmiller and OT Pita Elisara made 74 when Druckenmiller went to camp with the Colts in 2003 after writing letters to each team in the league, trying to get a break to get back in. He was close to signing witht the Chiefs in 2001 until they made a trade for QB Trent Green. Elisara, who played for the Demons, was a part of the Redskins practice squad in 2003.

Those who stuck through at least part of the season, for Las Vegas: LB Joe Tuipala (Jacksonville—played 27 games in two seasons, mostly on special teams), G David Diaz-Infante (Denver—played all 16 games in '01), RB Rod Smart (Philadelphia—played five seasons with the Eagles and Panthers; returned 78 kicks for a 22.2 average), WR Yo Murphy (St. Louis—played 27 games in two years), LB Mike Crawford (on Minnesota's practice squad) and LB Jonathan Jackson (New Orleans—played one game in '01); for San Francisco: S Kevin Kaesviharn (Cincinnati—still active in the NFL at this time, having started 59 games and picked off 17 passes since his time in the XFL; before the league, he was a substitute teacher in South Dakota) and FB Jamie Reader (Philly—played in all 16 games in '01); for LA: K Jose Cortez (S.F—played for six teams in five years, hitting 72% of his field goal attempts), WR Damon Gibson (Jacksonville—played two years, and was the Jags' main punt returner in '01) and QB Tommy Maddox (played five season in Pittsburgh and started all 16 games in 2003, and 11 in 2002); for Orlando: G Dan Goodspeed (Jets—was on the roster of four teams in four years, but was never got on the field), WR Kevin Swayne (Jets—played three seasons in the Meadowlands, catching 20 passes and one touchdown) and TE Lawrence Hart (played one game in '01 for Arizona); for Chicago: CB Corey Ivy (Tampa Bay's practice squad—still active today, has accrued eight NFL seasons with three interceptions and 9.5 sacks in 110 games), WR Fred Coleman (first player to play in XFL and get a Super Bowl ring, with New England in '01; also played in '02) and G Bennie Anderson (Baltimore—spent six season in the NFL, starting 73 games over that time); for NY/NJ: CB Damen Wheeler (Jacksonville—played in five games in '01) and P Leo Araguz (Detroit—kicked in nine games for three teams in three years); for Birmingham: RB Curtis Alexander (Buffalo's practice squad, but didn't play in a game). While they didn't make a team out of camp in '01, WR Mike Furrey (78 games in six seasons; 198 catches and 7 TDs and is still active), G Rob Murphy (three seasons and 27 games), RB John Avery (six games with the Vikings in '03), CB Kelly Herndon (six NFL season, starting 16 games twice and intercepting nine passes—holds Super Bowl record for longets Int. return for TD) and LB Paris Lenon (seven years in the NFL and has played all 16 games each year, starting every game his last three seasons; is still active) have made an impact as well. By my count, that's at least 10 players who have had a major mark on the NFL. To me, that's a good number of players, especially having three active today, eight years after the league went down in flames. All of the snooty columnists and NFL personnel men probably didn't forsee these numbers. If the XFL had a season two, they'd be getting a lot of publicity from newspapers doing articles on players trying to make it in the NFL, so they'd definitely stay in the news. And the more people read about these players being successful or at least taking the next step, perhaps they'd think twice about the XFL being a league for rejects that it had been seen as by so many people. The craziest thing is seeing guys who had little impact on their XFL teams, like Vegas WR Corey Nelson, who made just nine catches, sixth on the team, or backup RBs like Chrys Chukwuma, Rafael Cooper and Curtis Alexander get a chance with NFL clubs. Without the XFL, many of these guys wouldn't have had that one last chance at glory, even if they didn't make it onto a team for a regular season game. That's not to mention guys like Bills Pro Bowl P Brian Moorman and S Deke Cooper, a Chicago territorial selection who went on to play six NFL years, who were even cut by their respective XFL teams, and CB Lance Brown, who went on to play 14 games for the Bills in 2001, but wasn't even picked in the XFL's Supplemental Draft. But if the NFL was so much better, how can this be? With all the evidence given above, maybe, just MAYBE, the XFL wasn't second-rate football played by a bunch of hacks. Maybe it was more legitimate than anyone thought; unfortunately, it was too late to realize it.

One player who didn't get a chance to play in the NFL following the season was Hitment OT Troy Stark. Stark passed away on June 1, 2001, when a blood clot that formed after he had knee surgery, traveled to his lungs. Stark was injured playing for New York in the 2001 season and ended the year on injured reserve for the team. It was a grim reminder of the XFL less than a month after it folded.

It wasn't just players—coaches moved into the NFL too. But it took awhile for coaches to hook on, since most openings were filled by the time the league closed. While he would've returned for a second season, Haines was a little upset at how things went down. "(I) Absolutely would have returned. Loved that league and had so much fun. the timing of the folding of the league left coaches and players with little if any time to get anything else that year. There are no openings for coaching jobs when May rolls around. I am still somewhat bitter about how things were handled, I was looking forward to another year. There was absolutely no reason that the XFL should not have made it at least to another year or two, maybe longer.it (the league) could have made it especially if some competent people knew how to run it." The two that came from the NFL, Kippy Brown and Jim Skipper, made their way back into the league: Brown as a receivers coach for Houston and Detroit and was even assistant head coach of the Lions in 2008; and Skipper has returned to his running backs coach post, this time with the Carolina Panthers, and he too is assistant head coach. Keith Millard, the Demons Defensive Line Coach, went to the NFL with the Broncos and Raiders, coaching the same position. Hitmen RB Coach Joe Lombardi currently serves as QB coach in New Orleans. Xtreme QB Coach Tom Luginbill got out of the coaching profession and is now a national recruiting coordinator for SCOUTS Inc. and ESPN. Head coaches stayed in coaching for the most part, with Jim Criner moving to the high-school ranks, Al Luginbill coaches the Detroit Fury of the AFL in 2003, Ron Meyer worked as a football analyst for The Score in Canada, Gerry DiNardo now works for the Big Ten Network after coaching at the University of Indiana for three years, Rusty Tillman went back to working with Special Teams for a few years in the NFL, and Galen Hall spent one season as RB Coach with the Dallas Cowboys and now serves as the Offensive Coordintaor at Penn State. Even though it was only one year, many coaches still left their mark on players and coaches they worked with. Haines said of Meyer: "I learned so much from Coach Meyer. Whether it was knowledge of the game, management and organization, or his handling of players, he was a great coach in my opinion. I think he got a raw deal from the NFL and his winning percentage speaks for itself. I am a Ron Meyer fan." Many XFL players have gotten into the coaching game as well, from high-school to college. Included is Kerry Cooks (DB Coach at the University of Wisconsin), Jerry Crafts (OL Coach at Jacksonville University), and Jimmy Brumbaugh (DL Coach for Louisiana Tech).

In the year or two after the XFL, many players and coaches came out in defense of the league. Adrian, in the Daytona Beach News-Journal, called it "a lot of fun" and even liked some of the changes in the rules. Tommy Maddox, who returned to the NFL and shed the "bust" label he carried for some many years, said "The XFL was a great league for the players.(they) did everything first class." He even said that while the ratings were low, more people stopped to talk to him about the XFL then they did when he was in the NFL. Millard, a former NFL Defensive Player of the Year, told the Denver Broncos website that the league "was a good, short-lived experience). In a Q&A with the Birmingham News, Gerry DiNardo called his XFL experience "great" and said "I would do it all over again." He admitted that the Bolts struggled partly because of the early shake-up on their coaching staff and QB injuries. Jay Barker told the Toronto Sun that "it really was worth it for me," and he lauded the ability to work around players and an offense that he had a say in. "That's probably the most fun I've ever had playing this sport," Joe Tuipala told the Florida Times-Union; he also said he wouldn't trade his experience there for anything. He also credited the league for getting him a shot in the NFL. When Druckenmiller signed with the Colts, he showed appreciation for the league that got him back in the game, saying "Thank goodness for the XFL" in an NFL.com wire report. "I loved it (the league)" said Brad Trout to the Kansas City Star. The former XFL players seemed to be pulling for each other, playing with a chip on their shoulder to show everyone that the league wasn't second-rate; that players in the league could make it in the NFL. Former Outlaw WR Corey Nelson made it into the NFL thanks to his speed, and thanks to the Outlaws teaching him to play WR; his agent told ESPN.com's Greg Garber, "Corey Nelson wouldn't be in the NFL if it wasn't for the XFL." Enforcers DE Jason Chorak told the Seattle Times in 2004 that playing in the XFL was "10 weeks of Vince McMahon throwing a pretty outrageous party."

The most publicity the XFL got was long after it was dead and buried. In the 2004 Super Bowl, the Carolina Panthers were set to do battle with the New England Patriots. And the man who got arguably the most attention heading into the big game wasn't stud QB Tom Brady or the heart of Patriots, LB Tedy Bruschi; it wasn't Panthers star WR Steve Smith or Pro Bowl RB Stephen Davis. It was a little-used third-string running back.named Rod Smart. "He Hate Me" had made it to the Super Bowl, and it seemed every newspaper in the country took some kind of angle on the most popular player and most memorable image from the XFL not only making it in the NFL, but getting to play on the grandest stage of them all. But Smart wasn't all smoke-and-mirrors; he was more than a name. He finished with a 23.1 yard kickoff return average and also ended the season second on the team in special teams tackles with 14. In other words, he had some steak to go along with the sizzle.

Smart took his act to the NFL, having the time of his life and being, from most accounts, the life of the party at Media Day leading up to the Super Bowl. Reporters fell in love with him because he was everything the XFL had advertised to be: boisterous, in-your-face, flashy. He was the personification of the league, the league many of the critics who loved Smart, hated. Unlike most players, who were hesitant at first to join a league run by the pro wrestling kingpin Vince McMahon, Smart said he had no problem mixing it up if it was going to be a combination of football and wrestling. By this point, Smart had trademarked the "He Hate Me" moniker and was not running away from his time in the XFL and at one point, the one name the media used as an example as to why the league was, for all intents and purposes, garbage. Smart told reporters that he thought of legally changing his name to "He Hate Me" so it could go on his Panthers jersey, years before Chad Johnson followed through and became Chad Ocho Cinco. His alias made it onto the big screen, with famed director Spike Lee putting a twist on it in naming one of his movies *She Hate Me*, where a character in the movie even references Smart. His quarterback, Jake Delhomme, named one of his horses "She Hate Me" in honor of Smart as well. From noted columnists like Michael Wilbon, Ray Ratto and Dan Shaughnessy, everyone who was anyone wrote a column on Smart during Media Week. And in the actual game, it was Smart who had a chance to be a hero for the Panthers, returning the final kickoff with no time left, having a chance to really stand out and be remembered for all time. But he couldn't quite make it to the end zone. Because of all the attention paid to Smart, thanks in great part to his XFL exposure, perhaps it was Vince McMahon who got the last laugh.

A year after the demise of the XFL, columnist Kevin Modesti noted that the XFL hadn't left a legacy at all. Except for the players in the NFL that were vaulted there because of their time in the XFL. Then again, who is surprised the NFL didn't steal any of the XFL's ideas? The XFL went after the league because they were stodgy and complacent. Why would one think they'd parrot the XFL's ideas? The NFL wasn't going to change it's entire philsophy of what football was about. It would be tantamount to admitting the XFL did something right if they used the scramble for the ball or cameras on the field, and the NFL most certainly wouldn't go down that road, even if they were good ideas (and heaven forbid anyone admit that).

Because WWE was a publicly traded company, it was on their books that they had to expose how much exactly the XFL cost them. According to SEC filings, the XFL experiment set WWE back $46.9 million. It seems like a lot of money, but if they expected to lose money in their first few seasons. Plus, because of the business plan they formed, they would've made money after about year three of the league, so the only reason the number is inflated so much is because they only stayed in business one season.

CHAPTER EIGHTEEN

To me, there are three real reasons the XFL ceased existance. The first reason is because of the sub-standard play on the field, thanks in part to the short amount of time teams had to gel in training camp. I would venture to say that if the league started in 2002, rather than 2001, it would still be going today. One year was just too little time for teams to be created, acquire players, and learn to play together. Having several mini-camps and a longer training camps would offer teams time to steup up their game on the field, and this would especially be true for the several players in the league who were resurrecting their career after being out of football for some time. With that extra year, the rust would be off for the most part. It also would've given players more time to get used to the team's plays and how to execute them, as well as get used to the new wrinkles in the rules. Many players and league executives have offered a similar excuse, that perhaps the league was too quick to get things moving on the field. I think for McMahon and the XFL, they wanted to take advantage of the press they'd get and play in one year rather than two years from the announcement. If they began in two years, perhaps the feeling was they'd lose out on all that publicity, wouldn't be in the public eye as much and would lose that sense of being the "hot" brand in the marketplace. In the end, did taking the risk to play in one year outweight the idea that it would be best to wait an extra year? Since they aren't around anymore, I'd say no. The main reason people tuned out on that first week was because the play on the field didn't deliver. All the extracurricular stuff was for the most part as promised, even though most people could take or leave it, at least it was present. But the die-hard football fans who tuned in didn't like the sloppy play, tuned out, and never returned even when the play on the field picked up as the season went along. If the game in, say, week eight was played in week one, I don't think the ratings would've dropped as precipitously. While columnists and the media was all over the league, a lot of people were on the other end of the spectrum and didn't think the level of play was that bad. Kevin Iole was one of them. "I think the quality of play in the league was surprisingly good. It wasn't the NFL, but anyone who expected it to be the NFL was a fool and totally naive. I'll argue with anyone who says the quality of play wasn't good."

The second reason the XFL failed was because UPN dropped out. Had UPN stayed on as a network for the XFL, they would've had a season two. At least according to the XFL, the business plan for the league demanded at least one network television outlet air the games. Whether that meant in prime time or not, I'm not sure. UPN would've been in prime time, since each affiliate airs different things in the afternoon. While advertisers were leery of the league and the XFL did have to give away some ad time, I think a lot of the reason the advertisers stayed away included content and questions about the stability of the league. Returning for season two would've answered the stability questions, and all the XFL would have to do is show advertisers a tape of games in the later weeks to show them that the content isn't anything advertisers need be worried about. What interests me is that the XFL closed its doors the same day UPN said they wouldn't be airing games in 2002. That means either the XFL thought no other network would have interest, or already checked interest as a sort-of "safety net" and found that no one was willing to take on games. By mid-May, most 2001-2002 season schedules were set too, which left no room for a network to sneak the XFL onto the schedule. It just seems odd that they wouldn't keep the XFL around a little longer to see if they could hook on elsewhere. Because so many cable networks are owned by so few companies, it would've been tough to even acquire a second partner on cable—most affiliated with the NFL probably wouldn't want to rock the boat by acquiring the rights to what, right or wrong, many in the media perceived as a "rival" football company.

The third and final reason the XFL didn't survive was the amount the WWE Stock had dropped since the inception of the XFL. It was costing WWE money and prestige by keeping the albatross that was the XFL around. The WWE stock rose almost $1.00 in the day after it was announced the XFL was closing. It's no secret the league was doing harm to the stock. Also, WWE TV ratings were higer in 2001 than they have been the last few years; in the 5's and 4's then, and in the 3's and 4's now. If WWE's business was in a down-cycle in the, would WWE later cut bait on the XFL to make up some of the money they were losing out on with WWE? In other words, how long were they willing to stick with the XFL if they had past season one? If McMahon has been about anything in his career, it's been money, and seeing the WWE stock drop every day during the XFL season must've killed him. As far as NBC's part, I'm sure they were happy to get rid of the league and didn't put up a fight when McMahon ultimately made the decision. Their prestigious name was being dragged through the mud as the league lingered as well. If NBC did pull out of their ownership stake of the league, they'd likely have to pay a large fine to WWE, but then WWE itself would be on the hook to pay for the league for the rest of its running. As McMahon said in his statement when he closed the league: He does have a duty to his investors to do what's right for business, and to him, closing the XFL was right for business. McMahon wouldn't have conceded such a high-profile and public failing if he didn't absolutely have to; his ego wouldn't allow it. I always wonder if the league would still be running if WWE never went public on the stock market.

I think the media also had an impact on the league closing, but not as directly as those three reasons. Had they not given the league so much negative press throughout its run, I do think it could still be around today. The media is very powerful and people especially don't want to be a part of something that is considered "uncool," which the XFL was. Whether they hated McMahon, were just covering for the God-like NFL or whatever the reason, the media just did not give any leeway to this new entity trying to rise up and provide fans with football, and players, coaches and others with an opportunity to make a living doing what they love. Negativity sells more than positivity, that's for sure. I think I've provided enough examples to this point of the harm the media did to the XFL, much of which was irreperable.

Sometimes, I like to think of where the XFL would be if it were still around today or, at least, if it survived a few more seasons. The first thing that would need to be ironed out would be what networks the games would be on. NBC may have been out of the picture, but I still think a Saturday afternoon slot could've worked. TNN no doubt would've stayed, but it looked like UPN was on the way out. There's no other network they could've gotten on, with FOX, ABC and CBS both affiliated with the NFL and the WB not interested. Most of the other viable cable stations would've been out of the picture as well. FX would've been a great network for the XFL, but it's owned by FOX. USA would be out, as they split with WWE before Raw moved to TNN and I'm sure TNN wouldn't appreciate WWE teaming with another network of USA's standing. NBC later acquired the AFL, then just in the last few years, signed on with the NFL again. Who knows what would've happened had they kept the XFL and the NFL came up for bidding. UPN merged with the WB and formed the CW, while the affiliates who didn't move to the CW became MyNetwork TV. Not sure if the XFL would've survived that pare-down, as the CW wanted to focus on drawing more women, one of the reasons they let WWE Smackdown go to MyNetwork TV. Television is a fickle business and there would've been a lot of logistics to work out if they were to stick around. WWE later took its Raw show back to USA, owned by NBC, so there would even be problems there if the XFL was to survive. TNN later became Spike TV, where one would assume the XFL would fit perfectly, but after WWE left the network, would they be willing to do business with them to keep the XFL?

As for announcers, Craig Minnervini and Bob Golic likely would've stayed. I'm thinking that while Vince McMahon gave positive lip service to Jesse Ventura after the season, he wouldn't have been back for a second season. Sadly, I doubt Matt Vasgersian would've either. I think he was the right "voice" for the XFL, but he made some anti-XFL comments in a newspaper shortly after the league folded. Mike Adamle could've been kept in the color commentary role, perhaps with Chris Marlowe moving in with him, depending on how many networks they aired games on. Brian Bosworth got better as the season wore on, but he was a human likeness of the XFL: loud, abrasive but without a lot of substance. If the XFL wanted to be taken seriously, they needed to drop gimmicks like him.

Speaking of Adamle, he has had one of the more interesting careers since the XFL folded. In January 2008, he was brought aboard WWE as an announcer for their product. His start was very inauspicious debut, mis-pronouncing the name of one of WWE's main-event wrestlers on air. Fans were all over him, knowing he had little to no knowledge of the product. Unfortunately, that's how Vince McMahon likes them. It was rumored that it was McMahon's partner in the XFL, Dick Ebersol, who pushed for McMahon to hire Adamle. Three months later, with Adamle not showing any real improvement as an interviewer, he replaced beloved ECW play-by-play man Joey Styles and took over announcing for the ECW brand of WWE. Adamle continued to make mistakes on the air and was even instructed by Vince to simply leave the announce desk with 10-15 minutes to go in the show. Tazz, his broadcast partner, was soon told to follow suit. No one really understood what it was about, as the situation was never really explained on TV, other than Adamle apologizing on the next week's show for getting up and walking out. In July, he was promoted yet again to storyline general manager of the Raw brand. Some of his stuff was pre-taped, and he didn't do too bad there, but he would have to come out in front of the live crowd from time-to-time to announce something. Often, he dropped the ball, even though he had a clipboard telling him basically what to say in front of him. It was painful for viewers and I'm sure Adamle as well. In October, Adamle resigned from his on-air position in storyline, but he never returned to WWE TV. It seemed McMahon had finally seen the light. He returned to his job as sports anchor in Chicago after his stint with WWE.

All of the teams and coaches would've stayed on for a second season, I believe. The fact that no coach stepped down immediately after the season would lead me to believe they were all in it for the long haul. As the XFL became less boisterous and bragadocious, I believe the NFL would've looked to them and give the league assistance, even monetarily or begin developing the XFL as a feeder league. While on one hand, it would seem that the XFL "sold out" to the NFL after all McMahon said about the big boys at the start, it would probably be the best option for the XFL in the long-term. The NFL plucked almost 80 guys off their roster at the end of the season, more than come from the CFL or AFL after any of their seasons, and I'm sure that idea wasn't lost on front-office NFL folks. In fact, they'd need a new minor-league affiliate after NFL Europe shut its doors in 2007, leaving the NFL without a league to send players to to get experience in the off-season. That would've left the XFL with an influx of better players as well, and with each passing year, I think the play of the league would've improved. Its stability would've drawn players who were hesitant to deal with what they saw as a fly-by-night league in the first place—they would also get more players who were recently cut by the NFL. Players would see all of the XFL players getting signed by NFL teams after the season, and they'd certainly view it as the best way to get back into the big leagues. Speaking of broadcasts, on the off-chacne WWE would've had the same lineup of networks and games for season two, they really should've utilized the regional game schedule. It would'v helped ratings and also helped fans in those areas get closer to their teams since they could see them on TV every week, rather than having one game shown to the entire national audience.

Would the XFL have been able to top themselves in the "bringing fans closer to the game" department? Going into the locker rooms at halftime turned out to be a bust, but they did get some good pre-game and halftime clips they were able to show on tape, before the third quarter began. That also helped with the problem of having so many bleeps. Microphones on the field were a success, and the coach-to-QB communication was worthwhile when you had someone in the booth to explain the meaning of some of the stuff to the lay fans at home. The use of women, like Carol Grow and Dara Torres, who interviewed fans and others on the sidelines, disappeared after the first few weeks. I though they could've found more for the ladies to do, to fill the sex appeal quotient, but to not make it as obvious as half-naked cheerleaders. Something else that went away was the overhead camera on the zip line that was used excessively in weeks one and two. It could've been good for replays, but just wasn't a good every-play option. Having the announcers sitting with the fans in the stands didn't really have a big effect on the viewers at home, except when the announcers made mention of the weather. That was more for fans at the stadium and for the XFL to continue to show it had an "every man" quality. Interviews on the sidelines were hit-and-miss. Cameras on the field provided some good views, but cameras now can zoom in for close-ups to make you feel like you're on the field anyway. The on-screen graphics left a lot to be desired in season one. Eventually, I'm hoping the XFL would've developed some even more interesting ideas and technologies to use. The overhead camera is used in the NFL today and for some NBA games, there are microphones in the huddle during timeouts. While sports were already trending toward these kinds of developments, it was the XFL who stood up first and tried them out, to varying degrees of success.

Being affiliated with WWE would cast the XFL in some negative light later on, from the death of Eddie Guerrero to the murder-suicide of Chris Benoit an his family. Plus, the McMahon controversy wouldn't die, as Vince was accused of sexual harrassment at a Florida tanning salon in 2006. In the end, no charges were filed, but all of his indiscretions that the media overlooks because he's only in the "pro wrestling" business would be magnified because he'd be in the "sports" business with the XFL. That black cloud would hover over the XFL because of its kinship with WWE. Another problem would occur when WWE changed its business strategy in the last year or two, focusing on drawing more kids in the younger bracket, rather than the coveted 18-49 demographic. The thinking is to "get'em early," and keep them hooked on WWE for the rest of their life. Smart business, but using violence and sex-appeal isn't their aim at this point as far as WWE goes, which would make it difficult to cross-promote the XFL and everything that it was billed as, at least in the first season.

The XFL is etched in history thanks to nods to the league in various forms of television entertainment. On *The Simpsons*, Homer was shown to be an XFL fan in the episode "The Old Man and the Key," which originally aired March 10, 2002. Homer was wearing an XFL shirt, hat and waving an XFL flag in front of a TV, waiting to see who would win the Million Dollar Game. Marge had to break the news to him that the league folded. The punchline was that she heard it from the league MVP, who sweeps up nails at her beauty parlor. On an episode of *The Drew Carey Show* titled "Drew and the Activist," Drew was asked by his girlfriend if there was anything he felt passionate about. Drew replied: "Yes— my hatred of the XFL." In real life, Carey was famously a Cleveland Browns fan. That episode aired in May of 2001. Even here in 2009, the digs at the league haven't stopped. On a recent episode of *The Colbert Report*, Stephen talked of sports and said the second season of Brett Favre's retirement watch was in effect, which has lasted more seasons than the XFL. When these shots first occured, I was offended, being a fan and all, but now, I just laugh along with it. Even though it was ranked among the worst TV shows of all-time by TV Guide, I did enjoy the league for what it was: Football, played by men who truly loved the game, with some extra technological advances thrown in to bring fans closer to the game. I'm sure that's how Vince McMahon would like the league to be remembered too.

A lot of the resources I used came from the XFL itself. Most of the training camp information was from press releases from teams or team website postings. For the personal profiles or for in-depth information about the players, I used team media guides (post-season included) and game-day programs that were made available for fans at stadiums during the games. The XFL also put out a pre-season preview magazine, put out by Triumph Books, that gave an overview of what to look for on a team-by-team basis. The league also put out a season-in-review pamphlet that was sent out to the media as well, and some of the end-of-year news I culled from this. Since the XFL no longer has information available, most of my double-checking came courtesy of all-xfl.com. Another XFL fansite, XFLboard.com was infinitely helpful. I also used information gained from the Pro Wrestling Torch newsletter (editor Wade Keller). Newsweek (Mark Starr and Devin Gordon), Playboy and Sports Illustrated's (by Leigh Montville) articles on the league and Vince McMahon also provided some information used herein. Other references:

-Arizona Republic and Norm Frauenheim
-The Associated Press (mostly from information in their game recaps)
-The Bergen Record and Jennifer V. Hughes, Randy Lange, Tim Leonard, Pete Caldera, Brett Hughett, Al Thompson, Kevin T. Czerwinski

-Binghamton Univesrity and Patricia Cohen

-Birmingham Business Journal and Gilbert Nicholson

-Birmingham News and Doug Segrest, Clyde Bolton, Kevin Scarbinsky

-Biz.Stats.com

-The Bloomberg News and Rick Westhead

-The Boston Globe and Dan Shaughnessy

-The Boston Herald and Karen Guregian

-Business Week and Ronald Grover, Tom Lowry

-Calgary Sun and Eric Francis

-Canadian Press

-Channel4000.com and Ryan Sirvio

-Chicago Sun-Times and Greg Couch

-Chicago Tribune and Scott Merkin, Rupen Fofaria, Jimmy Greenfield, Don Pierson, Adam Caldarelli, Aaron Ament, Avani Patel, Bob Foltman

-CNNSI.com

-The Contra Costa Times and Cecil Conley

-Daytona Beach News Journal and Ed Plaisted, Mike Scudiero

-Detroit Free Press and Staff Reports

-Detroit News and Mike O'Hara, John Niyo

-Edmonton Sun and Gerry Prince

-E! Online and Emily Farache

-ESPN.com and Ray Ratto

-Fredricksburg.com

-George Will (syndicated column)

-The Jacksonville Times-Union and Bart Hubbuch

-www.jblpro.com

-Jewish Defense League (JDL.org)

-Kansas City Star and Jonathan Rand, Adam Teicher, Steve Rock

-Knight-Ridder and John Branch

-The Lakeland Ledger and Mike Cobb

-Las Vegas Review-Journal and Joe Hawk, Kevin Iole, Norm Clarke, Clint Olivier, Bob Cefalo, Bob Legere, Gabrielle Stevenson, Chris Di Edoardo, Matt Youmans

-The Las Vegas Sun and Dean Juipe, Victoria Sun
-Las Vegas Weekly and Ben Saxe
-"Long Bomb" by Brett Forrest; Crown Publishing
-Los Angeles Business Journal and Chris Sieroty
-Los Angeles Daily News and Kevin Modesti
-Los Angeles Times and Larry Stewart, Steve Irvine, Bridget Byrne
-Mankato Free Press and Charlie Potts
-Media Life Magazine and Kevin Downey
-Memphis Business Journal
-Memphis Commercial Appeal and Marlon W. Morgan, Geoff Calkins, Don Wade, Ron Higgins
-The Mercury News and Laurence Miedema
-The Milwaukee Journal Sentinel and Bob Wolfley
-Minneapolis/St. Paul Star Tribune and Conrad deFiebre
-Minnesota Public Radio and Michael Khoo (news.mpr.org)
-New Haven Register and Wayne Travers Jr.
-Newark Star-Ledger and Colin Stephenson, Pat Borzi, Steve Politi
-Newschannel 2000, WESH Orlando and Tim Kaiser, Matt Mochow
-New York Daily News and Adam Rubin, Julian Garcia, W.G. Ramirez, Bob Raissman, Michael O'Keefe
-New York Times and Richard Sandomir
-Nichi Bei Times and Azusa Miyoshi
-"On The Record With Bob Costas" (HBO TV Show)
-Orange County Register and Michael Lev
-Orlando Business Journal and Alan Byrd
-The Orlando Sentinel and L.C. Johnson, Scott Andrea, Adam Wilson, Andrew R. Tripaldi, Dan Tracy, Jerry Greene, Brian Schmitz
-Phillynews.com and Bill Fleischman
-Pittsburgh Business Times and Suzanne Elliott, Patty Tascarella
-Pro Football Weekly and Andy Hanacek, Joel Buchsbaum
-Rocky Mountain News and B.G. Brooks
-St. Petersburg Times and Bruce Lowitt, Greg Auman
-Salon.com and Eric Boehlert
-San Antonio Business Journal and W. Scott Bailey

-San Francisco Chronicle and Mark Fainaru-Wada, Tony Cooper, Joe Garofoli, Kevin Lynch, Glenn Dickey, David Steele, John Crumpacker, Bruce Adams, Henry Schulman, Carolyn Jones

-San Francisco Weekly and Mark Athitakis

-Seattle Post-Intelligencer and Angelo Bruscas

-Seattle Times and Jose Miguel Romero

-Silicon Valley/San Jose Business Journal and Andrew F. Hamm, Tom Anderson

-SLAM! Sports and Jon Cook

-The Sporting News

-Sportsline.com and Len Pasquarelli

-The Sports Network

-The Tennessean and Chip Cirillo

-Topeka Capital Journal and Rick Dean

-The Toronto Sun and Perry Lefko, Mike Ulmer

-The Washington Post and Michael Wilbon, Sally Jenkins, Leonard Shapiro

-Washington Times and Eric Fisher, Rick Snider

-"The Waterboy" by Bob Ackles; Wiley Publishing

-Zap2it.com